ALBANIA'S ECONOMY IN TRANSITION AND TURMOIL, 1990-97

Albania's Economy in Transition and Turmoil, 1990-97

Edited by
ANTHONY CLUNIES-ROSS
University of Strathclyde
PETAR SUDAR
University of Tirana and University of Strathclyde

Ashgate

Aldershot • Brookfield USA • Singapore • Sydney

Published by
Ashgate Publishing Ltd
Gower House
Croft Road
Aldershot
Hants GU11 3HR
England

Ashgate Publishing Company
Old Post Road
Brookfield
Vermont 05036
USA

HC
402
.A634
1998

British Library Cataloguing in Publication Data
Albania's economy in transition and turmoil, 1990-97
   1. Albania - Economic conditions
   I. Clunies-Ross, Anthony II. Sudar, Petar
   330.9'4965'04

Library of Congress Catalog Card Number: 98-73406

ISBN 1 84014 563 3

This research was undertaken with support from the European Commision's Phare ACE Programme 1994.

The book contains selected passages from studies submitted for a project entitled 'Economies in Transition - A Case Study of Albania' which was carried out in the context of the European Commission's Phare ACE Programme 1994. Their content does not, however, express the Commission's official views. Responsibility for the information and views set out in the papers lies entirely with the editors and authors.
Original papers: © European Communities, 1996.

Printed in Great Britain by The Book Company, Suffolk

Contents

List of Tables   vii
List of Contributors   x
Preface and Acknowledgments   xii
List of Abbreviations   xv
Note on Albanian Place Names   xvi
Note on Albanian Pronunciation   xvii
Map: Albania's Districts and Neighbours   xviii

1   Introduction: Puzzle and Paradox   1

2   Albania's Distinctiveness   7

3   Land, Regions and People   31

4   Politics, 1990-96   52

5   Liberalization   72

6   Privatization   82

7   Stabilization   107

8   Safety-Nets and Social Security   122

9   Institution-Building   139

10   Changes in Production and Trade Patterns   150

11   Public Finance   161

12   Labour and Employment   175

13   Financial Institutions   189

14   Foreign Resources   208

15 Events of 1997   227

16 Prospects and Priorities   245

Bibliography   250

Index   254

vi

List of Tables

Table 3.1   Land in Albania by potential use, 1990   32

Table 3.2   Farmland area per agricultural worker, late 1980s   33

Table 3.3   A comparison of agricultural productivity among
             East European countries, 1988   33
Table 3.4   Demographic indicators in Albania, 1950-1992   35

Table 3.5   Territorial and administrative units of Albania, 1995 38

Table 3.6   Employment by sector [industries], 1994-1995   40

Table 3.7   Employment by sector [ownership], 1989-1995   41

Table 3.8   Distribution of private enterprises, local and foreign,
             end-1995   44
Table 3.9   Environmental 'hot-spot' areas by district   46

Table 6.1   Privatization of small and medium enterprises,
             1994-1996   93
Table 6.2   Information on enterprises privatized in the first
             rounds of mass-privatization, 1995-1996   93
Table 7.1   Growth rate of real GDP, and inflation, 1989-1996   113

Table 7.2   Nominal and real bank lending rates, 1992-1996   114

Table 7.3   Income-velocity of money, quarterly, end-1991
             to mid-1996   115
Table 7.4   Nominal and real exchange-rates of the lek,
             1992-1997   116
Table 7.5   Albania's balance of payments, 1989-1996   118

Table 7.6   Albania's balance of payments, 1995 to June 1997   119

Table 9.1   Progress in transition, Central Europe and the CIS,
             1996   143
Table 10.1   GDP by sector of origin, 1990-1995   152

Table 10.2	Composition of foreign merchandise trade, SITC groups, 1990, 1993-1997	153
Table 10.3	Composition of foreign merchandise trade, alternative categories, 1989, 1995-1997	155
Table 10.4	Output of various agricultural products, 1989-1996	156
Table 10.5	Livestock numbers, 1989-1996	157
Table 10.6	Increasing per-animal productivity, milk and eggs, 1989-1996	158
Table 11.1	National-accounting and budgetary aggregates ---mainly expenditure---1989-1996	164
Table 11.2	Budgetary aggregates---mainly revenue---1989-1996	165
Table 11.3	Budget balance as percentage of GDP, certain CEE countries, 1989-1994	166
Table 11.4	National-accounting and budgetary aggregates ---mainly expenditure---1996-1997	172
Table 11.5	Budgetary aggregates---mainly revenue---1996-1997	172
Table 12.1	Selected labour-market indicators, 1989-1997	178
Table 12.2	Fall in employment and rise in unemployment, 1989-1995	181
Table 12.3	What unemployment rates would have been on certain assumptions, end of 1994 and 1995	183
Table 12.4	Sectoral breakdown of the fall in employment, end-1990 to end-1994	184
Table 12.5	Sectoral shares of employment, year-ends, 1994-1997	185
Table 12.6	Average monthly rates of flow into and out of unemployment, by gender	186
Table 13.1	Formal institutions of the financial system, end-1996	190
Table 13.2	Further capital required by banks, mid-1997	196
Table 13.3	Banking institutions: balance sheet, 31/12/1995, 31/12/1996	196
Table 13.4	Banks: structure of non-government deposits	197
Table 14.1	Aid commitments received, by function, 1991-1996	210
Table 14.2	Companies involving FDI, to 1995	213

Table 14.3   FDI value (excluding trade, offshore exploration),
              1991-1996   213
Table 14.4   Sectoral breakdown by value of major foreign direct
              investments, 1991 to July 1995, ACFIP data   213
Table 14.5   FDI from tax registrations (sample 2), 1991 to
              September 1995   215
Table 14.6   Size of firm and foreign capital per firm (sample 2),
              1991 to September 1995   216
Table 14.7   Firms with foreign investment, by size of firm
              (sample 2), 1991 to September 1995   217
Table 14.8   Foreign investments by country of origin (sample 2),
              1991-1995   220
Table 14.9   Foreign investments by country of origin (sample 2),
              1991 to September 1995, in US$ current prices   221
Table 14.10   Foreign investments by country of origin, 78 larger
              investments, ACFIP source, 1991 to July 1995   221
Table 15.1   Exchange-rates and price-levels, 1997   239

List of Contributors

John Bachtler, Co-director, European Policies Research Centre, University of Strathclyde.

Spiro Brumbulli, General Administrator, National Commercial Bank of Albania; formerly Faculty of Economics, University of Tirana.

Anthony Clunies-Ross, Department of Economics, University of Strathclyde.

J.R.Davies, Department of Accounting and Finance, University of Strathclyde.

Rajmonda Duka, Department of Economics, Faculty of Economics, University of Tirana.

Stewart Dunlop, Fraser of Allander Institute for Research in the Scottish Economy, University of Strathclyde.

Roy Grieve, Department of Economics, University of Strathclyde.

Servete Gruda, Department of Economics, Faculty of Economics, University of Tirana.

Sulo Haderi, Department of Economics, Faculty of Economics, University of Tirana.

C. Paul Hallwood, University of Connecticut.

Pavlos Karadeloglou, European Central Bank; formerly Bank of Greece and University of Athens.

Neil Kay, Department of Economics, University of Strathclyde.

Ilia Kristo, Department of Marketing, Faculty of Economics, University of Tirana.

Dhori Kule, Dean, Faculty of Economics, University of Tirana.

Niall Levine, Department of Human Resource Management, University of Strathclyde.

Shyqyri Llaci, Head, Department of Management, Faculty of Economics, University of Tirana.

James Love, Head, Department of Economics, University of Strathclyde.

Ronald MacDonald, Department of Economics, University of Strathclyde.

Ahmet Mançellari, Department of Economics, Faculty of Economics, University of Tirana.

Luljeta Minxhozi, Head, Department of Economics, Faculty of Economics, University of Tirana.

Hasan Mytkolli, Department of Mathematics, Statistics and Computer Science, Faculty of Economics, University of Tirana.

Douglas Pitt, Dean, Strathclyde Business School, University of Strathclyde.

Stefan Qirici, Ministry of Foreign Affairs, Albania.

Mary-Louise Rooney, European Policies Research Centre, University of Strathclyde.

Genc Ruli, Professor, University of Tirana; President, Albanian Institute of Contemporary Studies.

Neritan Sejamini, Founder, Albanian Institute of Contemporary Studies.

W.J.Stewart, Department of Economics, University of Strathclyde.

Chrisostomos Stoforos, Department of Economics, University of Athens.

Omer Stringa, Department of Mathematics, Statistics and Computer Science, Faculty of Economics, University of Tirana.

Petar Sudar, Department of Finance and Accounting, Faculty of Economics, University of Tirana; currently Research Scholar, Department of Accounting and Finance, University of Strathclyde.

Halit Xhafa, Department of Finance and Accounting, Faculty of Economics, University of Tirana.

Yaping Yin, Fraser of Allander Institute for Research in the Scottish Economy, University of Strathclyde.

Preface and Acknowledgments

This book is one outcome of a project devised in 1993-94 by Gramoz Pashko and the late Jim McGilvray---after several years of cooperation between the Faculty of Economics of the University of Tirana and various departments of the Business School of the University of Strathclyde in Glasgow.   Gramoz Pashko was at the time a Member of the Albanian National Assembly and was on the staff of the Tirana Economics Faculty, and he had been Deputy Prime Minister in the first post-Communist Government of Albania in 1991.   Jim McGilvray was Chair of the Economics Department at Strathclyde; was a former Director of the Fraser of Allander Institute for Research on the Scottish Economy; and had been extensively involved in academic cooperation with countries in Eastern Europe.

The project was to devise a series of studies on various aspects of the Albanian economy during its 'transition to the market'.   On each study one or more Albanian scholars would work in cooperation with one or more foreigners.   The aim would be multiple: to assemble a body of information for outsiders interested in Albania; to provide locally-based teaching material for use with Albanian students of economics; and to clarify policy issues.   Alexandros Panethimitakis and Pavlos Karadeloglou, economists at the University of Athens, joined with Pashko and McGilvray in backing the project, which was adopted for financing by the European Commisssion under its Phare programme in 1994.   Contact was made between a number of Albanian academics and workers of corresponding interests in Greece and Scotland.   But the completion of the project, already somewhat behind schedule, was thrown into jeopardy by the sudden death of Jim McGilvray in November 1995 and the difficulties faced by Gramoz Pashko as a prominent oppositionist---difficulties that led him to leave Albania for a considerable period until after the election of 1997.   It was suggested in the latter half of 1996 that Anthony Clunies-Ross should step into Jim McGilvray's role as 'Coordinator' in order to bring the project to completion by the last day allowed under the contract with the European Commission.   At Gramoz Pashko's request, Genc Ruli, another distinguished former-Minister---he had held office as Minister of Finance in both the first coalition government and the first Democratic-Party-led government---agreed to be the Tirana Partner; and Pavlos Karadeloglou was prepared to continue as the Athens Partner.   The imminence of the final date meant that the great bulk of the writing had to be completed during the extremely disturbed first half of 1997.

Nevertheless eleven studies were completed, and parts put into Albanian.

After the traumatic events of 1997, it seemed more than ever important that Albania's highly distinctive experience of 'transition' from Stalinist hermit-kingdom should be recorded and presented in perspective. This book attempts that task, drawing on the work of the thirty-two people listed above as Contributors. It would have been unsatisfactory to present the original eleven studies, however edited. They were diverse in character. They had a teaching brief which did not quite fit the present purpose, and some of them were too specialized for the kind of readership at which we could aim. There were also gaps which it now seemed possible to fill.

So what we try to do here is to give a unified account of the political economy of Albania from 1990 to 1997. An attempt at overall interpretation of the experience is made in chapter 2. Chapters 5 to 14 deal topic by topic with what happened in economic institutions and performance from 1990 until 1996. Chapters 3 and 4 give accounts of some of the background to these events. A section in chapter 15 deals with the economic developments of 1997. There is a Summary at the end of each of these chapters. Lessons that might be drawn, especially from the 1997 events, are outlined in the Summary at the end of chapter 15. Priorities for policy, as we see them now in 1998, are recorded in chapter 16. Anyone aiming to get the gist of the book's message might read chapters 1, 2, and 16 and the Summaries at the ends of the other chapters.

The eleven original studies have been extracted, sometimes *verbatim*, and in these cases no quotation-marks or source-references to them have been given. The authors of those studies are in effect the joint-authors of this book. However, some of the studies are cited in the text for further information, and all are listed, with asterisks, in the Bibliography. Petar Sudar has acted as Co-editor with Anthony Clunies-Ross. Though as far as possible Contributors have been given a chance to comment on drafts of the chapters that draw on their own work, it would have been impossible to issue the book as representing the agreed views of thirty-two people from opposite ends of Europe or to have them all check every assertion made. So we as Editors take full responsibility for the opinions and interpretations expressed in it and for any and all inaccuracies. We regret that the character and length of the book have meant that we have had to omit valuable elements in the studies, including some of the most original work.

Acknowledgments

We pay tribute to Gramoz Pashko and Jim McGilvray, scholars and initiators of broad vision, who conceived the project. Anthony Clunies-Ross, as its residual 'Coordinator', expresses sincere thanks to all the

Contributors---among them many good friends---for their cooperation, often under great difficulties, especially to the Tirana and Athens 'Partners' in the project, Genc Ruli and Pavlos Karadeloglou, for their forbearance, and also to Neritan Sejamini, who acted as a genial trouble-shooter on Genc Ruli's behalf. He has been grateful for the support of the two most recent Deans of the Tirana Faculty, Omer Stringa and Dhori Kule, and has depended considerably, for both encouragement and many-sided practical help, on his own Dean, Doug Pitt, and Head of Department, Jim Love. Dauphine Sloan, who was the Brussels contact for the Phare programme, regularly found ways by which the exigencies of the Commission's rules could accommodate themselves to the difficulties that the project faced. One source, so far unpublished except as a discussion paper, we have cited (with permission) so extensively in the chapter on privatization that particular thanks are due to its authors, Iraj Hashi and Lindita Xhillari. There has really been no substitute for their paper on privatization. Mrs Milva Ekonomi, Director of the Institute of Statistics, Albania, several times provided valuable help amid the pressure under which she and her institute were working. A number of other senior Albanian officials have generously made time to give interviews. Fatmir Mema kindly gave a copy of his book on privatization. Mimosa Manxhari acted repeatedly as guide in Tirana, deploying her marvellous capacity for arranging interviews with anyone from traditional-medicine practitioners to Government Ministers. Niall Levine helped, among many other tasks, by proof-reading; and Kirsty Hall put the finishing touches on the copy when the task exceeded the older Editor's word-processing ability.

*****

Albania is different. That makes its story interesting---and perhaps instructive. We hope that some of the interest is here conveyed.

Anthony Clunies-Ross, Petar Sudar
Glasgow, Midsummer 1998

List of Abbreviations

AAS	Annual Agricultural Survey
ACFIP	Albania Centre for Foreign Investment Promotion
AO	Albanian Observer
BCCI	Bank of Credit and Commerce International
CEE	Central and Eastern Europe
CIS	Commonwealth of Independent States
CPI	Consumer Price Index
CSCE	Council for Security and Cooperation in Europe [later the OSCE; see below]
DA	Democratic Alliance
DP, DPA	Democratic Party of Albania
EBRD	European Bank for Reconstruction and Development
EU	European Union
FDI	Foreign direct investment
GDP	Gross domestic product [value of what is produced within the borders of country over a period, net of material inputs but gross of depreciation of capital goods]
IMF	International Monetary Fund
INSTAT	Institute of Statistics, Albania
MNF	Multinational Force
NAP	National Agency for Privatization
OECD	Organization for Economic Cooperation and Development
OSCE	Organization for Security and Cooperation in Europe
PIP	Public Investment Programme
PLA	Party of Labour of Albania [the former ruling party.]
PSA	Socialist Party of Albania
SII, SSI	Social Insurance Institute, Social Security Institute
SYA	Statistical Yearbook of Albania
VAT	Value-added tax
WDR	World Development Report

Note on Albanian Place Names

All Albanian nouns have two sets of forms---indefinite and definite. This applies to proper nouns, such as place-names, as well as to common nouns. When Albanian place-names are used within discourse in other languages, neither form is clearly more appropriate than the other. With one (inconsistent) exception we have aimed to use the indefinite form of place-names. So we write *Shkodër, Elbasan, Durrës*, and *Vlorë*, and not *Shkodra, Elbasani, Durrësi*, and *Vlora*---which would be equally correct. The inconsistent exception is over the capital of Albania. Where we are referring to it mainly in a geographical context (as in chapter 3) we call it *Tiranë*, and we use that (indefinite) form also for its District. But mostly (when for example we are mentioning it as capital or as scene of historical events) we use the definite form *Tirana*, by which the city is commonly known abroad.

Note on Albanian Pronunciation

Albanian spelling, having been standardized quite recently, is highly phonetic. The following hints are designed for English-speakers, merely to guard against the worst mistakes.

a, e, i, o, and **u** are pronounced roughly as in Italian or Spanish: *very* roughly like the vowel-sounds in English *car, care, key, core, cool.* But they may be long or short.

y is pronounced like the French *u* or Gernman *ü.*

ë is pronounced as an 'indeterminate vowel': like the *e* in *terrific;* but, when it occurs at the end of a word, some speakers make it silent. When it occurs at the end of a word, it is said to lengthen the sound of the previous vowel.

With the following exceptions, most consonants (and combinations) are pronounced very roughly as in English.

c is like the *ts* in *bits.*   **ç** is like the *ch* in *chew.*

dh is like the voiced *th* in *then.*   **th** is like the unvoiced *th* in *thin.*

gj is like the initial consonant sound in *due.*

j as consonant is pronounced like the English y, never like the English *j.*
   aj or **ai** *is* like the vowel in *ply;* **ej** or **ei** like the vowel in *place.*

l and **ll** are treated as different letters, as are **r** and **rr**, and pronounced differently, but English-speakers will not readily notice the difference.

q is like the initial consonant sound in *tune.* **x** is like the *dz* in *adze.*

xh is like the *dg* in *edge.* **zh** is like the final *g* in *garage* or *arbitrage.*

Map: Albania's Districts and Neighbours

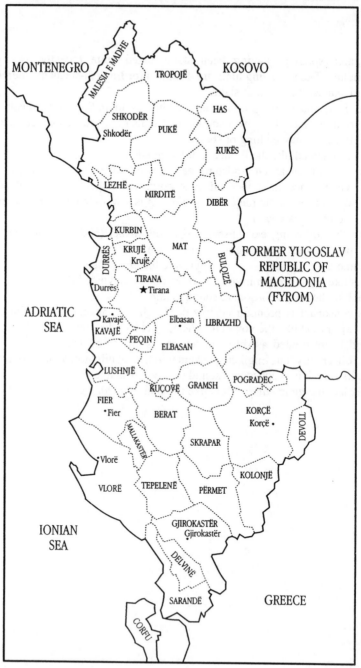

1 Introduction: Puzzle and Paradox

Albania was a maverick in Cold War Europe, and it has continued to be a maverick among the 'transition economies'. But the paradoxes begin here. Ending the 1980s as the poorest country of Communist Europe, the most isolated and autarkic, and the most extreme in its Stalinism, and then (at least among countries outwith the former Soviet Union) suffering the most severe disruption to production in the first couple of years of its transformation, it appeared by late 1996 to have become the most successful economically over the previous few years.   It had been especially quick to achieve a stable floating exchange-rate and fairly stable domestic prices.   It seemed set to overtake its 1989 level of production earlier than any of the other European and ex-Soviet transition economies apart from Poland and perhaps Slovakia and Slovenia; and, alone among them, it had apparently experienced growth at 'East Asian' rates for four years.   Advocates of *shock-treatment* as the best recipe for transition to the market could plausibly cite Albania in support.

But then, with the collapse of a booming informal financial sector in the early days of 1997, all went into reverse.   Much of the productive capacity and many social facilities were physically destroyed, as much of the country fell, more or less briefly, into anarchy.   Understandably, in view of these experiences, informed Albanians have varied in their outlook at the start of 1998 from high optimism to extreme gloom.

The immediate causes of the collapse of 1997 are clear enough.   The deeper causes---why a financial system of that especially precarious character grew so fast; why there was no official response to the danger-signals; why the multilaterals and foreign aid-givers were not able to make warnings heard; why people reacted so destructively to the collapse; why state control broke down---must remain subjects of puzzle and debate. The lessons are not nearly as clear as we should like them to be.

Equally the success of the years 1993 to 1996 raises puzzles of its own.   If the key to success was the early shock-treatment applied, the question arises *why* politically such radical policies *could be* followed in Albania rather than elsewhere.   We believe that there are plausible answers here that remove some part of the mystery.

1

Transition Economies

This book tries to see and evaluate Albania's experience in the 1990s against that of the other *transition* economies.   We need to explain how exactly we are using the term.

No one had heard of the transition economies before 1990.   They were the product of the extraordinary events of the last two months of 1989.   At first the term referred to the Soviet Union and those eight countries within Europe that were, or had once been, members of its alliance.   Transition meant the move from a largely-command to a market economy.

China was not normally included because the timing of its (spectacular and economicallly successful) transformation was so different.   The process started in China about 1978, but gradually and without an explicit goal, and it encountered nothing much like the painful shocks that have characterized the transition economies of Europe.   Vietnam, Laos and Cambodia are also not included.   Vietnam, like China, has not so far given up the form of one-party rule.   Mongolia, however, to that point a genuine Soviet satellite, which changed direction at about the same time as most of the rest, might naturally be classed with its European brothers.

From 1992 the number of transition countries had multiplied, with the fragmentation of the Soviet Union and Yugoslavia.   East Germany had joined West Germany in October 1990, and Czechoslovakia had broken into two at the start of 1993.   Since the Soviet Union divided into fifteen and Yugoslavia into six, this would give (without Mongolia) a total of twenty-eight.   However, we shall follow for convenience the list used by the European Bank for Reconstruction and Development, and (ignoring Bosnia-Hercegovina, Serbia and Montenegro, as well as Mongolia) treat the transition economies for purposes of comparison as twenty-five.   They are divided into the twelve within the CIS (the Republics of the former Soviet Union minus the three Baltic states) and the remaining (non-CIS) thirteen, which we shall call 'Central European'.   There is no particular logic about this list.   Five of the CIS twelve are just as completely outside Europe as is Mongolia.   Confining the comparisons to the twenty-five is a matter of convenience.

The Processes of Transition

Transition from state- and collectively-owned command-economy to market may be seen primarily as a matter of *liberalization* and *privatization*.   But these processes require that new techniques for stabilization should be adopted, since the old necessarily tend to be abandoned with liberalization.   So we can see *stabilization* under the new conditions as the third key process involved.

On the face of it **liberalization** is easy.   It means simply removing restrictions.   But, given the assumption that these are not all removed *at once* (as they seldom if ever are), the sequence in which this happens is of some importance.   Getting the sequence wrong might mean not only introducing new distortions but also disturbing production and income, and destroying enterprises that had every reason for surviving. Liberalization from the extremes of a command economy paradoxically requires new forms of regulation and supervision.

Privatization raises difficult questions throughout.   In what units will state or collective property be transferred, to whom, for what price and on what conditions?   Should former private owners or current workers or occupants have any priority over the rest of the public in the acquisition of particular assets or enterprises or dwellings?   Should relevant experience be a requirement for coming into possession of particular types of property? Should the rich have priority in obtaining privatized assets (as is almost inevitable if the assets are auctioned for cash)?   In the absence of open auctions, can favouritism be avoided?

Stabilization in transition may also be a delicate matter.   In the face of liberalization, there is typically a conflict between saving existing enterprises and jobs on the one hand and preventing the excessive issue of money on the other.   So in the short term maintaining output and real income is likely to compete with price stability.   Numerous groups will be battling to save their particular interests; and yet if all vocal forces are to be satisfied the rest of the public will suffer.   There will be the consumer-burdens of inflation, which will also aggravate all the uncertainties of the situation to the detriment of useful investment and enterprise, and in addition spending on important public purposes will probably be neglected. The quest for price stability has to be pursued with some attempt to limit collateral damage, and against political pressures that have the potential for threatening the position of a government and even endangering civil order.

Apart from these esssentially *transitional* problems of stabilization, there are questions to be decided about a *continuing* stabilization regime--- what disciplines over fiscal, monetary, exchange-rate and wage variables should be followed in order to combine price stability with steady income growth.   Getting the best trade-off here requires judgments of how the particular economy behaves: whether real wages in the private sector, for example, adjust rapidly to clear labour markets or whether they have an institutional life of their own; whether accordingly relative prices tend to return to their previous alignment after some change in the nominal exchange-rate or in world prices.

A further need in transition to the market is for the development of new **safety-nets** to provide a rudimentary living for those displaced from work by the changes.

But the creation of a functioning market economy goes well beyond liberalization and privatization and the stabilization measures and safety-nets that must accompany them. There is also a need for what is broadly called **institutional development:** that is for systems of formal and informal rules, together with the organizations to develop, interpret and enforce them, and also what might be called habits of mind---perceptions of how the new environment works and of what reactions are appropriate within it.

What is needed is not merely commercial statutory law appropriate to such an economy (general law on business organizations, contracts and civil wrongs), but also courts and practitioners that can interpret the law, and agencies to police it. There must also be laws to impose taxation on private economic agents. Also needed with more or less urgency are laws and agencies to regulate the production or delivery of particular kinds of service where the consumer or user needs guarantees of safety, reliability, or quality; or where competition may be deliberately limited; or where (as in financial institutions and markets) apparently rational behaviour on the part of a number of individual participants may risk systemic collapse. These laws too need their interpreters and enforcers. In some cases the state (within a basically market-led economy) may need to set up, or deliberately to foster, certain types of essentially commercial institution, such as particular forms of financial intermediary.

More subtly, and not directly within the gift of the government, a market economy needs some understanding among members of the public of how such a system may be expected to work. It also needs certain norms of personal behaviour if it is to operate efficiently. A measure of trust and trustworthiness must exist and some readiness to respect the law. There needs to emerge a recognition of the distinction between legitimate and criminal ways of pursuing pecuniary self-interest.

The Dubious Success of Transition to Date

The record of economic growth or recovery so far across the transition countries taken together has not been especially encouraging. If policy-makers in early 1990 could have seen the EBRD's recent Table (1997a, p.7) estimating changes in GDP between 1989 and 1996 in the twenty-five that we are considering, they might well have hesitated. In only one of the twenty-five (Poland) was estimated GDP in 1996 higher than in 1989, and in only two others (Slovenia and Slovakia) was it 90% as high or more. In Albania it stood at 87%. In the twelve CIS countries GDP altogether in

1996 was at only 51% of its level in 1989, and in the remaining thirteen taken together it stood at 91%. If the outcome could have been foreseen, a strategy likely to see GDP *reduced* by a half, or even by 9%, over six or seven years could hardly have seemed an attractive one.

Let us admit that GDP comparisons of periods between which a country's price-system has radically altered must have an arbitrary element; and also that GDP in and after transition may be under-stated in relation to GDP before, both because the unrecorded economy will probably have expanded and because what is produced conforms more closely to what people want. Yet the gap for the *CIS* economies (except Uzbekistan) and for some others is so huge that these reservations are not much consolation. For the peoples of many of the transition countries, living standards have become not only less secure and more unequal, but also *far lower on average*.

While it would no doubt be difficult to reconstruct what advisers, from Western countries and the international organizations, typically expected at the start of the decade, it now seems likely that they often over-rated the speed of adjustment to changing incentives and the degree of reform that could be accomplished by simple processes of transferring property rights and removing restrictions, and that they often underestimated the institution-building that would be necessary and how difficult it would be.

Albania and its Record in Transition

We consider, in chapters 5 to 9 below, the Albanian experience of liberalization, privatization, stabilization, safety-nets, and, as far as we are able, institutional development. Particular faults may arguably be picked with certain aspects of the first four processes. Privatization in 1996 was not yet complete, though quite advanced by the usual standards of transitional economies at the time. The wisdom of opening the economy so abruptly to world competition is at least debatable, though many would defend it vigorously. But on the whole, in the perspective of the mid-1990s, there appeared to be far more to commend than to criticize. In a number of respects (to adapt the English proverb) the proof of the pudding seemed very well attested by the eating. That things eventually (if briefly) went so badly wrong we have, by elimination, to attribute to a failure or failures in institutional development. This diagnosis possibly raises more questions than it answers. In particular, it does not tell us whether the failures were those that any government, with reasonable human foresight, could have remedied.

So, viewing the scene in 1998, we must try to explain both spectacular success and a spectacular setback. In the next chapter we shall consider a number of the features that have made Albania unique or at least distinctive, and we shall begin to speculate on how these might fit together in such a way as to resolve the paradoxes.

2 Albania's Distinctiveness

Albania's distinctiveness among the transition economies may be seen in its starting-point; in the policies adopted; and in the responses of the people taking part, as reflected by the economic outcomes.   We shall outline these various elements and then tentatively suggest how they might fit together.

Starting Point

Barring the Caucasus, Albania still holds an undisputed place as the poorest country in Europe.   It is also, by conventional GNP-per-capita measures, one of the poorest of all the twenty-five transition economies---surpassed in 1995, according to the World Bank (*WDR 1997*, pp. 214, 248), only by Tajikistan, Azerbaijan and Georgia (all of them recently theatres of war). Albania's GNP per head cited for that year is US$670.   There is no estimate on a purchasing-power-parity basis.   Yet we guess that the *hidden economy* in the 1990s has borne an unusually large ratio to the recorded economy on which this estimate is based, so that true GNP per head (even translated conventionally by the exchange-rate) may be substantially greater.   By the mid-1990s *inward transfers*, moreover, added an amount probably equal to about 20% of GNP to what is called *national disposable income* (what the population and government actually have to consume or save).   So the very low GNP-per-head estimate is almost certainly misleading as a pointer to potential living standards.   However, Albania is definitely *classed* as a **low-income country**.

Fitting with this ranking is Albania's **high proportion of workforce in agriculture**.   This is given by the World Bank for 1990 (*WDR 1997*, p. 220) as 55%, much higher than in any other of the transition economies in that year and comparable to Pakistan or Indonesia.   Inferences from figures provided internally would put it slightly lower, at 50.5% (36.7% in collectives and 13.8% in state farms).   Official estimates of the share of the net *value of output* coming from agriculture in 1990 put it at 39%.   This proportion of GDP from agriculture *even in 1990* would match with some of the poorest countries if measurements used are comparable.   The World Bank's estimate *for 1995* (*WDR 1997*, p.236) makes the proportion of GDP originating in agriculture 56%, higher than for *any* of the 47 other low-income countries listed except Georgia and two of the very poorest countries in the world, Tanzania and Ethiopia.

7

But does the picture of Albania as a low-income country, like Malawi or Chad or India, really hold up?   Certainly the **health and education indicators** do not fit very easily.   Its life-expectancy at birth of 73 years (1994) is more typical of upper-middle-income countries; its infant-mortality (31 per 1,000 in 1994) suggests a middle-income country; and its primary-school and secondary-school enrolment rates would also not be out of place among upper-middle-income countries.   Such divergence between rankings on official GNP per head and rankings on health and education indicators is not unusual: China and the State of Kerala in India have shown similarly high ratings in spite of apparently low average income. But Albania's record in health and education has provided an important benefit to its people and a productive asset which talk of the country's material poverty should not obscure.

In its *command-economy* period Albania enjoyed all the typical institutional features of **Stalinism,** if anything **in an extreme and rigorous form**: collective and state farms, with a very small part of arable land in private plots; state-owned industry; a ban on private trade and enterprise and on commercial investment from abroad; centrally-directed allocation of labour; state management of all external transactions; domination by the single Party of all spheres of social life.   After the completion of the collectivization of land in 1967, if not before, the market mechanism must have been virtually unknown except in illicit transactions.   There was no system of justice independent of the government; and civil courts had a very limited range.   There was a fairly rigorous distinction between peasants and others; a person classified as a peasant needed a settlement licence to relocate in a town, and, unless there was some official reason for the move, this was extremely hard to get.   Moving into or out of Albanian territory was banned, except in rare privileged cases (until *inward* tourism began to be allowed in the mid-1980s), and unauthorized attempts were severely punished.

In all this Albania might seem to have been extreme rather than unique among Communist countries.   But there was a further combination of factors that made it truly distinctive.   This is the combination of **smallness and political isolation**.   The famous bunkers that still dot the Albanian countryside in their hundreds of thousands, facing prospective enemies from every direction, are a reminder that the country was a self-proclaimed Ishmael among nations---its hand against the hands of all men.   After Tito's break with Stalin in 1948, all its immediate neighbours were enemies.   From soon after the death of Stalin in 1953, Enver Hoxha's ideological doubts about the USSR, added to differences over trade strategy, led to a gradual breakdown in relations to the point at which, soon after the Sino-Soviet split of 1960, aid and trade were sharply interrupted (Brancati, 1996, pp.86-87).   After that, there were no states in Europe that

Albania could regard as well-disposed to its experiment.   Its remaining ally, China, was thousands of miles away to the east and could have been of no military help in case of attack.   And then, from 1971, over a period spanning the death of Mao in 1976, relations with China too gradually deteriorated to the point of a complete break by 1978 (Brancati, 1996, pp.91-93), after which Albania had no allies at all.   Though there were kind words still for Vietnam and Cuba, all the ruling Communist parties of the world were by then in Hoxha's view revisionist.

Hence, for much of the forty-five-year period after the Second World War, Albanians could not even take advantage of the controlled movement of people among Communist countries that prevailed over the rest of Central and Eastern Europe. There were also no Western tourists until the mid-1980s.   Receiving broadcasts from the rest of the world was severely punished, though quite a lot of it went on surreptitiously---there was a thriving underground trade in devices to help reception of Italian television. Yugoslav television was often jammed by the authorities.

Moreover, because of the smallness of its population, Albania's withdrawal from the world must also have been far more crippling to science and scholarship than the same degree of isolation would have been for say the Soviet Union, with about a hundred times as many people. Given that only an extremely privileged few were allowed to study abroad, scholarly and scientific transfer from the rest of the world took place almost entirely through publications brought in---and then only in safe disciplines. Even foci of underground dissent would surely have found it much more difficult to sustain themselves in a rather small and intimate Tirana than in Budapest or Prague, let alone such a huge city as Moscow.   It was a common saying that the authorities knew the state of the teeth in your mouth.   With virtually no travel either way until 1985 and no approved neighbours, the introduction of any unauthorized publications into Albania must also have been extremely difficult.

All religious activity was banned, under severe penalties, from 1967 (Harxhi, 1995, p.15), so that another potential source of critical thought and outside influence was, as far as possible, eradicated.   If the aim of policy had been to keep Albanians knowing very little of the rest of the world, it must probably be rated as successful as any such policy in an age of telephones and radio and television can be.   That is to say it did not leave Albanians entirely unaware of contrasts between their own life and the life of their neighbours, but, because it virtually eliminated *dialogue* with outsiders or any *public dispassionate examination* of these differences, it probably presented them in distorted form.

Yet it is perhaps significant for later events that collectivization of agriculture was not complete until 1967 (Brancati, 1996, pp.82-83), more than thirty years later than in the Soviet Union and a decade later than in

China.   There seems in Albania to have been reluctance, if not passive resistance, toward collectivization, which at least delayed the project in spite of the strong commitment of the regime to it.   Hoxha had after all promised during the War to give land to those who worked it, not to take it away from them, which is what collectivization seemed to mean.

Beside limitation of contact with people and ideas from abroad, there was also a strong tendency toward **autarky** in Albanian trade policy. The aim was that, as far as possible, the country should be self-sufficient.   One of the grievances against the USSR in the Khrushchev period was over its attempt to have Albania specialize in certain primary products (Brancati, 1996, p.86). The pursuit of autarky meant that, judged by the criterion of comparative advantage, resources were unduly directed into 'heavy industry' (capital goods and semi-processed materials) and, within agriculture, into field-crops and particularly wheat.   From the 1970s or earlier, attempts were made to carry cultivation to the hilltops (Brancati, 1996, p.89).   Some of the effects of that enterprise are highly visible in Albania today, with olive-trees growing on steep places and summits where you would expect forest or rough grazing.   Exports were virtually confined to minerals with a fairly low degree of processing and some farm products.   Minerals made up about 60% of export value in 1970 and 1980 (Brancati, p.97).   Albania's low labour-costs were not exploited so as to permit it to specialize internationally in labour-intensive manufactures.

As was common among Communist countries, the **direction of foreign trade** was politically conditioned, but in Albania's case this had extreme effects as the Hoxha regime switched its allegiance to and from the major Communist powers.   In 1950 it had no import or export trade except with Comecon countries, 62.7% of its exports going to, and 37.4% of its imports coming from, the USSR.   Though in 1960 these percentages were still 49.9% and 56.3%, there was by then some trade with China and a trickle with non-Communist countries.   But from 1970 until the late 1980s (indeed apparently from about 1961) there was *no trade at all with the USSR*.   In 1970, 25.9% of export trade and 56.9% of import trade was with China, but then in 1980 there was *no trade with China either way*.   Non-Communist countries (industrial and developing) accounted for more than half of both import and export trade in 1980, but markedly less, both proportionately and absolutely, in the mid-1980s.   (Details can be found in tables labelled Figures 12 and 13, in Brancati, 1996, pp.114-115.)

Albania's **population growth** between 1980 and 1990, at 2.1% a year, though not specially high for a low-income country and lower than in the previous decades, was very fast by European standards, and above (mostly well above) those of the other future transition economies.   The age structure meant that the population of working age was growing faster than the population in total.

To summarize: by the standards of the transition economies, Albania started the decade very poor though with fairly good health and education indicators; with an exceptionally high proportion of both workforce and output agricultural; strongly Stalinist in its economic organization; its population small and exceptionally isolated in terms of interaction with outsiders; highly inward-oriented in its trade, with an unusual degree of zeal for self-sufficiency and a consequent bias towards heavy industry and foodgrains; having a history of repeated disruptions in its trade direction because of changing political allegiances; and undergoing a high rate of population and workforce growth.

Important to developments in the 1990s were also the **neighbours** that Albania happened to have: to the south and southeast, to the northeast and north, and across the Adriatic to the west---Greece, Yugoslavia and Italy respectively.

Transformation Policies

The most striking feature of Albania's transformation policies is the speed with which a number of critical reforms were accomplished. They have to be seen against the fact that Communist (Party of Labour of Albania, PLA, PPS) control was not popularly challenged until late in 1990, and the Communist monopoly of government was not ended until two months after the election of March-April 1991.

Albania's authorities lost no time in **liberalizing**, especially after the installation of the Democratic Party government that followed the election of March 1992. The state monopoly of foreign trade was ended in 1991, and quantitative restrictions on imports and exports were largely removed from the 15th September of that year. Thereafter, though duties on imports were introduced, and until 1994 there were export duties (and until 1995 export-licensing requirements) on certain goods (Muço, 1996, p.57), Albanian products had to compete on price in home and foreign markets with those from other countries. By the start of 1996, there were no quantitative restrictions or embargoes on either imports or exports other than for health, environmental, and public-order reasons. State enterprises were subject to hard-budget constraints by late in 1992. In August 1992, prices of a number of goods, said to cover nearly 75% of all prices (Muço, 1996, p.56), were either raised or freed. Most price controls and subsidies on basic consumer-goods were removed by 1994 and even the control on bread prices by 1996. At the end of that year the only subsidized goods and services (other than in health and education) were electricity, rural water, rail and urban-bus transport, and school-books. Other utilities' prices remained controlled but not subsidized.

The foreign-investment law of the 2nd November 1993 treated foreign enterprises in the same way as domestic, except that they were required to be incorporated and that foreign individuals and companies were at first allowed to lease land but not to own it (EBRD, 1994, p.16). Since July 1995, they have even been able to buy land provided they are committed to a sufficient investment on it (EBRD, 1996, p.136). Wages in the emerging private sector (including privatized state enterprises) have not been controlled, except that it appears that the official minimum wage applies by law to private firms as well as to state-owned enterprise and government (ACFIP, 1997). Housing and agricultural land, once privatized, were (apart from a very brief and unenforced control on change of use of farmland) subject to no official restrictions on use or on rents charged. Housing could be bought and sold---as, after July 1995, could farmland by law (EBRD, 1996, p.136), though the legal requirements have so far made sales of farmland extremely difficult in practice (IMF, 1997, pp.35-36). The foreign-exchange market was virtually uncontrolled from the date of institution of a floating exchange-rate at the midpoint of 1992, though the targeting of the rate required of course control of domestic credit. A floor was set to bank deposit-rates, and, until late 1995, there were directives on bank lending-rates; but, as was to prove momentous, borrowing institutions *not* registered as banks or in any other legally-defined category (in fact being arguably illegal after early 1996) were in fact subject to no official control whatever until late in January 1997.

Privatization in certain important areas was also extraordinarily prompt and thorough. It started officially in March 1991 with transfer of the ownership of some small shops and service establishments, mainly to their workers.

Privatization of the land of the collective and state farms into about 450,000 family-size units (sources differ over the exact number), begun 'spontaneously' by 1991, was almost complete under official auspices by the end of 1993. It would appear that, among the other transition economies that inherited collective or state farming or both, only Romania had privatized land to anything like the same extent at that time (inferences from EBRD, 1994, pp.16-41). We are not aware that the kind of popular pressure for privatization of land that pushed matters forward---manifest in the original spontaneous privatizations---was matched elsewhere, except again possibly in Romania. It may perhaps be linked to the comparative recency and unpopularity of the collectivization.

Albania was also unusual, if not unique, among transition economies in a prompt and radical privatization of urban housing, which again was almost complete by the end of 1993. Here it would appear that only Georgia and Moldova had done anything at all comparable by that date (again from EBRD, 1994, pp.16-41). Since rural people received land and urban people received houses or flats, and a number also were given whole or part ownership of shops, it is likely that most households in the country had acquired some important pieces of state or collective property less than three years after the end of the Communist political monopoly. Thus most people quite early became stakeholders in the new order.

The rest of privatization was not so easy. Disposal for cash by auction suffered from lack of reputable native buyers; sales by negotiation were subject to suspicion of favouritism. Like about half of the other transition countries, Albania used vouchers to distribute shares to the public. The vouchers were used in what was called *mass-privatization*, begun in September 1995. But major sectors still remained to be privatized at the end of 1997. However, because land was so important in its economy, Albania appeared by mid-1996 as the transition country deriving the equal-highest proportion of its output from private enterprises---at 75%, equalled only by the Czech Republic (EBRD, 1996, p.11).

Stabilization moves also came comparatively fast. In the midst of the period of extreme disruption covering late 1991 and 1992, during which inflation reached quite high rates (a 237% rise in consumer-prices over 1992 according to EBRD, 1996, p.185), the authorities arranged a last drastic step-devaluation of the lek on the 1st July 1992, and thereafter took the gamble of allowing it to float, while targeting by domestic monetary measures a rate of around 100 lekë to the US dollar. Capital transactions, other than for repatriation of profit and capital by foreign investors, have been technically subject to exchange controls (EBRD, 1994, p.17), but in practice the foreign-exchange market appears to have been left free, with only rare interventions by the authorities in the market (IMF, 1997, p.16). Currency trading goes on openly in respectable Tirana shops and on the streets, indeed virtually in the shadow of the central-bank headquarters. The rate followed by the banks is set in the Tirana street market (*ibid.*).

This policy (combined, we must assume, with the measures of liberalization taken) seems to have been quickly and strikingly successful--- in the sense of stabilizing domestic prices while giving no ground for thinking that it significantly inhibited the recovery of output. A brief idea of how this came about will be given in chapter 7. But essentially the authorities stabilized the exchange-rate while abandoning direct control of it; and they also stabilized prices while at the same time removing by stages direct price-controls.

On rough comparisons we can say that, among all the transition economies, only the Czech and Slovak Republics, the three Baltics, FYR Macedonia, and Slovenia, achieved as much stability or more in their dollar-exchange-rates over the four years 1993-96 as did Albania (inferences from EBRD, 1996, pp.185-209).

Exchange-rate floats of various kinds have become not uncommon among the transition countries, but the combination of (i) a float (that is, allowing movement without any announced rate or rule), *and* at the same time (ii) a fairly stable rate as a result, seems to have been unusual, at least by 1993-94.   Central Europe had commonly opted for some form of peg (that is, an announced or clearly implied rate, or limiting band or rule, at any one time): the Czech and Slovak Republics, a peg to a basket of currencies; Poland and Hungary, a crawling basket-peg; Latvia, what is in effect a fixed peg to the SDR, though unannounced; the other two Baltics, pegs supported by currency boards which require full reserve backing for the issue of base-money.   Romania and Bulgaria had floats, but neither had achieved much stability in the exchange-rate by 1994.   Slovenia and FYR Macedonia probably came closest to the Albanian policy and experience. A number of the CIS countries had floats, more or less managed, but their rates over 1993-96 were mostly much less stable than Albania's (EBRD, 1994, pp.16-41; 1996, pp.185-209).

To fit the new order, in which unemployment was an important emerging reality, the main new **safety-nets** added were Unemployment Benefit and what was called Social Assistance or Family Protection, both introduced in 1992.   The former provided for wage-workers during the first year of unemployment and was in principle to be part of the contributory social-insurance system inherited from the old regime and modified in 1993.   The latter dealt with people otherwise without means of support.   Its maximum amount has been only slightly less generous than Unemployment Insurance.   It is clearly supposed to be means-tested.   The importance of these benefits is indicated by the fact that, at the end of 1994, 145,000 households were receiving Social Assistance and about 50,000 individuals Unemployment Benefit.   Thus it would seem that something approaching 200,000 families were getting one or the other.   On the face of it, rural people were much less favourably treated under these benefirs than urban; and, even for towndwellers, there had been some decline in the adequacy of the two benefits by the end of 1996.

Even before transition there had been difficulties over applying social-insurance to the large farm population on the same basis as to urban and other state employees, and there were consequent anomalies.   The causes of these difficulties have not disappeared.   This highlights what is remarkable about these social-security provisions.   It is at least extremely unusual for a complete social safety-net, in the form of cash benefits from the state bureaucratically administered, to be applied *in a low-income country*.   Such systems of social security were developed in affluent societies at a time when most active workers could be assumed to be employees, as indeed they probably are today in all of the transition economies---apart from Albania.   In Albania, it seems, over half of all workers are members of self-employed farm families. Social-security *contributions* after the changes of the early 1990s have gone nowhere near to covering the outlays they are supposed to meet, even excluding those for Social Assistance. In these conditions, the attempt to rig up such a safety-net in Albania seems heroic, even if politically or morally unavoidable.

It becomes much more difficult to talk about the peculiarities of *policy* in relation to **institutional development**. But Albania's position on the periphery of Europe before the Second World War, and its isolation since 1945, might have signalled that this would be a source of peculiar problems. It would not be surprising if Albanians, at comparable levels of education and sophistication, had even less knowledge and inner understanding about the workings of a highly specialized market economy than most others in Central Europe. What is remarkable perhaps is that there was so little clear evidence of major socioeconomic problems specifically attributable to such institutional peculiarities until the latter days of 1996. In fields in which small-scale organization was adequate, the adaptation to the market and to new freedoms seemed to have worked astonishingly well. It was when novel challenges arose, which demanded concerted public action but to which there were no directly importable antidotes, that the unprepared character of Albanian social machinery became painfully evident.

One field in which Albania did *not* at first entirely succeed in establishing institutions generally considered part of the package in transition was the maintenance of an open, law-governed society following the rules of democratic politics. If we exclude Croatia, Serbia, Montenegro and Bosnia as special cases and leave a question-mark over Slovakia, the reigning government in Albania over 1993 to 1996 went further than others in Central Europe in using its power to incapacitate its main political opposition.

Responses and Outcomes

Albanians' unique reponse to the stresses and opportunities of the new order was mass **emigration**. This has happened to a degree quite unmatched elsewhere in the transition economies. The only emigration of workers in the last three decades that seems to be of comparable importance for the source population, is from Mexico to the United States; even the huge absolute movement from certain Middle Eastern and South and Southeast Asian countries to the Arab Gulf states cannot be proportionately anything like as significant for any of the countries of origin. Albanian workers have gone mostly to Italy and Greece, but overwhelmingly to Greece. As far as is known, most have not gone with any definite intention of staying away permanently. Some have gone for only a few months at a time and made frequent visits. Since many have entered Greece or Italy illegally, there are no adequate records of numbers. But the number of emigrants of working age in the mid-1990s absent at any one time (as derived from Greek government estimates and the inferences that can be made from the demographic statistics) was probably at least 300,000, possibly 400,000 or more, and it may well be greater after the events of 1997. At 300,000 it would equal about a sixth of the working-age people remaining in Albania.

Closely connected to emigration is another phenomenon that distinguishes Albania from most of the other transition economies. This is that the substantial growth in unemployment has *not* (as elsewhere) been accompanied by a fall in the male rate of labourforce participation. The participation rate of women has fallen but not of men. It would appear that, instead of dropping out and ceasing to look for work, men have emigrated.

Emigration not only relieved unemployment but also produced a considerable inflow of cash **remittances** available for consumption or investment. Acording to one official source, the amounts of private inward transfers, as roughly inferred by subtraction from other external-payments items, was in 1994 and 1995 US$374 million and US$386 million respectively---about US$10 a month for each person remaining in Albania, that is an amount of the order of 20% of GDP, or, for every woman, man and child remaining, 15% of the average monthly wage as it stood at the end of 1995. Resident Albanians in the mid-1990s may on the whole have been poor, but many must have been *substantially less so* than they would have been without the readiness of their relatives to take the risks and inconveniences involved in seeking work in Greece.

Together with direct foreign investment (rising to 1995 and 1996), and aid (highest in 1992 but not much lower in 1996), which overlapped with foreign borrowing (highest over 1992-94)---but, at their 1994-95 level, probably more important in scale than these other inflows added together--- remittances made it possible for the value of imports of goods and services greatly to exceed that of exports. Merchandise-import payments were more than three times as high as merchandise-export receipts in 1995, more than four times as high in 1994, more than five times as high in 1993, and more than seven times as high in 1992. Yet Albania's gross international reserves (excluding gold) *rose* in each of those years as a proportion of current-account outlays other than transfers (EBRD, 1997a, p.35), and indeed the reserves rose in dollar terms over each year from 1992 to 1997.

The emigration is a striking example of the adaptation that Albanians have been prepared to make, and it has provided an extremely important social safety-valve and inflow of resources.

A further feature that seems distinctive is the large number of **very-small-scale inward direct investments**, mainly from neighbouring countries, and this time especially from Italy. Overall inward investment per head from 1989 to 1996 was not particularly large by the standards of Central European transition countries, indeed somewhat below the median ---though well above that entering the CIS countries (apart from Azerbaijan, Kazakhstan and Turkmenistan, all three rich in natural resources) (EBRD, 1997a, p.12). But the character of the small investments, often in joint ventures with Albanians, may have been well suited to stimulating and supporting Albanian entrepreneurship in the very areas in which it was most likely to be productive. It is believed that the new export sector in clothing and footwear owed much to smallish-scale Italian investment.

Unrecorded of course, but widely attested, is that there has been considerable income earned through the use of Albania as a **transfer route for smuggling**, especially to the new Federal Yugoslavia until late 1995 while it was under UN trade sanctions, and especially of petroleum. US Intelligence officials in May 1995 accused Greek oil companies of shipping thousands of barrels of oil a day to Yugoslavia through Albania 'which was reportedly importing some 9,000 barrels per day more than was necessary for domestic purposes. The fuel represented about 50 per cent of oil consumed in Yugoslavia' (*Keesing*, 40512). Beside petroleum, consumer manufactures also came in from Albania, many of them in transit from Turkey and elsewhere. Weapons, barred by UN resolution from import into all parts of the former Yugoslavia, must also have provided a fertile field. Beside sanctions-breaking, which necessarily ceased when these sanctions were lifted in the wake of the Dayton Agreement of November 1995, there were undoubtedly other forms of illegal transit trade, notably the movement of banned drugs into Western Europe. It seems there was also unofficial, if not strictly illegal, transit of arms to the Middle East. Less well attested for obvious reasons, but highly plausible, is that Albania, with a large unregulated informal financial sector run partly by registered companies and for a time paying enormous rates of interest (and also a number of foreign-owned private banks with little local business), was a prime site for *money-laundering*. (For some testimony on this, see the end of chapter 13.) These activities seem to have flourished because of the combination of Albania's geographical position with its low level of law-enforcement. None of this necessarily makes Albania unique, but it was specially well placed to profit in this way.

Another peculiarity---unplanned, but probably harmless or even benign---has been the widespread use of the US dollar as a **parallel currency**. Prices may be quoted in lekë or in dollars. The oscillation of the exchange-rate for four and a half years around the rate of 100 lekë to the dollar led this to be the rate that most people had in mind, the true rate as they saw it, so that those exchanging money to help their customers, rather than as a business activity in itself, might use the 100-to-1 rate even when the current market rate would be more to their advantage.   Banks did much of their accounting as if this were the actual fixed rate of exchange.

The speed with which relative **price-stability** was achieved in Albania is not extreme but must nevertheless have been highly encouraging in the contemporary scene.   Inflation was brought under control fairly rapidly in 1993, almost certainly in large part as a result of the measures taken to stabilize the dollar-exchange-rate.   It was reduced from 237% over 1992 to 6% over 1995, though it then rose somewhat in 1996.   This put it very low by Central European transition-country standards in 1995, and below the median inflation-rate of those countries in 1993 and 1994.

What is remarkable is that this fairly quick move to price stability did not appear to be associated with any depressing effect on **economic growth**.   On the contrary, estimates of GNP published early in 1997 have it growing at an average rate of 9.5% a year over the four years 1993 to 1996: *high by even East Asian standards.*   In each of those years the rate was *well* ahead of that of *any* of the other transition economies, with the single exception of Georgia in 1996, which is recorded with a rate of growth of 10.5% in that one year.   Indeed to put it this way *understates* just how exceptional the Albanian growth record was.   In each of these four years a number of the transition economies had negative, often large negative, rates of growth (20, 13, 11, and 6 of them respectively in the four successive years).   In 1993, when Albania's rate was given as 9.6%, the next highest was Poland's at 3.8% (EBRD, 1997a, p.7).

There is one more unique feature that deserves mention.   That is the **collapse** of 1997.   It is important to be clear what this entailed and what made the whole story so unusual.   The fall of the informal financial institutions ('funds'), mostly taking place in the first weeks of 1997, was different, in what might be called its strictly economic impact, from events such as the US stockmarket crash of 1929, or the Korean and Southeast Asian crises of late 1997.   In these latter cases the collapse of credit in one institution readily *led to* similar dificulties in others, not just because of panic but also because of credit-multiplier (and income-multiplier) effects: assets derived directly or indirectly from what had been borrowed from one institution had been lent to another.   Where much money consists of bank deposits, this effect is specially acute.   But in Albania any credit-multiplier effects were probably small.   Indeed it is possible that the government could have acted quickly in such a way as to undo much of the damage. However, once the crisis had broken, there was little time to think. Foreign advisers, being unfamiliar with precisely *this* kind of problem, probably had little pertinent to say at the critical moments or made stereotyped recommendations designed for different contingencies.

We have to presume that most of the funds (those that were not or had not always been simply 'pyramids', certainly all those that had been operating for several years) had been funding activities (legal or not) that generated substantial income for Albanians, largely from sales to foreigners. Money was of course brought in as a result of these activities. But technically, since *deposits with them* would not be counted as part of the money supply, the funds' activities themselves would not directly *create* money. Correspondingly, the collapse is unlikely to any great extent to have in itself reduced the money supply. *In response* to the collapse, or *in anticipation of* it, some funds may have been withdrawn from the country, but *the money supply* is unlikely to have fallen significantly *simply as a result of the collapse of credit*. (M1 and M2 measures of money-supply, as recorded in *International Financial Statistics*, were each almost exactly the same at the end of February 1997 as two months earlier, and each then rose somewhat in every month until June.)

What the funds did was to give people the impression that their *wealth* was much greater than it turned out to be. For the true pyramids, this was inevitable because they were founded by definition on an illusion. For some of the other funds, it is arguably possible that collapse may not have been inevitable (at least not in early 1997) if a panic had not set in, putting undue demands on their *liquidity*. It is not out of the question that some of them may have had assets (generously interpreted) that exceeded their liabilities. Some of the depositors must in fact, over the life of their deposits, have made enormous returns. It is more than likely that quite a large number of Albanians, not only the promoters of the funds and indeed many people who were not in any way criminal or fraudulent, became rich, or at least for a while enjoyed an enhanced standard of living, at the expense of the rest of the population, and that some of the proceeds were transferred overseas. Many others were seriously, objectively, impoverished. The important political point is that all except the most perceptive had their expectations seriously disappointed. The fall in the wealth that people believed they possessed would in itself have reduced spending, and therefore income, in the economy in the absence of compensating measures. Nevertheless---if that had been all there was to it---with prompt initiatives and time to work them out, the worst of the effects on individuals and on the activity of the economy could have been mitigated.

The real damage was done not by the financial collapse itself but by the popular reaction to it, which was to destroy much social property and productive equipment and to institute a state of anarchy, which lasted for varying periods in different parts of the country.   This had the effect of cutting off much internal and external trade, no doubt rendering many people unemployed or otherwise deprived of cash income, at least temporarily; it reduced the flow of revenue to government in the first half of the year, and in one quick blow it made many people and the country at large considerably poorer.

Any explanation of the tragedy must be largely in *political* terms.   Yet it does not fit readily into familiar categories.   It was not a revolution in the usual sense: despite noises made by some gang and committee leaders in the south, there was no organized body poised to take over by force from the existing government.   It was definitely not a civil war: a civil war requires two or more militarily organized sides.   It might have *developed into* either a revolution or a civil war, but did not do so.   It did not comprise ethnic or religious or class riots.   It was not a fight over territory. Some vendettas were pursued; gang-rule was enforced more extensively and brutally than usual; negligent and accidental and personaly-motivated killing was perpetrated---all with the pretexts and opportunities for violence that anarchy gives among a heavily armed populace.   A commonly quoted figure for those killed is 2,000 (Rama, 1997).   Yet, considering the immense dissemination of guns, the widespread disappearance of government authority from many towns and communes, and the prevalence of criminal gangs, there was *surprisingly* little killing, in fact minimal killing judged by the standards of Balkan civil wars.   The destruction was mostly of things not people.   But people certainly suffered.

Tentative Interpretation: Putting the Picture Together

How do the distinctive starting-point and policies explain the outcomes, especially the very fast growth of 1993-96 and the unique setback of 1997? Though *special cultural characteristics of the Albanian people* may play some part in the true explanation, we shall try to give an interpretation that depends *as little as possible* on such debatable premises.

The main explanatory factors that we shall cite for **the successful growth record** are the initial poverty that prompted action of some sort and made migration attractive, the importance of farming and farmers, the neighbouring countries with their own peculiarities, the swift creation of so many stakeholders, the dash for stabilization and the way it was done, the moderately *laissez-faire* approach to the private labour market, and more dubiously the social-security safety-net.   We should probably also add the weak or non-existent law-enforcement in certain spheres, regrettable as that may have been on other grounds and even obstructive to growth in a longer perspective.   The neighbours contributed heavily to intermediate terms in the explanation: the emigration, mainly to Greece; the small-scale inward investment, mainly from Italy; the sanctions-breaking, mainly to Montenegro and Serbia; and the opportunity for illicit or unofficial transit trade in drugs and weapons, probably in the main between the Middle East and Western Europe.

For the collapse we have to look to what might be called the fall-out from the processes generating growth, and also inevitably to institutional peculiarities.

Remember that one of the elements to be explained is how a people capable of quite destructive protest (as 1991-92 and 1997 showed) could accept so easily a radical and almost textbook liberalization and stabilization that entailed a big reduction in employment---why the protests came mainly *before* the radical liberalization rather than immediately after, and, when they did come again, did so over quite a different issue.

First then, a large part of the outcome is explained by the low incomes of Albanians combined with the accessibility of Greece.   On the information gathered by Mançellari *et al.* (1995, p.8), Greece, though one of the poorest countries of the EU, had an average *daily* wage in 1993 equal to about half the average *monthly* wage in Albania in the same year. Unemployed men, or dispensable farm workers, could migrate, enjoy a higher level of consumption than at home, relieve their relatives (or the state) of the responsibility of supporting them, and still send back significant remittances.   Greece, rather like Britain in the 1950s, had plenty of potential unskilled jobs available for wages and conditions that native workers were decreasingly willing to accept---an ideal situation for migrants coming from a much poorer environment.   And all this was virtually within walking distance.   Despite prejudice in Greece, and the real possibility that illegal migrants could be shot at the border or forced back under humiliating conditions, by and large the Albanians were accepted; not too many awkward questions were asked about legal niceties; many no doubt came to seem indispensable as cheap workers; and on the whole, despite some indignities, they do not seem to have complained of their treatment.   The remittances (in foreign exchange too) allowed those remaining in Albania to enjoy significantly higher consumption and investment than would otherwise have been possible.   (Apartment-blocks were going up fairly vigorously in Tirana at the end of 1996, largely paid for with cash *in advance* by prospective occupants.)   And much of the grievance that might have arisen from the big reduction in employment was no doubt mitigated by the fact that many of the most vigorous young men had taken themselves off.

Second, in an important respect Albania was closer in structure to China than were the other Central European and CIS transition economies. Maybe this has some part in explaining the fact that its growth rate for a while came to resemble China's.   Politically of course things were very different.   China kept Party control with little regard for liberal immunities and democracy from below.   Yet Albania, like China, has had a majority of the workforce in agriculture.   Like China around 1980, and even more suddenly, it liberated them to make their own decisions about what they grew, freed the prices that they received (again more quickly and radically than China), and let them enjoy as individual households the proceeds of their work and enterprise. It is very likely that *these* elements of liberalization almost entirely *benefited* the families involved, *and they were the majority of the population.*   They responded too by very rapidly increasing output.   Starting from the depressed base of 1991, the agricultural-output index in one version increased by 54.0% over the next four years (figures personally communicated from bank sources), an annual rate of increase of 11.4%.   (And remember that agricultural net output came to comprise more than half of GDP.   So an 11% increase in *farm* output would mean something like a 6% increase in *overall* output even if all other elements in production remained static.)   Though outputs of wheat, maize, sugarbeet, and most treecrops, fell from their 1990 levels, outputs of the other main products increased, some of them explosively. So, like typical peasant families in China in the early 1980s, Albanian farm families received what were generally *higher prices* in real terms than their collectives had done; they had *more output* either to sell or to consume directly (mostly the latter); and they gained *much greater freedom* to take their own decisions. It was a bonus (typically an immense bonus for those that had access to it) that family members might also go for periods to Greece or Italy to add more again to the family's income, and another bonus that the range and quality of consumer-goods available increased. With minute holdings on average in country much of which is inhospitable, farm incomes were and are still extremely low by European standards.   In some mountainous areas of the north, such as Mirditë and Malësi e Madhe, conditions are strikingly harsh and methods primitive.   But farmers have been at least free to make the most of what the land offers, not obliged to grow wheat or olives because planners in Tirana like the idea.   And farm families, comprising more than half the population, must in the great majority of cases have become detectably better off.

Third, as has been suggested, the rapid privatization of land and housing, together with that of small shops and service establishments, made most households in the country, urban as well as rural, into stakeholders. That high proportion of town residents lucky enough to acquire ownership of their dwellings in 1993 (for little or nothing) now had valuable assets that they could sell or let at market rates or use for business purposes. Hence many, even of those who were hard hit initially by liberalization, had acquired *a stake in the country* and, at least potentially, opportunities that had not existed before.

Fourth, apart from fitfully enforcing the requirement for social-security contributions and maintaining (probably rather half-heartedly) the minimum wage, the authorities did little to regulate or burden the labour market in the emerging private sector. This, together with liberalization of product prices and overseas trade and possibly other features of the economy, has probably helped to keep the price system flexible. Evidence is cited in chapter 7 that relative prices, as measured by the *real-exchange-rate,* have tended to be *fairly* quickly restored after what might be called monetary shocks. This characteristic, admittedly not uncommon in the Central European transition economies, together with others mentioned in chapter 7, goes some way to explain why the measures instituted in 1992 to stabilize domestic prices (by targeting a stable nominal exchange-rate through monetary policy) accomplished their task for practical purposes so quickly and at the same time allowed real output to start growing at speed. If low inflation can be had on those terms, it is an unquestionable boon. Low inflation and a stable exchange-rate encourage confidence in the currency and in the economy, and their political dividends are considerable. The authorities acted quickly to stabilize prices, and they did so in conditions that were likely to make their policy successful.

Fifth, a social safety-net was put in place, despite the doubts that must have been entertained over whether this might be overburdening the public finances and despite the problems of applying a workable means-test. The payments, though meagre and arguably failing to cover a large segment of the population, must have mitigated much misery that would otherwise have been unavoidable. It is plausible that they helped to dispel dissatisfaction with the programme among the many urban families who were its victims.

Sixth, it does seem that a number of smallish Italian entrepreneurs (and some from Greece and Kosovo) used contacts made in part through Albanians abroad (assisted in some cases by having a common language) to bring knowledge and small amounts of capital into joint ventures. This process remains to be systematically studied. (For some evidence, see chapter 14.) Probably Italian business, with a lot of its production small-scale, was specially suitable for playing this role. In that case, it was good luck that Italy happened to be near, that a number of Albanians had moved there, and that the Italian language was not altogether unknown in Albania itself.

Seventh, neighbours again: given that there was considerable smuggling and sanctions-breaking into Serbia and Montenegro, this could explain another big source of purchasing-power in the years covering the Bosnian war. But the opportunity for sanctions-breaking could last only as long as the sanctions themselves. The general trade sanctions on Serbia and Montenegro were removed, and the weapons embargo on the whole of former Yugoslavia began to be phased out, on the 22nd November 1995 (*Keesing*, 40831). Whether on a longer view the special circumstances of Montenegro and Serbia at this precise time should be regarded as *good or bad fortune* for Albania is debatable. It may be that over-reliance on this source of income played a part in the growth and the 1997 collapse of the informal financial institutions. The widely attested illegal drugs and weapons trade also owes much to Albania's geography. It is generally presumed that the drugs go from the Middle East to Western Europe and the weapons in the opposite direction.

Eighth, much of the smuggling and sanctions-breaking clearly depends on the fact that the Albanian authorities do very little to stop it. In the longer term poor law-enforcement in these realms may well be a handicap. Yet it probably is one of the factors contributing to the growth of 1993-96.

Ninth, in spite of the self-denying ordinance adopted above over invoking national characteristics, we may perhaps be allowed to suggest that Albanians showed themselves specially resilient and adaptable. *Possibly* any other people would have done the same in similar circumstances: equally squeezed economically and at the same time equally highly educated and living so close to one of the richest parts of the world. But this must be speculation.

To summarize: a form of shock treatment, probably encouraged by advisers from the multilaterals and from rich-country financial and economic circles in the early 1990s, was applied rigorously and in conditions which favoured both its public acceptance and its success; and some of the special twists given by the Albanian authorities in the early stages assisted the process. Probably half or more of the population gained detectably and pretty quickly, in income and autonomy, from the combination of liberalization and privatization. Almost all households acquired valuable assets. Emigration provided a safety-valve for political purposes, an ameliorant to living standards, and a source of investment. The additions of 1992 to the social safety-net also helped to mitigate conditions for the sufferers and very probably to mollify discontent. Inflation in the circumstances obtaining could be, and was, tamed quickly without impairing growth. The three sets of neighbours provided their peculiar contributions to the process, as did the virtual lack of any suppression of illegal overseas trade.

So much for the spectacular growth. What about the **collapse**? Partly we can see it as a result of some of the elements that contributed to the success of the mid-1990s. The funds would presumably not have grown up if there had not been *plenty of cash around*. The fact that there was cash around is no doubt partly due to the remittances but also partly to the sanctions-breaking and other illegal trades, which were probably important contributors of resources for growth.   The income from sanctions-breaking and similar activities probably added a further element in being *unreliable.*   The Dayton Agreement happened to come at just about the time that the older funds, which had at least been earning income from their assets, were hit by the arrival of the pure pyramids.

Beyond that, however, there are at least four questions to be answered. How were the funds possible in the form in which they appeared?   Why were they not officially suppressed?   Why did they fail?   And why did their failure lead to disastrous mass-action?

What is *not* surprising is why people lent to them, given the interest-rates that they paid by 1996 and the fact that some of them seem by common report to have been paying out high (though not continually nearly *such* high) rates for *four years* before the collapse.   Towards the end of 1996, even one of the oldest (and therefore presumably most safe-seeming) funds, which gave the *lowest* rate of interest, would have allowed a family that had obtained a single sum of US$1,000 from a son or brother in Greece to earn US$80 a month continuously in interest, well above the average monthly wage, and, even at 10% inflation, equal to 129% a year *in real terms.*   Whatever fears you might have about lending money to *any* institution, whatever unanswered questions about how the money was invested and what kinds of business could possibly guarantee such a rate of return in perpetuity, the fact that something like this had been going on month after month at increasing rates for three, three-and-a half, four years, would make its continuance begin to seem as certain as the rising of the sun.

First, how was it possible?   Remember 8% *a month* was merely the lowest of the interest-rates in late 1996.   Further attention will be paid to this question in chapter 13.   What seems likely is that some of the institutions (inevitably short-lived specimens---principally Xhaferri and Populli, which appeared only on the national scene late in the day, and probably Sude and Gjallica), were genuinely and only *pyramid-funds.* The rest, certainly those that had been running longest, must have been *investment institutions* of a sort, most of them not simply fraudulent, but it is hard to explain the very high rates that they paid, even in say 1994, without supposing that they were *extensively* financing illegal practices to keep up the returns on their assets.   (This is discussed near the end of chapter 13.)   Sanctions-breaking, as we have suggested, was probably only one of the activities involved.   Albania with its wild terrain, its coastline, its large number of neighbouring states, several of them far from stable in the 1990s, its patchy policing, would form an excellent staging-post for all kinds of forbidden articles. Money-laundering too might be highly remunerative for an outwardly respectable private company whose financial activities were unregulated.   There was of course no transparency about the activity of the funds.   But it is hard to believe that people in the thick of events did not have some *theories*, if nothing stronger, about how they made their money.

Second, why was nothing done to check lending to the funds?   A popular view of course is that too many of those in authority had personal stakes of one sort or another in the continuance of the funds.   This may be part of the story, but it is not a *necessary* part of the explanation.   Even if there had been a desire in government *to avert the collapse* (a collapse which to many in high official positions must have appeared likely), what could politicians have done?   Once the mania had taken over in 1996, it may have seemed far too late to start regulating.   To sow doubts might have brought on the collapse that was feared.   Moreover, the funds were understandably popular; the ruling party had even vaunted or pretended an association with them in the May 1996 election campaign; some had been given free advertizing time on state television.   To have started investigating them in advance of overt failure, or to have limited their rates, or to have closed any of them, might have brought forward the disturbances of 1997---with extra bitterness directed at those who were spoiling the fun. We can see this---even though it is clear now (and must have been obvious then to anyone who thought about it) that the earlier the crisis was precipitated the less damage would have been done.   In the political fray it is often convenient to overlook what with hindsight seem inescapable truths.

Outsiders must have felt and expressed concern, but by mid-1996, when the danger was evident, what advice could they have given that would have appealed to the ruling politicians?   In modern experience this particular kind of infatuation, at least in its extent and universality, was probably unprecedented.   Few foreign experts would have had memories extending back to the South Sea Bubble or the Darien Scheme.   There had been pyramid schemes in Russia and Poland and elsewhere.   But in Albania funds that always were, or eventually became, pyramid schemes seem to have enticed a majority of households in the country.   By the time the genuine craze was in full swing, say after the May election of 1996, policy-makers were trapped.   It would have taken courage and conviction to collapse the house of cards before it fell of its own accord.

Third, why did they fail?   The pure pyramid funds of course were doomed to fail since their continuance depended on an unceasing and fast accelerating receipt of new deposits.   And any jolt to confidence could bring on the end precipitately.   But what of the others?   If sanctions-busting was a large part of the deal with the longer-running funds, it is easy to see why the party may have had to come to an end not long after the Dayton Agreement.   It is quite possible that a number of their other high-return activities were similarly precarious.   The IMF view (see chapter 13) is that the onset of the true pyramid funds forced the pre-existing investment funds to offer unsustainable rates---in effect, to become pyramid funds themselves. Any initial jolt to confidence here (such as the suspension of payments by one important fund in December 1996) probably meant that depositors would soon have started trying to withdraw their funds. Even the less crooked promoters would have been obliged to stop payment. The more crooked possibly cleared out with what cash was left. At least one, possibly two, of the large funds finished with no traceable liquid assets---in one case apparently no assets at all.

Fourth, why the destructive reaction? Apart, we must assume, from some of the more sophisticated depositors (who would be aware of the risks) or perhaps the more cynical and crooked promoters of the funds, almost everyone involved suffered at least some *serious disappointment of expectations*. The majority of depositors who had come in late suffered the most in the sense that their total transactions with the funds were very likely to be negative. They were the real losers. But almost all depositors, even those who objectively had gained far more than they had lost but had become used to a correspondingly high standard of life or expectations of future wealth, found themselves with a much lower expected present value than they had supposed a short while earlier and probably had to cut their consumption or their plans drastically. Half the inhabitants of whole townships, we are told, had sold their houses and now found themselves without their main asset and with nothing in exchange. Though doubtless many people had had expectations that anywhere else would have been rated highly unrealistic, those who had lost everything could understandably conclude that someone else had gained at their expense. (Many seem to have believed that the government must be backing the funds, and that belief is understandable.) Just as most of the farm population had made both real and symbolic gains from liberalization and privatization, so a very large part of the population of Albania had endured symbolic losses and punctured hopes and could expect sharp falls in actual or expected living standards. Of these probably quite a large number (all the late-comers) had made objective, and sometimes catastrophic, losses--- as a result of forces that they could not fully understand (just as we do not fully understand them even in retrospect).

What could be more natural than to suspect foul play on somebody's part? No one had warned them. The governing party had even tried to get on the funds bandwagon. So the government, specifically the President, became the target of anger. But how to vent your anger on the President? Since there was no satisfactory rational answer (until the 1997 election came to solve that problem), the responses were irrational. The anarchy that ensued suited gangsters and all those who needed to work outside the law. But, where it continued to prevail or spread its influence, it bore extremely hard on most ordinary people.

There is another special factor, on which great stress is laid by Rama (1997). This is that those in power in Albania over 1993 to 1996 had gone well beyond those in other Central European countries in prosecuting or otherwise penalizing people who had held high office under the Communist regime and in suppressing opposition. This meant that many of the political class felt deprived of potential access to power or even under personal threat. Politically-minded people from the Socialist Party, and some others, inevitably saw the anarchy in the south as having potential for rescuing them---whether or not they had had any part in initiating it.

Where was the institutional failure? One possible answer is that it lay in characteristics that were beyond the reach of policy-makers in Albania. It was intrinsic in the situation. Albania adopted a policy model that had worked more or less elsewhere. To a point it showed brilliant results, a number of coincidental factors and some sound common sense conspiring to that end. But then a phenomenon appeared that was not in the book. For various reasons connected with greater experience of the market economy, it would not have appeared in Switzerland or Belgium or Greece. If it came to be known that any institution in these countries with a public face was paying 100% or 20% or even 8% *a month* in interest, professional investors, the press, the authorities, would want to know *why*. If the answer was naivety, or fraud, or criminal activities, this would become known, and the authorities would feel obliged to act, even if inaction seemed temporarily convenient. Authorities in modern industrialized market economies have permitted a number of frauds and idiocies in their financial systems---through blindness or lack of vigilance or corruption--- but nothing quite like this, so simple and blatant.

The public, the officials, the business community in those countries are probably no more moral, no more intelligent, no better at arithmetic, than their opposite numbers in Albania. It is just that a greater experience of market economies would have rung alarm bells with influential people early in the story if anything like the Albanian funds had appeared, and various institutions would have generated corrective action.

Individuals in every country make manifestly foolish investments, putting too many eggs in one basket. Reputable banks have made enormous mistakes which in retrospect seem to break all the rules of financial common-sense. Banking authorities in a range of countries have overlooked huge banking scandals such as that of the BCCI in the 1980s. Central banks and governments had not forestalled, or apparently foreseen, the disastrous debt crisis of many developing countries that broke in 1982, threatening the world financial system at the time and representing an enormous burden to the debtor nations for a decade or more later. Some people can be talked into putting money into anything that is alleged to be very profitable, with no questions asked.   But somehow we can have little doubt that, in any of the affluent West European societies *at large*, a combination of experience, a free and active press, and tacit or open rules about how people in certain positions should behave in such contingencies, would have scotched ventures *with the characteristics of the Albanian pyramid funds* as they emerged.   There are safeguards against at least *some* ways of fooling all the people all the time.

Yet in fact the phenomenon was so unprecedented that, *given that the danger-signals had not been sounded at an early stage*, the Albanian authorities were probably caught in the coils of the monster before they or any foreign adviser had time to devise preventive action.   *If it had ever come to this point*, governments in other countries might have found it equally difficult to ward off the catastrophe.   Then, as we can say with hindsight, collapse was inevitable.   No doubt, the prompter the action, the less the damage would have been; but it is an exceptional politician who would rush to precipitate a disaster on that ground.   *We can see now* that the authorities should have risked provoking the collapse much earlier, when its effects would have been less severe, and that they should have planned how to deal with the crash when it came.   But it is not surprising if they did not see it like this.

There is another area in which institutional characteristics helped to make the disaster worse.   In a more open and law-governed society, at least in Western Europe, once any *politician* had been widely suspected of being involved in financially dubious activities, the case would be investigated.   *Business tycoons* engaged in grossly fraudulent practices, as in one case recently in Britain, have for long periods been able to scare the press off with libel writs, but *politicians*---no!   There would be plenty of people eager to discredit even the head of government, and they would see that charges were not overlooked.   This means that the general public would have some ground for thinking that they knew *which if any* leading politician should be under suspicion.   They would have some idea *who* was worthy of their indignation, and by implication who was not.   They would also have means of investigation.   And they would have ways of dislodging or punishing the guilty party that did *not* involve burning down hospitals or wrecking food-processing plants.   But Albania at the end of 1996 was not a fully open, law-governed society in that sense.

Non-enforcement of certain laws and international commitments, we have suggested, was a precondition of *part* of the successful economic growth of 1993-96, growth that was possibly even faster than the official figures suggest.   Non-enforcement of these and other laws *possibly* helped the longer-running funds to burgeon and collapse as they did.   Whether that is so or not, a general climate in which ruling politicians and their enforcing agencies were believed to be above the law and beyond investigation gave occasion to the tragic destructiveness of the reaction to the collapse.

This destructiveness was very probably enhanced by another element of the behaviour of the government in power that departed from liberal and democratic norms.   This was its persecution of its main opposition.   A number of political figures could not help seeing the anarchy as a way out of enforced impotence and the risk or actuality of imprisonment.

Summary: The Paradox Restated

The paradox with which we started is that Albania, apparently the transition country with least initial resources for making a success of a market economy, quickly achieved a growth rate unheard-of among the other transition economies or indeed elsewhere in Europe.   Then, at the apparent peak of success, there was an orgy of physical and institutional destruction that undid much of what had been achieved.   The Albanian people, who had submitted patiently to the shock and disruption of very fast liberalization, rose up in wrath and temporarily dismantled their state, at a point at which the real economy had been booming and showing every prospect of continuing rapid material improvement.

Our solution to the puzzle has been briefly that there were in fact a number of favourable conditions in Albania that enhanced the success and mitigated the suffering of liberalizing shock-therapy, and that policy-makers took a number of the right options sensibly and quickly.   The collapse and its destructive aftermath can be put down to institutional features, in particular: first, failures in law-enforcement, which, though perhaps contributing to growth, also probably played a large part in its nemesis; second, lack of widespread experience with a market economy which allowed certain danger-signals to go unheeded; and third, the absence of a truly open and law-governed political society that would have encouraged open debate about what was happening and, by observing the rules of the democratic game, would have made possible cooperation in emergency among the the main factions of the political elite.

This illustrates one of the intrinsic problems with *transition*.   Many of the elements that make a market economy work more or less efficiently may be simply adopted by a stroke of a pen.   Others, some of the more institutional features---including habits of mind and of behaviour---need to be gradually acquired over a period.   Albania provided an example of what may happen when the institutional features---some perhaps unavoidably, some as a result of wrong political decisions---lag behind the enacted reforms.

3 Land, Regions and People

Population, Area and Land Resources

Albania has a little over 3 million people, much the same number as Wales, New Zealand, Lithuania, Armenia or the Irish Republic.   Its area of 28,748 sq. km, however, though about 50% larger than that of Wales and much the same as for Armenia, is less than half that of Lithuania or the Irish Republic, and about one ninth that of New Zealand.   This makes its density of population, at 114 to the sq. km., just slightly higher than in France, higher than in Greece, Croatia or FYR Macedonia, and about half that of Germany or the United Kingdom.

What is remarkable about this density is that more than half the 'employed' workforce in Albania are reported as living from farming (55% in 1990 according to the *WDR 1997*, 66% in 1995 according to the Institute of Statistics), as compared with (in 1990) 5% in France, 4% in Germany, and 2% in the United Kingdom, and with 23%, 15%, and 22% respectively in Greece, Croatia, and FYR Macedonia.

The contrast with Northwestern Europe is even more stark when we take into account the topography of Albania.   Much of the country is mountainous.   This is certainly the prevailing impression as you fly over it. Land over 1,000 metres in altitude (about 3,300 feet) comprises 28.6% of the area, and land over 600 metres 51.6% (*SYA [Statistical Yearbook of Albania] 1991*).   There are various forms of describing the pattern.   Some agricultural accounts divide Albania's land into three zones: Lowland, Foothills, and Upland.   In 1995, just over half the farm population, and just under half the farms, were in the Upland Zone (*AAS [Annual Agricultural Survey] 1995*).

A simplified account of the topography of Albania, probably according roughly with this threefold division, might run as follows. There is a narrow strip of lowland (below 200 metres) along the Adriatic and Ionian coasts, very narrow in the south, broadest in the centre, where it extends as far east as the cities of Tiranë and Elbasan.   Next further east is an irregular strip loosely described as 'foothills', and mostly between 200 and 1,200 metres in height.   But something like half the country, along its eastern and northern borders, is described as upland or mountainous; much of this is more than 1,200 metres above sea level.   (Information is largely based on the maps at the end of World Bank, 1992.)

Table 3.1 gives the proportions of total land area in 1990 devoted to various uses.   Of the 704,000 ha. represented there as arable land, only 435,700 and 431,100 ha., about 15% of the country's total area, were reported as *under crops* respectively in 1994 and 1995 (*AAS 1995*), which works out as about 1.0 ha. per farm---not large, even by South Asian standards, and minute by the norms of much of Europe.   It was recognized in the mid-1990s (Kunkel, 1996, pp.3, 4) that there had been a considerable decline (around a third) in area *cropped* since 1990.   This may have been in part a result of the destruction of irrigation facilities and fruit-trees in the disruption around 1991 and in part a rational reaction to the over-extension of cultivation under the old regime.   The total *arable and pasture* reported in Table 3.1 for 1990 would represent about 2.6 ha. per farm in 1994-5.   But it is worth noting that as much as 18.5%, even of the land regarded as arable, was 'mountain land', with slopes of 25% or greater, and a further 37.5% was 'hilly', with slopes between 5% and 25% (World Bank, 1992, p.168).

Table 3.1 Land in Albania by potential use, 1990

	Area (000 ha.)	% of agricultural land	% of total land
Total land	**2,875**		**100.0**
Total agric'l land	**2,230**	**100.0**	**77.6**
Land under water	62	2.8	2.2
Meadows & pastures	417	18.7	14.5
Forests & other	1,047	46.9	36.4
Arable land	704	31.6	24.5
Field crops	*579*	*26.0*	*20.1*
Orchards	*125*	*5.6*	*4.4*
Waste, urban, industrial	**645**		**22.4**

Source: Adapted from World Bank, 1992, p.171

FAO figures for the late 1980s (World Bank, 1992, p.173), given in Table 3.2, seem to indicate that the area per agricultural worker was very low by Central European standards, roughly a third that in Poland or a quarter that in Romania.   Albania's usable land is extremely crowded.

Table 3.2   Farmland area per agricultural worker, late 1980s

Country	Farmland per agricultural worker (ha.)
Albania	1.5
Yugoslavia	5.6
Poland	4.4
Romania	5.9
Bulgaria	10.5
Hungary	9.8
Czechoslovakia	8.3
The Netherlands	8.3

Source: World Bank, 1992, p.173

In spite of these high ratios of workers to land, which might suggest its more intensive use, yields *per hectare* still seemed to be lowish by Central European standards.   As Table 3.3 shows, not only did Albanian cultivators have much less land each to work with than their fellows in neighbouring former-Communist states; they also tended to use these meagre areas less productively---whether because the land was intrinsically less fertile, or because they were provided with less of other inputs per hectare, or because of lower X-efficiency.

Table 3.3   A comparison of agricultural productivity among East European countries, 1988 (tons per hectare)

Commodity	Albania	Bul-garia	Czecho-slovakia	Hungary	Poland	Rom-ania
Wheat	3.20	4.01	5.28	5.45	3.48	3.58
Potatoes	5.41	9.73	20.64	-	18.60	-
Sunflower	1.00	1.57	-	-	-	1.51
Sugar-beet	17.19	16.08	18.60	39.34	34.13	11.36
Milk per cow (litres)	1,274	3,397	3,777	-	-	2,074
Eggs per bird	96	170	247	-	-	154

Source: World Bank, 1992, p.173

The upshot by the mid-1990s of this extremely poor endowment of land for the farm population is what might be called a subsistence-plus-pension form of support, that is if pensions can be taken to include remittances from family-members abroad.   In 1995, according to the *AAS*, only 77 % of farm households had any on-farm cash income at all; and only about 25% by value of farm produce was marketed.   Of the estimated US$2,000 worth a year income in cash and kind per household, off-farm cash income accounted for US$820 (say 41%), on-farm non-cash income (that is direct use of the farms' own product) for US$950 (47.5%), and on-farm cash income for only US$230 (11.5%).   (Of course the precision is spurious.)   Of the on-farm cash income less than a fifth came from crop sales, the rest mainly from livestock.   The off-farm cash income came roughly 70% from remittances and 20% from government payments. (Kunkel, 1996, pp.5, 6.)

In 1990, about 60% of arable land (9% of total land area) was reported as accessible to irrigation, but, with the disruption and destruction of the first years of reform, the proportion had fallen to 50% two years later (World Bank, 1992, pp.170, 244, 248).

Mineral Resources

Albania has exploitable reserves of chromium, copper, iron, nickel, lignite, oil and natural gas.   Between them raw and semi-processed forms of these commodities provided 54-60% by value of Albania's exports in the late 1980s (*SYA 1991*).   The forms of export were bitumen, coal, chromium ore and concentrate, ferrochrome, blister and cathodic copper, copper wire and cables, iron ore and concentrate, and iron-nickel ore.   There has also been exploration for zinc and gold.   Production of most of these materials (chrome, copper, lignite, petroleum) fell off sharply in the 1990s, apparently in response to liberalization.

According to a consultancy report of 1995 (HEMA CONSULT, 1995), Albania's known deposits of nickel (with a nickel content of a million tonnes) are the third largest of any country's (surpassed only by those of New Caledonia and the Dominican Republic). Nevertheless nickel production virtually ceased in 1992, when a Chinese-built nickel-cobalt refinery in Elbasan was closed, partly on environmental grounds.   The known remaining petroleum deposits, according to the same source, amount to about 500 million tonnes (roughly 3,500 million barrels). This, if correct, would mean that Albania had about 0.35% of the world's proven oil reserves, equal to about a fifth of the proven reserves of Western Europe, not by any means negligible.   At the rate of extraction of 1990 they would last about 500 years, but Albania was not self-sufficient in oil at that rate.   Duka (1992, p.33) gives the oil reserves as 300 million tonnes. However, a UN source makes the reserves a tiny fraction of what this would imply: 22 million tonnes (about 154 million barrels) of petroleum and liquid natural gas (UN, *Energy Statistics Yearbook 1994*, p.485).

For other minerals, Duka (1992, pp.30-33) cites reserves of 37 million tons for chrome (22 million of them 'industrial reserves' at the time she was writing, about 18 to 22 years' supply at the rates of extraction of the early 1990s); 60 million tons for copper (60 years' supply or more);   260 million tons of ferro-nickel (215 to 260 years' supply); and 750 million tons of coal-lignite (158 million 'industrial', which would be about 50 to 75 years' supply).

On the face of it, there are substantial exploitable mineral resources. There has been some not very spectacular involvement of foreign investors, but most of the privatization remains to be done.

Population Structure and Growth

Following the pro-birth policy of the communist regime, Albania in the early Hoxha period had one of the world's fast-growing populations, which rose from around 1 million after the Second World War to over 3 million at the end of the 1980s. The annual growth rate slowed from 2.86% in the 1950s to 2.01% between 1979 and 1989, but this was still about 5 times as high as the European average (Carter and Turnock, 1996, p.9).

Table 3.4 Demographic indicators in Albania, 1950-1992

Years	1950		1960		1969		1979		1989		1992[a]	
Life-expectancy	50	50	61	61	60	62	66	71	68	74	70	76
Change (%)			22	23	-2	2	9	13	4	5	3	3
Change (%)			22	23	-2	2	9	13	4	5	3	3
Infant mortality 0-12 months	142	143	90	102	112	111	74	73	45	40	34[b]	
Change (%)			-37	-29	24	9	-34	-34	-39	-45		
Child mortality 1-4 years	96	128	50	73	25	31	16	16	15	15	11[b]	
Change (%)			-48	-43	-50	-58	-36	-48	-6	-6		
Adult life-expectancy	54	58	58	62	55	60	58	63	58	64		
Change (%)			8	7	-6	-4	4	6	1	1		

a Institute of Statistics
b 1994 Ministry of Health Operative Statistics
Source: UN, *Human Development Report Albania 1995*

Migration to and from Albania was not permitted under the government at the time. The increase in the population growth rate from pre-War sprang from both an increase in gross fertility rates amongst women and an increase in life-expectancy. Fertility remained high at 2.9

children per woman in 1991 compared to a European average of 1.7. But it had fallen in Albania from around 6.5 children per woman in 1960.

As Table 3.4 indicates, there have also been significant increases in life-expectancy in Albania. These have mainly come about because of investments in primary-health-care and improvements in sanitation. Life-expectancy rose from 50.4 years for males and 49.5 years for females in 1950 to 70.0 years for males and 76.3 years for females in 1992. At the same time there were huge improvements in infant mortality, which fell from an average of 142.5 per thousand in 1950 to 42.5 in 1989.

The female/male ratio is almost unity at 1:1.02 (INSTAT, 1995a, p.3).

The political events that began in Albania in 1990 have had a significant effect on the demography of the country. For, in 1990, a period of mass emigration began, which was spurred by the poor living standards and made possible by the political and economic transition which was beginning. It was particularly evident in southern Albania where there is a Greek-speaking minority, some of whom (together with many others) moved over the border to Greece; others travelled to Italy. The Albanian population fell from 3,282,000 in 1990 to 3,190,000 in 1992 and further to 3,167,000 in 1993: the first reductions in the population for many years. Then, between 1993 and 1994 the population increased by 1%. This is high in comparison with the EU average of 0.3%, and is five times as high as the 0.2% increase in Italy and ten times as high as the increase of 0.1% in Greece. However, even that represents a big fall in population growth from the usual rates of increase that had prevailed since the end of the Second World War. In part the slowing, even as late as 1994, probably still reflects net emigration, the striking demographic phenomenon of the 1990s.

As has been made clear, a large proportion of the Albanian population live in rural areas. On one estimate, only 36.7 % of the population lived in urban areas in 1991, which is probably the lowest proportion in Europe (excluding the Caucasus), the next lowest being that of Moldova with 47.3% (UN, *Demographic Yearbook*,1994). At the census date in 1989 there was only one town with more than 100,000 inhabitants, and this was Tiranë with 238,100. Of the rest, only five---Durrës, Elbasan, Shkodër, Vlorë and Korçë---had populations of over 50,000 (*SYA 1991*).

Prior to 1990, some internal migration was permitted, but the process required permission from the authorities and so did not take place on a large scale. As a result, the spatial distribution of the population had not changed much for a number of years before 1990. The subsequent lifting of the restrictions on internal migration, however, is widely believed to have resulted in large rural-urban movement of the population. There is a lack of data to support this claim, and there are widely conflicting accounts of changes in the rural workforce including evidence in Agriculture Ministry figures of some reversal of the rural-urban movement after the privatization of farming was complete. Ministry figures would imply a net rise in agricultural employment of about 30,000 between end-1990 and end-1995: a fall to 1992 and 1993, followed by a quite large recovery to 1994. Institute of Statistics [INSTAT] figures, drawn from the Ministry, show an increase in agricultural employment between 1993 and 1994 of 159,698 or 27.0%, an increase equal to 15.2% of total employment in 1994. However, some estimates put the *net* shift of people in the five-year period after the start of the transition as being rather *from countryside to town*, to the extent of 6% of the population. It seems very likely in fact that there was considerable movement both ways, the removal of restrictions drawing many from country to town, and the loss of urban employment pushing others in the opposite direction, especially after farm privatization was largely complete. Certainly Tiranë has gained considerably in population, but it is not impossible that losses in other towns on balance have been comparable or even greater since 1989.

Within Albania there are marked regional differences in demographic variables, despite government by a socialist regime which advocated uniformity among the population. There is very little statistical evidence on the subject, but in general the mountainous and rural areas appear to have the most 'adverse' demographic indices (high fertility, mortality, and infant mortality). The northeast region of the country, and some eastern and south-central districts such as Librazhd, Gramsh, Skrapar, and Tepelenë, represent the least economically and socially developed regions that traditionally have had higher birth rates as well as higher levels of infant mortality.

Tiranë, and other districts dominated by large towns (Durrës, Korçë, Shkodër and Vlorë), have generally had a lower rate of natural population increase than the Albanian average. This is attributed to the influence of modernization and industrialization, as well as related factors such as housing shortages. The southern districts of Albania also recorded lower levels of natural increase, but there are no concrete indicators as to why this was. The new regional organization of 1992, changing the number of districts, has made it more difficult to compare territorial phenomena over different periods. Religious traditions and out-migration (which, although it was not permitted in the Communist period, may have taken place across the Greek border) possibly contributed to the south's lower-than-average population growth, all of which was recorded as low natural increase.

Territorial Structure and Administration

Before the Second World War, the territorial and administrative organization of Albania divided the country into 10 prefectures, 39 sub-prefectures, 116 communes and 2,711 localities. The prefectures, which were the equivalent of regions, were Berat, Durrës, Elbasan, Girokastër, Korçë, Kukës, Shkodër, Tiranë and Vlorë. Sub-prefectures were the equivalent of districts and comprised communes and localities. This structure was changed in 1947, when the system of prefectures was abandoned and replaced by 39 districts, which two years later, in 1949, were reduced to 26 districts; these included the capital city Tiranë with the special status of a city district.

Between 1953 and 1958 this territorial administrative structure changed again several times, culminating in a division of the country again into 26 districts. The city of Tiranë was a free administrative unit until it became part of the Tiranë district. By 1969, with a few minor changes, the system again comprised 26 districts, with 104 localities, 315 'united villages'· (units smaller than localities and created where there was a close economic relationship among villages), 56 cities and 2,545 villages. This structure remained more or less static, with the late addition of one further district, Kavajë, until the 1992 reforms.   A city or town (*qytet*), even one that was the administrative centre of a district, might have as few as 3,000 people at the time of the census in 1989 (*SYA 1991*, p.38).

Table 3.5 Territorial and administrative units of Albania, 1995

Prefecture name	Districts	Population
Berat	Berat, Kuçovë, Skrapar	221,413
Dibër	Dibër, Bulqizë, Mat	210,715
Durrës	Durrës, Krujë	222,843
Elbasan	Elbasan, Gramsh, Librazhd, Peqin	362,458
Fier	Fier, Lushnje, Mallakastër	381,798
Gjirokastër	Gjirokastër, Përmet, Tepelenë	139,891
Korcë	Korçë, Pogradec, Kolonjë, Devoll	306,241
Kukës	Kukës, Tropojë, Has	144,093
Lezhë	Lezhë, Mirditë, Kurbin (Laç)	165,687
Shkodër	Shkodër, Malësi e Madhe, Pukë	286,969
Tiranë	Tiranë, Kavajë	469,130
Vlorë	Vlorë, Sarandë, Delvinë	251,787
Total		**3,163,025**

Political and economic liberalization brought a new administrative structure in 1992.   A further nine districts (Kuçovë, Bulqizë, Peqin, Mallakastër, Devoll, Kurbin, Has, Delvinë, Malësi e Madhe) were created (to add to the existing 27 districts), generally in remote areas.   The 36 districts were grouped into 12 prefectures, each containing between 2 and 4 districts and most with a population of 200,000-300,000 (Table 3.5).

The prefecture is the organ of central government at regional level. Locally, there are three main popularly elected bodies: the district council, the municipality council (urban) and the commune council (rural), the two latter at the same levèl. District councils have various competencies and powers including the coordination of municipalities and communes; review of lower-council proposals; and approval of socio-economic development programmes, over which the district councils have the role of supervisory authorities. The power to raise local taxes and duties also lies with them, as does the establishment of economic institutions, and social, cultural and medical centres, catering for the needs of their districts.

Communes and municipalities are the smallest units in the Albanian local-government system, both having the same organisation and competencies. Municipalities cover cities and surrounding areas that are not parts of communes. Their functions include the collection of taxes and duties; the management of public properties; and the monitoring of employment, housing and environmental-protection measures in the areas which they cover. A commune normally contains several villages.

Every district, municipality and commune has its own local budget. Each budget consists of two parts: an independent part and a 'conditional' part. The independent part of the budget has revenues derived from local sources such as local taxes, service tariffs, and fines. The conditional (mandated) part is provided out of the central budget, and its use is pre-determined centrally, though it is administered by the local-government organs.

Under the system of central planning, local institutions had no authority with regard to economic planning and were purely executors of the centrally formulated policy. The decentralization represented by the new structure is a new direction for Albania.

The establishment of the new districts has helped reduce the previous size and development disparities between districts. However, some of the new peripheral districts created since the last reorganization (Has, Kurbin, Peqin, Kuçovë, Mallakastër, Delvinë, Devoll, Malësi e Madhe), as well as some that already existed, do not have the material and human resources necessary for their effective organisation and administration. One suggestion is a reduction in the number of districts from 36 to 16, defined to reflect the geographic, economic, traditional, political and social situation.

Some of the prefectures legitimated in 1992 were still (in 1997) not functioning, even though they were designed to play an important role in the administration of the territories that they covered. It has been suggested that a reduction of the number of prefectures from 12 to 7 or 8, together with the reduction of the number of districts to 16, might be accompanied by a transfer of some government competencies to local administration, which would increase the independence of the new administrative units.

Distribution of Employment, Industry and Foreign Investment

In 1995, the employed workforce was 1.156 million. The agricultural sector was the largest for employment, with 760,000 people recorded in Table 3.6 as employed in it---66% of the employed population. (There are inevitably definitional questions over which of the working-age adults living on family farms are presumed to be 'employed'. The Albanian definition seems to have been highly inclusive.) The sector providing the greatest opportunity for new jobs in 1995 was trade, where employment between 1994 and 1995 increased apparently by 57.8%. The construction industry also increased employment significantly, rising by 16.7% between 1994 and 1995.

Table 3.6   Employment by sector [industries], 1994-1995

Activity	1994	1995
Agriculture	758,782	760,205
Fishing	20,830	17,766
Extraction industries	20,480	20,982
Manufacturing	81,357	64,811
Electric energy and water	9,044	9,100
Construction	18,235	21,286
Trade	32,286	50,961
Hotel/restaurant	10,067	10,882
Transport	27,563	29,926
Education	54,715	53,410
Health	32,247	25,817
Other	95,940	89,300
Total	1,163,540	1,156,441

Source: UN, *Human Development Report Albania 1996*, p.52

Job losses occurred mainly in the low-paid state sector. Manufacturing job losses amounted to 16,500 (20%) as state enterprises continued to close down sections, while the private sector in manufacturing was still taking its first steps.

The labour force in Albania has increased at a rapid pace since the war. This increase matched the large increase in population. Between 1969 and 1994 the labour force rose by over 700,000 (INSTAT,1995a), in spite of losses through emigration at the end of this period. Enterprises and agricultural co-operatives under the old regime were under obligation to do their part in achieving a full-employment economy. The result was a labour-intensive economy which, coupled with a lack of modernization and technological development, helped to keep the labour force in full-employment.

The Albanian economy, until the end of 1990, had two main sectors of employment: the public sector, which was based mainly in urban centres, and a cooperative sector that was concentrated in rural areas. In 1987, according to one set of figures, the main source of employment was agriculture, which employed 52% of the working population. The next largest sector of employment was industry with 22.9%. (Other sources give a larger proportion to industry.)

The breakdown for the whole country in 1992 and 1995, in comparison to the situation in 1989, is shown in Table 3.7, the most noticeable development being the huge decrease in public-sector employment, a direct result of the changing political structure.

Table 3.7 Employment by sector [ownership], 1989-1995 (000s)

	1989	1992	1995
Total employment	1,440	1,095	1,154
State-sector employment	889	615	276
Cooperative employment	551	420	0
Private agricultural sector	0	0	750
Private non-agricultural sector	0	60	128

Source: INSTAT, *Albania Human Development Report 1996*, p.49

The fact that Albania has one of the highest proportions of rural population in Europe is broadly reflected in the pattern of employment. In all of the districts, with the exception of Kuçovë and Tiranë, the proportion of the working population employed in the private agricultural sector has recently been greater than in the public and private non-agricultural sector. The highest proportions of agricultural employment in 1994 were in Devoll and Dibër with 82% and 85%. The more urbanized regions have a smaller agricultural sector and a larger public sector, most noticeably Tiranë with a public-sector-employment level of 46% and Kuçovë with 47%. Peripheral regions such as Malësi e Madhe, Dibër and Devoll tend to have the largest proportions of employment in the agricultural sector and the least in the non-agricultural private sector.

Industrial production is concentrated in certain districts. Tiranë is the main industrial centre, producing around one sixth of all industrial output. The three largest industrial centres, Tiranë, Durrës and Elbasan, together account for around 40% of industrial production. Primary and extractive industries also tend to be regionally concentrated. Oil extraction and processing takes place mainly in the south and southwest of the central region; engineering, timber and paper production, in the central area; and coal/lignite extraction around Tiranë and in the centre-south of the country. Metal extraction and processing is based in the north-east and south-east of Albania. Light industry and the foodstuffs industry have been distributed throughout Albanian territory, their distribution based to some extent in the past on political and ideological criteria but no doubt also reflecting the distribution of the Albanian population which has constituted most of their market.

During Albania's period as a command economy, all investments were state-controlled, and, until 1978, all long-term capital inflow came from other communist countries. On the break with China in 1978, all entry of foreign capital into Albania was halted. Thereafter, it was only in 1992, when the country became relatively stable politically, that significant foreign investment started to arrive.

According to the *Reporter of Economic Enterprises 1991-1995*, in late-1995 there were 890 wholly-foreign-owned firms in Albania. There were also a number of joint ventures between Albanian and foreign firms, mainly from Italy and Greece. It has been estimated that one half of all joint ventures were with Italian companies, while one fifth of joint ventures were with Greek partners. Italian foreign investments are concentrated in Tiranë, Durrës and Vlorë, whilst Greek investments are high in Korcë and Gjirokastër. (See chapter 14 for further details.)

So, as is to be expected, foreign investment is not uniformly distributed across Albania. The districts receiving the highest levels of foreign investment are Tiranë, Shkodër, Elbasan, Korçë and Durrës. Tiranë has the best infrastructure. It also has the biggest domestic market, because it is wealthier than other districts and has a greater concentration of population. Durrës and Korçë are attractive for Italian and Greek investors respectively because of their proximity to these countries and their traditions of trade relationships.

Another factor which attracts foreign investors to particular areas is the specialization of some districts, inherited from the time of the planned economy. Shkodër, for example, produced ready-made clothes and shoes, a factor which is now attracting foreign investors in these fields into Shkodër. Similarly, Elbasan has drawn foreign investment in timber, and Bulqizë in mining. Smaller and more rural districts with poorer infrastructure, such as (according to Table 3.8) Dibër, Has, Kolonjë, Krujë, Kuçovë, Mat, Pukë and Tropojë, have apparently received no foreign investment.

State of the Physical Environment

Current environmental problems evident in Albania include soil erosion; soil and water contamination mainly from chemicals used in agriculture; and pollution as a result of toxic gas (*PIP*, March 1996, 41). As has been typical in former-Communist countries, serious environmental degradation has been one of the consequences of the economic policies which placed emphasis on output with little regard to the effects on the environment of the methods of production. Elbasan has been especially affected, with much of the vegetation around it destroyed. Vlorë, with its PVC factory, has also been seriously degraded, as has Pogradec.

The urban centres, particularly Tiranë, Shkodër and Korçë, have serious levels of atmospheric pollution that are due to heavy concentrations of industry. The types of industries which have contributed to environmental degradation in these centres include an oil- and lignite-burning power station in Tiranë and a copper-wire factory at Shkodër, and especially the mineral-concentration plants in the north-eastern area. Other sources of contamination have come from the cement industry, which emits cement dust out of unfiltered chimneys. There are four such plants in Albania, but operations have stopped for periods in all four. The chemical industry---which produced mainly soda, PVC, nitrogenous and phosphate fertilisers, pesticides, pigments and paint---generally used old Chinese and Albanian equipment and was one of the contributors to pollution.

Off the coast, marine pollution, originating from Italy, Greece, and former-Yugoslavia, is beginning to affect the marine environment (Carter and Turnock, 1996). Table 3.10 shows areas most affected by pollution.

Economic circumstances in Albania before the transition period created conditions for households which were favourable to the environment. Albania became economically isolated in 1978 when its alliance with China came to an end. This led to a need for self-reliance because Albania no longer received any assistance from other countries. One result was that material waste was kept to a minimum as low consumption and the 'shortage economy' made people more aware of the necessity of re-using whatever was possible. Although this was not intentionally an environmental policy, it nevertheless kept at bay some forms of environmental harm which occur in other countries through high levels of waste and low levels of recycling.

Transport Infrastructure

Since 1990 there have been considerable increases in both goods and passenger traffic. The road, air and sea sectors have dealt with most of this increase, while the railways, which are particularly in need of investment, have lost out. In general, all of the transport sectors require a great deal of

Table 3.8 Distribution of private enterprises, local and foreign*, end-1995

Districts	Total	Domestic firms	Joint-ventures	Foreign firms
Berat	291	267	22	2
Bulqizë	30	28	1	1
Delvinë	34	28	4	2
Devoll	11	6	5	-
Dibër	48	48	-	-
Durrës	581	419	100	62
Elbasan	224	203	16	5
Fier	315	272	40	3
Gramsh	57	57	-	-
Gjirokastër	257	152	99	6
Has	16	16	-	-
Kavajë	110	97	10	3
Kolonjë	25	25	-	-
Korçë	275	176	76	23
Krujë·	94	92	-	2-
Kuçovë	63	63	-	-
Kukës	126	124	2	-
Kurbin	n.a	n.a.	n.a.	n.a.
Lezhë	144	135	8	1
Librazhd	80	75	2	3
Lushnje	155	138	16	1
Malësi e Madhe	155	154	1	-
Mallakastër	14	11	3	-
Mat	96	96	-	-
Mirditë	15	13	2	-
Peqin	16	14	1	1
Përmet	92	91	1	-
Pogradec	79	67	11	1
Pukë	85	85	-	-
Sarandë	263	224	36	3
Skrapar	56	53	3	-
Shkodër	805	733	50	22
Tepelenë	81	78	3	-
Tiranë	4202	2495	964	743
Tropojë	92	92	-	-
Vlorë	414	360	50	4
Total	**9500**	**7078**	**1532**	**890**

*   The Albanian partner in a joint-venture is often the Albanian government.
Note that, though the numbers of foreign and joint-venture firms given here fit with details in chapter 14, the implied number of locally-owned firms is much smaller than that cited in chapter 6.

Source: INSTAT, *Reporter of Economic Enterprises 1991-1995*, July 1996

investment, not only to be able to cope with further forecast increases in use, but also to compensate for years of under-investment.

Albania has 18,000 km of road, 7,650 of which is national roads and 1,000 km local roads. The most important axes in the road network are:

- Han-i-Hoti / Shkodër / Lezhë / Tiranë / Durrës, which runs from the border with Montenegro down the western coast of the country
- Qafë-Morinë / Kukës / Fushë-Arrëz / Pukë / Shkodër, which cuts across the northern part of Albania from the border with Serbia to the west coast

- Durrës / Kavajë / Tepelenë / Gjirokastër / Sarandë, which runs from the central coastal area down to the border with Greece
- Tiranë / Elbasan / Progradec / Qafë-Thanë which runs from the east to west, up to the Macedonian border.

The highest levels of road density are in the coastal and lowland areas of Albania. The districts with the highest densities of road are Shkodër, Lezhë, Durrës, Elbasan, Tiranë, Lushnje, Fier and Vlorë, which hav an average density of 0.14 km/km^2 , whilst the regions of Dibër, Tropojë, Kukës, Mirditë, Kolonjë, Përmet and Skrapar have an average road density of only 0.07 km/km^2. However, even those districts with higher road densities are likely to face future problems dealing with traffic levels because of the combination of poor quality of roads and increase in road usage.

The quality of the road network is very poor. However, there are plans for improvement to make the road system compatible with the development of the market economy. The priorities involve mainly upgrading work, the principal focus being on the main corridor roads. Among those already planned is the upgrading of the west-east Durrës / Tiranë road. There are also plans for work on roads which are thought to be particularly attractive for the tourist trade.

The railway network in Albania covers 677km of track. Of these, 447km are main lines and 230km are secondary and branch lines. The main lines run north-south (Durrës / Han-i-Hoti) and east-west (Durrës / Pogradec). The railway is in extremely poor condition. In some parts, train speeds have been reduced to 30-50 km/h by the poor state of the wood ties. The World Bank has been helping Albania to make plans for the future development of the railway system. Options that have been considered range from developing the service to its complete closure (*PIP*, March 1996, 55). However, the less extreme option being considered in late 1996 was operating it as a commercial railway, which would involve reducing the number of passenger services.

Rinas, the airport near Tiranë, is the only civil-aviation airport in Albania. It was built in 1958, and has suffered from a lack of investment. Its infrastructure, facilities and equipment are all outdated. Since its creation, very little reconstruction has taken place. As a result of its lack of modernization, planes using it are limited to 150 tonnes. With increasing traffic, it may be necessary to up-grade and possibly expand the civil-aviation infrastructure. The Ministry of Defence has a further 10 small airport runways throughout Albania, four of which have the potential to be used as civilian airports.

Table 3.9   Environmental 'hot-spot' areas by district

District	Environ-mental damage (1)	Soil erosion (2)	Chem'l contam-ination (3)	Industr'l pollution (4)	Oil pollution (5)	Toxic gases (6)	Loss of diversif-ication (7)
Berat	C	**	**	**	**	*	*
Bulqizë	C	*	*	**	*		
Delvinë	M	*	*	*			
Devoll	M	*	*	*			
Dibër	S	*	**	*	*		
Durrës	C	***	***	**	*	**	*
Elbasan	C	***	***	***	**	***	**
Fier	C	***	***	***	**	***	**
Gramsh	C	**	*	*			
Gjirokastër	M	*	*	*			*
Has	M	*	*		*		
Kavajë	C	**	***	**	*	**	*
Kolonjë	M	*	*	*			
Korçë	C	*	**	**	*	**	*
Krujë	C	*	**	*		**	*
Kuçovë	C	***	*	**	*	**	*
Kukës	C	*	*	*	*	***	**
Kurbin	C	*	**	**	**	***	**
Lezhë	C	*	**	*		**	*
Librazhd	C	**	*	*	*	*	*
Lushnje	C	***	***				*
Mal. e Madhe	M	*	*				
Mallakastër	C	**	*	*	**	**	*
Mat	C	*	*	*	*		
Mirditë	C	*	*	**	*	**	*
Peqin	S	***	**	*			*
Përmet	S	***	**	*			*
Pogradec	S	*	**	*	*		*
Pukë	S	*	*	*	*		*
Sarandë	S	*	**	*	*		*
Shkodër	C	**	***	**	*	**	
Skrapar	M	*	*	*			
Tepelenë	C	**	*	*			*
Tiranë	C	***	***	**	*	**	
Tropojë	M	*	*	*			
Vlorë	C	***	***	**	*	**	*

Key: (1)   Environmental damage level: M = Moderate; S = significant; C = critical
  (2)   Soil erosion
  (3)   Contamination from agricultural chemicals
  (4)   Surface water pollution from industrial discharges and domestic waste
  (5)   Contamination of soil, groundwater and surface waters from mines, oil and gas fields
  (6)   Emission of toxic gases
  (7)   Loss of biodiversity
   *   moderate
   **   significant
   *** critical

Source: Bachtler and Downes, 1994

A programme has already been devised to develop civil aviation. Repairs to runways and upgrading of airport equipment form part of the plans. The programme includes funding from Germany. The development of further airports is an option under consideration.

The main maritime ports in Albania are Durrës, Vlorë, Sarandë and Shëngjin, the largest of these being Durrës, which handles around 85% of maritime traffic.   In 1994, with financing from the Kuwait Fund, redevelopment of the port of Durrës began, involving the installation of modern equipment and infrastructure repairs.

The Albanian People and State

Who are the Albanian people?   They are identified first of all by their language.   Though a member of the Indoeuropean family, the Albanian language has no close surviving relations, with no specially strong links to the Greek, Slavonic and Romance languages that surround it.   It is generally believed to be descended from the Illyrian language of Roman times.   'Albania' and words related to it go back apparently to the second century AD, and Albanians themselves at one time used them, but since the fifteenth century they have called the language *shqip*, the people *shqiptarët* (the Albanians), and the land *Shqipëri* (Zymberi, 1991, p.1).   *Shqiponjë* means an eagle.

If we regard all native-speakers of Albanian as constituting the Albanian nation, then nearly half of that nation lives beyond the boundaries of the Albanian state, most notably the roughly two million Albanians who form the overwhelming majority of the population of Kosovo, politically a part (until 1989 an autonomous part) of Serbia.   A further 400,000 or so form about a fifth of the people of FYR Macedonia (23% according to a census, but some allege that the numbers are greater).   There are smaller groups who are long-standing residents of Greece and Montenegro; and then there are the emigrants of the 1990s, mainly in Greece and Italy, maybe another 400,000.   Within the boundaries of Albania there are Greek-speaking and Slav-Macedonian-speaking minorities: in 1989 about 59,000 and 5,000 respectively, altogether about 2% of the population, according to the official figures (*SYA 1991*), but it is commonly believed that the Greek minority is very much greater, perhaps 400,000.   There are small numbers of others, such as Serb speakers.   As with much of the Balkans, language and political divisions do not correspond.   The domestic Greek minority has had what is in effect its own political party, whose name declares its dedication to human rights, but voting has been by no means entirely along ethnic lines.   Such friction as there is over the Greek minority has been largely a result of unhelpful statements from both governments.   By 1995, they had both come to take a more moderate approach, with the Greek government accepting that there were armed dissidents aiming to disrupt the south of Albania with the idea of having it secede to Greece, and the Albanian government committing itself more explicitly to minority rights.   There is also a partly assimilated Romany minority not separately counted officially, whom the Hoxha regime did its best to render sedentary.

Two main dialects of Albanian are described---Tosk traditionally said to be spoken to the south of the Shkumbin River (which runs past Elbasan), and Gheg to the north, including Kosovo.   The differences between the two are very largely in vowel pronunciations, which, because Albanian spelling is strongly phonetic, are fairly clearly represented in writing.   In fact there seems to be more like a gradation of forms of speech than a sharp division between two homogeneous dialects.   Though the capital lies well to the north of the traditional dividing line between Gheg and Tosk, the official literary language, standardized by the early 1970s after a long process of negotiation in which the Kosovars were fully involved, has much more in it of Tosk than of Gheg.   (See Zymberi, 1991, pp.3, 235-236.)

Though there were periods in which various Albanian groups fought side by side, there had never been what could be called an Albanian state before the twentieth century.   The Albanians were under the Roman Empire for five centuries, under the Byzantine thereafter, with links from time to time with Venice; and eventually for more than five centuries under varying degrees of control from the Ottoman Turks.   If they are to be identified with the Illyrians, they provided four Roman Emperors, including the very notable Diocletian; and they also gave birth to twenty-five Ottoman Grand Viziers, and a Pope.   It seems, however, that, like other mountain peoples, they often operated in semi-independent clans and lordships, at least between the high point of the Roman Empire and the centuries of firmly established Ottoman rule.   The Empire that claimed to be in charge might have rather tenuous control---as in neighbouring Montenegro, and in the Scottish Highlands until the mid-eighteenth century.   Notably it was an Albanian with a Turkish official title who became a hero of his nation and of Christendom for his twenty-five years of resistance to the Turks in the middle of the fifteenth century, a period covering the fall of Constantinople: the name Skënderbej (Skanderbeg) by which Gjergj Kastrioti is usually known is a corruption of his Turkish designation, Iskander Bey. Another highly independent Albanian with a Turkish title was Ali Pasha, at one time the self-made tyrant of much of the Balkan Peninsula.   Through the centuries, under varying intensities of foreign rule, the Albanians retained a distinctive tradition, symbolized by the code of law and behaviour associated with the name of the fifteenth-century lord, Lekë Dukagjini.

By religious heritage, present-day Albanians are roughly 65-70% Muslim, somewhat over 20% Orthodox Christian (mainly in the south), and 10% Catholic Christian (mainly in the north).   Yet there is no recent history of persecution by any one of these religious groups of another, and consequently none of the inflammable suspicion that characterizes relationships between the religious traditions among the South Slavs. Foreign journalists tend to make much of divisions between north and south or between Gheg and Tosk. Albanians recognize the differences and admit that they can sometimes have political relevance, with a tendency of northerners to think of themselves as neglected and of power as being concentrated in the south (though in fact of the country's three strong men in the present century two, Zog and Berisha, came from the north-centre and north). But the divisions seem to be rather complicating factors than of primary political importance.

The Albanian state was created after the First Balkan War by a declaration of Albanians at Vlorë on the 28th November 1912. It was recognized by the powers the following year, but they awarded Kosovo to Serbia. Albania's independence was blatantly precarious at various points between then and the 5th April 1939, when Italy invaded. Enver Hoxha's fear of the outside world, though in retrospect exaggerated, was perhaps understandable.

But now there is no retreat. Engagement with the world has been chosen. That being so, a question that inevitably concerns the Albanian state and the Albanian people is that of Kosovo. The past position, apart from being morally repugnant, has proved to be simply not sustainable politically. To recognize this does not depend on romantic notions of a Greater Albania. The two main branches of the Albanian people may well work out their futures under different flags provided each has its autonomy and they can communicate as equals. A war over Kosovo is in no one's interest. But internal war at the time of writing has already begun. There are risks for Albania both in being provocative and in doing nothing. Serbians' historical fixations are political facts. But so is the need for Kosovars to be able to live their life with dignity. All possible ways have to be explored of reconciling these conflicting demands. The Albanian state, which has been the patient for much of the 1990s, will have to play a part as the therapist. Indeed the approach for the most part of Berisha when he was in power, and later of Nano, has been to intercede tactfully for Kosovo's autonomy without giving prominence to any desire to join it to the Republic of Albania.

Summary

The population of Albania forms little more than half of the Albanian people, inheritors of a unique language and tradition, able eighty-five or so years ago, after two millennia of fitful involvement with the empires of the region, to form a small and precarious state.

Albania's population density is similar to that of France in spite of having 55% to 66% of the workforce in agriculture by contrast with France's 5%. Hence the farming households of the country have been extremely densely settled---and on land of which much is mountain and only a smallish proportion arable. Such land as *is* available for cultivation, despite the very large numbers available to work each hectare of it, has been unproductive even by the standards of Communist Central Europe. As a result farm families in the 1990s have been living largely by eating what they grow themselves and on remittances and state benefits, and only to a minor extent from sale of produce.

Albania's mineral resources are by no means negligible and provided more than half the value of its exports in the 1980s, but extraction of almost all has fallen sharply during the 1990s.

The population grew very fast by European standards in the post-War period, tripling in size over forty-five years, though with some retardation in the 1980s, and the resident population fell, partly because of emigration, in the early 1990s. It was about three times as large in 1990 as in 1945. Life expectancy rose, and infant mortality fell, considerably under Hoxha's rule, to approach affluent-country levels. Demographic patterns vary across the country, with the poorest and most remote areas tending to have higher fertility and mortality and infant-death rates, and the larger towns lower rates of natural increase.

There is a three-tier system of local administration with representative institutions at the two lowest levels. The reorganization in 1992 was designed to give genuine local autonomy at these levels. It also increased the numbers of entities in the two highest layers; but there are doubts about whether the new prefectures (the highest level) and districts (the middle level) have the resources to function effectively.

Because of the low degree of urbanization, and possibly also because of deliberate location of industry under the old regime, population is more evenly distributed across regions than in many European countries. As a legacy of the planned economy there is a fairly high degree of imposed specialization by region in the various branches of secondary industry, and since the opening of the economy foreign investment in these branches has tended to go to where they are already established.

Albania's low level of industrial development might be expected to preserve it from the more industrially-generated forms of pollution; yet, as in other ex-Communist countries, such industry as there is has tended to work overtime at producing noxious emissions, and indeed there have been problems with toxic gases. However, urban-industrial pollution, especially after the collapse of so much heavy industry, falls far short of what is experienced in the more industrialized ex-Communist countries. Albania has also suffered soil-erosion (probably a by-product of state and collective agriculture and of some specific policies), soil and water contamination from chemical fertilizers, and marine pollution (largely by courtesy of its Adriatic-Ionian neighbours).

Much greater demand has been put on transport since the change of regime, and infrastructure of road, rail, air and sea is lagging. The railways are in such a poor state that doubts arise whether they should be continued.

Albania has a substantial Greek, and a much smaller Slav, minority. These groups give rise to very little friction when governments do not generate it.   There is a Romany minority, partly assimilated.   Among themselves the ethnic-Albanians of Albania have differences of religious tradition, of dialect, and (subjectively at least) of regional levels of education and influence.   The last of these may have some political importance, but only as a complicating factor in other issues.   There are few *inherited* causes of conflict among cultural sub-groups of the population.

However, the Albanian state is inevitably involved, whether it is active or passive, in the affairs of the other main branch of the Albanian people, across its northeastern border in Kosovo.   The very real possibility that lethal conflict there will continue and extend unless there are radical changes must be a matter of great concern for the rest of the world but especially for the residents of Albania.   Beside all its domestic burdens, the Albanian state is faced with the external task of seeking what is the only means of avoiding such conflict, which is to achieve effective and dignified autonomy for the people of Kosovo.   At the time that this book goes to press, a major tragedy in Kosovo is under way.

4 Politics, 1990-96

'Transition' in Central Europe has been taken to entail not only movement toward a market economy but also the establishment of an open, democratic, pluralist and law-governed society.   The two do not necessarily go together, though historically there has been some association between them.

It has sometimes been argued that illiberal regimes have been able to make the market work more efficiently by keeping the masses in order and resisting demands for over-regulation of wages and conditions that might distort the employment of labour.   Yet there is also a case for saying that open traffic in information and opinion is an important safeguard against official corruption and plunder, official negligence and ignorance, the abuse of market-power, and various forms of financial imprudence and chicanery. So, beside desiring an open and law-governed society for its own sake, we may also value it as helping to ensure that the market works effectively to achieve the objectives expected of it.

There is a further point to be made in favour of the open society for today's Central European nations.   They are now tending to seek safeguards for their continuity and integrity not in maintaining fully independent states that cling to traditional concepts of sovereignty but in the interdependence entailed by the network of European institutions. Here national security is sought through openness rather than secrecy and there is a balance between autonomy and the acceptance of common rules. (See, for analysis on which this statement is partly based, Cooper, 1996.) Most of them rightly consider that the safest place to be, and on the whole the most favourable economically, is in the heart of the system: to be members not only of the OSCE and the Council of Europe but also of NATO and the European Union.   But *de facto* there are conditions for such full membership, among which in very broad terms is democratic openness and the rule of law.

For these reasons the extent to which Albania became an open, law-governed society in the 1990s is quite possibly relevant to its economic performance and prospects; and it is of interest to explore the bearing of any deficiencies that the country may have had in this respect either on its economic success or on the setback of 1997.

Also of interest is the political process by which the country became committed to 'transition'. There is variation among the Communist countries in the extent to which the initiative for change came from above or from below---from the higher circles of government and the ruling party or from expressions of public discontent. With the earlier attempts at radically changing the Communist system---in Hungary and Poland, 1956, and Czechoslovakia, 1968---there had been interplay between reformers above and radical aspirations among the populace below. Poland's 1970 and 1980 movements had been more exclusively from below. But, before the decisive events of November-December 1989, the Soviet Union, Poland and Hungary had all three launched into cautious moves toward pluralism, engineered in each case from above. But the first moves in East Germany, Czechoslovakia, Bulgaria and Romania were primarily from below, certainly not from the highest levels of power. Gorbachov had signalled to the satellites the end of what was called the Brezhnev Doctrine: the Soviet government's claim to a right to interfere in their affairs if they moved away from the lines it had laid down. Once the East German regime had given way in early November, without Soviet interference, to free movement between East and West Germany, revolutions from below were allowed their head in Czechoslovakia and Bulgaria. Finally, Romania, less of a pure satellite than the others, went down to a popular movement on to which even second-level leaders had jumped.

Albania's starting-point was different. It was not, and had never been, a satellite. Its Communist regime did not depend on outside backers. That fact, and other elements of its political history, perhaps help explain why its course was different from that of all the rest.

Constitutional Legacy to the Albania of the 1990s

The first twelve years of the life of the Albanian state, from late 1912 to early 1925, were uncertain and unstable. A foreign nonentity was imposed by the powers as king and fled after a few months. Then came the First World War, in which Albania was a battleground and the infant state was almost inevitably associated with the Central Powers Those that came nearest to being its protectors turned out to be on the losing side. Yet it survived Versailles. Without much reliance on popular democracy, the early 1920s were a time of jockeying, principally between two factions: a more liberal one led by Fan Noli and a more traditionalist feudal one led by Ahmet Zogu. Zogu was elected as President of the Parliamentary Republic proclaimed in January 1925, and thereafter ruled, from September 1928 as King, until Mussolini's invasion of April 1939.

There followed nearly six years of Italian and German occupation, challenged by three (competing) resistance groups: the supporters of Zog; *Balli Kombëtar* ('the national front'); and the Communist Partisans (*Partizanët*). That the occupying powers were expelled by November 1944 depended in part on events in the rest of the world, but the victory of Enver

Hoxha's Partisans over the other two was their own work and owed little to outside help other than from the Yugoslav Partisans, at that time their allies.   So, like the Communists in Yugoslavia, but unlike those elsewhere in Central Europe, Hoxha's team had no need to be Stalin's satellites. Both Yugoslavia and Albania broke with the Soviet Union---Yugoslavia in 1948, Albania finally in 1961---but they did so on different grounds and remained ideologically at opposite extremes.   From 1948 Hoxha's government expressed intense hostility and fear toward that of Tito, the Albanian Partisans' former mentor.

Twelve years of uncertainty, fourteen of fairly autocratic rule by Zog, and five to six years of fascist occupation, were followed by forty-five of home-grown totalitarianism of the most extreme kind, with an all-intrusive party, suppression of most forms of individual initiative save in accord with party direction, and an adulated and increasingly paranoiac leader who imprisoned or killed many of his closest comrades and lieutenants and gave privileges to his family and those few others in special favour. Even after Hoxha's death in 1985, Ramiz Alia continued his system with only minor relaxation until 1990.

So, in contrast to Czechoslovakia or Hungary, there was in 1990 virtually no living memory of 'normal' constitutional politics.   Hungary had a constitutional tradition that went back, at least interruptedly, to the Dual Monarchy Compromise of 1867, and in 1990 its political parties revived with echoes of the pattern before the start of Communist rule more than forty years earlier.   Czechoslovakia had had its inter-War republic and it too had had a brief time of constitutional rule after 1945.   Albania had virtually no comparable memories.   In this respect it may not have been unique, but it was toward the extreme end of the present Central European transitional economies.

Six Periods

There are several turning-points that can be used to break up the seven years from the start of 1990 to the end of 1996.   We shall divide it into six highly unequal periods.

The first stage lasts from the beginning of 1990, just after the wholesale collapse of the satellite regimes, until the start of the riots of December, a period in which the economy was declining, unrest was bubbling up, the need for reform of some sort was dawning, but only rather tentative change was made.

The second lasts from the legalization of independent parties during the December 1990 demonstrations until the election at the end of March 1991, a time of emerging hardship and serious uncertainty, during which, in response to mass attempts at emigration and much unrest, there was a sense of serious crisis but no clear direction.

The third stage is that between the election of March 1991 and the election of March 1992, when a number of reforms were started under one or other of the three governments of the period, while unrest continued and living conditions grew rapidly worse to reach what was probably their nadir in the 1991-92 winter.

The fourth interval covers the first fifteen months or so of Democratic Party rule until mid-1993, when there was a clearer direction and rapid comprehensive action in all the main aspects of transition; unrest had died down; it came to seem likely that economically the corner had been turned; and by the end of the period a number of the technically easier (and, as it turned out, politically and economically most rewarding) aspects of the reform were well under way.

The fifth we count from about the time of the arrest of Fatos Nano in July 1993 until shortly before the election of May 1996, when the political focus of the party in power had clearly changed from that of joining forces with others in quelling popular dissatisfaction to one of weakening its opponents; and there was at the same time continuous rapid growth and increasing price-stability.

The sixth runs from May to December 1996, when, amid the euphoria created by the 'funds', the government party had clearly shown its determination to stay in power by whatever means were necessary, and it appeared not to be seriously challenged.

In the background to these events of strictly domestic politics, the government was ending Albania's unique isolation by establishing relations with other countries and with the international organizations. In the first few years it had repeatedly to negotiate for economic aid. It was also responding to frequent disputes with its three land-neighbours, especially Greece, with whom there were the two issues of the Greek minority (and alleged terrorist movement) and Albanian migrants. Albanian-Greek relations had greatly relaxed by the time of the visit of the Greek Foreign Minister in March 1995 (*Keesing*, 40466) and on the whole continued to improve.

Signs of Unrest and Piecemeal Reforms, January to December 1990

Since Albania, like Yugoslavia, was not part of the Soviet bloc and owed nothing to it, it is perhaps not surprising that its ruling party did not, like the others of Central Europe, give up its exclusive claims in the last months of 1989. Yet Albanians were well aware from television of what had been happening then, and so were their rulers. So far from being the wave of the future, Stalin's legacy readily came to seem more like a thing of the past.

Demonstrations in the Shkodër area occurred from late December 1989. There were foreign reports that they were put down very brutally, but no official account (*Keesing*, 37195-6). Then on the 1st July 1990 there were 'unprecedented anti-government street demonstrations in Tirana' which were, according to the report, 'brutally broken up by the security forces' (*Keesing*, 37618-9). Finally and critically, starting on the 9th December 1990 in Tirana, mass protests spread to Shkodër, Durrës, Elbasan and all the main cities. The demands were an end to one-party rule, multiparty elections, and changes in the economic structure (*Keesing*, 37924). A week after the start of the protests, troops with tanks were sent into Tirana to restore order. Of the demonstrators 157 were convicted, and they were given sentences of up to 20 years.

But there were also positive responses on the part of the authorities. In spite of the suppression of these demonstrations, a corner had been turned. What happened in December 1990 would have been unthinkable a few years earlier. At least the demonstrators were not simply mown down. Opposition, though risky, was now possible. The spell was broken and the rules had changed. The public had witnessed what the crowds had accomplished in Prague and elsewhere. The leaders had seen what had happened to the Ceaucescus.

But, once the reins are loosened, the old disciplines no longer hold to keep people doing what they are told and to stop them taking what they want. A system that depends on obedience to central commands and the moral authority of the state, and links self-interest to productive activity only through the rewards and penalties that the hierarchy of government and party can give, breaks down once the populace no longer believes in the power of the government and party, or accepts their moral authority. Output had already fallen fairly drastically in 1990. It was to fall much further in 1991.

What of reforms before the events of December 1990? As early as 25th January 1990, Ramiz Alia, the First Secretary of the Party and head of state, had announced modest changes which in the context were nevertheless quite startling: there would be more popular election of officials; more reliance on incentives and less central planning; less subsidies; free sale of agricultural surpluses; and permission to people to build their own houses (*Keesing*, 37195-6).

Early in May 1990, the People's Assembly approved changes to the penal code; an end to the ban on religious propaganda; the citizen's right to a passport; increased autonomy for enterprises; an end to the prohibition of seeking foreign capital or investment; and a provision that unauthorized emigration or agitation against the state should no longer carry the death penalty (*Keesing*, 37463). On the 12th July it was announced that private enterprise would be allowed in services and handicrafts, provided there were no paid employees; and on the 31st July the Presidium of the Assembly approved a decree allowing demonstrations by citizens in public places and another decree allowing foreign investors to repatriate profits and to hold foreign-currency accounts (*Keesing*, 37618-9).

Apart perhaps from explicitly allowing demonstrations, the reforms so far had probably not gone beyond what some other Communist states had permitted fairly routinely years or decades earlier. It was not till the 16th November 1990 that the first public religious service since 1967 was held: an open-air Mass at Shkodër attended by thousands. (The Et'hem Bey Mosque in central Tirana held its first service the following January.) Early in November Alia called for a change in the Constitution to 'redefine' the leading role of the Party and to allow religious freedom; and on the 14th the Assembly approved a draft electoral law providing for secret ballot and the possibility of independent candidates to stand against those of the Party (*Keesing*, 37864, 37972-3).

In April 1990, Alia had announced Albania's readiness to restore diplomatic links with the USSR, the USA and EC countries, and also to join the CSCE, to which virtually all of the rest of Europe, as well as North America, belonged. Ambassadors were exchanged with the Soviet Union in July. In October, Albania entered the IMF and began negotiations to join the World Bank (*Keesing*, 37385, 37618-9, 38462).

This was where reform stood when the mass protests mentioned above began in Tirana on the 9th December.

Crisis and Lack of Direction, December 1990 to March 1991

On 11th December 1990, two days after the start of the Tirana protests, the public was told that independent political *parties* would be allowed, and the next day, a week before the Assembly had passed the necessary law to permit it, formation of the Democratic Party of Albania (*Partia Demokratike e Shqiperisë*, DPA, PDS) was announced. On the 11th there was also a purge of hardliners from the Politburo, and on the 20th, Hoxha's widow, Nexhmije, was removed as President of the Democratic Front, the umbrella organization that embraced the ruling Party. On the 23rd, the trades-union federation announced that it would thenceforth be pluralist; and on the same day a human-rights-monitoring group was formed. On the 28th, the DP was given permission to publish its own paper (*Keesing*, 37924). Within a few days Albania had become officially, and to a point actually, pluralist.

On the 23rd, Fatos Nano, who was to have a major role in what followed, was brought into the government for the first time as Secretary to the Council of Ministers (*Keesing*, 37924).

In January two further parties were formed, the Ecology Party and the Republican Party. On the 5th January came the first mass release of political prisoners, a process that was to continue until all political prisoners had been pardoned by the 2nd July (*Keesing*, 37972-3, 38351).

The period was marked by repeated attempts at mass-migration---only a few months after unauthorized exit had ceased to be a capital offence. In January 1991, the flow of workers to Greece was said to have risen to a flood, with 3,500 leaving over the two days at the turn of the year alone. More visible for obvious reasons was movement to Italy. On the 9th February there were riots at Durrës by would-be emigrants trying to board a ferry for Italy. In the first seven days of March, 20,000 Albanians arrived by ship in Italian ports, and on the 7th troops took control of Durrës to stem the tide (*Keesing*, 37972-3, 38016-7, 38105-6).

Demonstrations and riots also continued. February was marked especially by attacks on the cult of Enver Hoxha. A boycott of classes started on the 6th at what was then the Enver Hoxha University in Tirana. Strikes by students began in various other cities. On the 18th, 700 students and academics at Tirana began a hunger strike. On the 20th, the statue of Hoxha on Skanderbeg Square in Tirana was pulled down, and Hoxha's statue in Durrës was also attacked. There were clashes with the police in Tirana, but also reports that some police had sided with the demonstrators. On the 21st, Hoxha's works were assailed in a Tirana bookshop (which was then burned out), and an attempt by demonstrators to storm the Military Academy was repulsed with loss of life. On the 28th it was announced that 58 people had been arrested because of attacks on monuments (*Keesing*, 38016-7).

In February for the first time the ownership of cars and the wearing of beards were legalized (*Keesing*, 38016-7).

In an attempt to deal with the disruption, which was also seriously affecting the economy, Ramiz Alia on 20th February declared presidential rule. On the 22nd he named a provisional government under the chairmanship of Fatos Nano, and also, to advise himself, a small Presidential Council, on which among others were included the Chairman of the Supreme Court and two respected academics (one of whom, Rexhep Mejdani, was more than six years later to become President himself) (*Keesing*, 38016-7). It was no doubt evident that fairly fundamental action needed to be taken. But further reform seemed to have been suspended until after the election, with, it appears, one important exception. The first privatizations were authorized in March 1991, when workers in some small shops and service establishments were first allowed to buy the enterprises in which they worked (Hashi & Xhillari, 1996).

Early in March food and other aid began to arrive from Italy. On the 18th, all food distribution was put under police control (*Keesing*, 38105-6).

Major Change Begun in Uncertain Hands, April 1991 to March 1992

The parliamentary elections of 31st March and 7th and 14th April 1991 were contested by at least seven parties or groups. They constituted arguably the first fully democratic election in Albania ever, but the governing party (the PLA) was alleged to have used its control over the media to its own advantage, denying access to the opposition; and its influence was widely believed to have been deployed in other ways. The DP seems to have dominated in the major cities, but the PLA won heavily overall, with about two-thirds of the vote, gaining 169 seats to the Democrats' 75. The only other parties to be represented were Omonia (the association of the Greek minority) with 5 and a Veterans' Party with 1 seat.

On the 29th April the new Assembly passed a Law on Major Constitutional Provisions, in effect an interim Constitution of fairly standard liberal-democratic character that has remained in force until the time of writing in 1998. This provided for a directly elected People's Assembly of members elected for a four-year term, and a President elected by the Assembly for five years. The Assembly also was to approve the Council of Ministers.

In accord with the new law and on the day after it was passed, Ramiz Alia, though he had been quite decisively defeated in a Tirana constituency by a DP candidate, was elected by the Assembly as President of Albania. In this position he had power to nominate the Prime Minister, and on the recommendation of the Prime Minister to appoint and dismiss members of the government (though all subject to the approval of the Assembly). He also had power in certain circumstances to dissolve the Assembly, or to declare an emergency, a mobilization, or, if the assembly was not sitting and Albania was attacked, war; and he was commander-in-chief of the forces.

The President's role envisaged in the interim Constitution was probably more on the Italian or German than on the post-1958 French pattern; but the first two Presidents of Albania under these rules were distinctly more active participants than Italian and German Presidents are expected to be.

The election of the Assembly for four years and the President for five made it quite likely that there would from time to time be what the French call 'cohabitation', with the President of a different party from the Assembly majority, but presidental resignations in 1992 and 1997 have so far prevented this from happening.

The previous government continued in office for the first few weeks of the new Assembly's life, and on 3rd May Nano was named by the President as Prime Minister once again, with a new government composed of members of the PLA, the old ruling party (*Keesing*, 38105-6, 38160, 38208).

On the 4th April, in between rounds of the election, the government had issued decrees on privatization. A Committee for Reorganization of the Economy had been set up. It was to decide by the end of April which enterprises should be privatized, an over-ambitious asignment suggesting that the difficulties of privatization were under-rated. In recognition of what was widely occurring, Albanians were permitted to be employed abroad (*Keesing*, 38160).

On the 4th June, two months after the election, the new government resigned 'against a background of strikes, continuing unrest and soaring prices', says Harxhi (1995, p.16). A 'Government of National Stability' took office on the 12th, under Ylli Bufi of the PLA as Prime Minister, with Gramoz Pashko, Parliamentary Leader of the DP and an economist with international credentials, as his Deputy and Minister for the Economy, and another DP economist, Genc Ruli, as Minister for Finance. Altogether there were seven DP members in the government. Three smaller parties were also represented (though apparently without members in the Assembly). Among the government's first acts was to make a no-strike agreement with the unions (there had been a hunger strike by miners shortly before) and to control some prices and liberalize others. The Party of Labour of Albania was re-formed as the Socialist Party of Albania (*Partia Socialiste e Shqiperisë*, PSA, PSS) on the 13th June. Nano resigned from his post in the new government on the 14th in order to take office as the party's chairman (*Keesing*, 38302-3).

Some of the main economic policy measures of the coalition government were: a land-privatization act passed at the end of July; then on 1st September establishment of a National Agency for Privatization; increasing the independence of the State Bank; allowing Albanians to have hard-currency accounts and to receive remittances from abroad; the linking of the lek to the ECU at an initial rate of 1 ECU to 30 lekë (it fell to US$1 to 30 lekë about six weeks later); the lifting (14th September) of most quantitative restrictions on imports and exports; the creation of a Foreign Investment Agency, which started operations on the 1st October; a bill at the end of October for financial help to the unemployed; and on 1st November the removal of price controls on the products and services of heavy industry and transport. Most of the property of the former ruling party was taken over by the state (*Keesing*, 38400, 38448, 38539, 38583).

Demonstrations, riots and strikes continued, the strikes reaching a pitch in November. The President warned on 3rd November that police would intervene to stop strikes. Some of the demonstrations were directed specifically against the remaining influence of members of the former ruling party. Some were supported by the DP. Around the end of November there were food riots, in one of which 35 people died as a result of a fire ignited when there was an attempt to storm a storehouse (*Keesing*, 38448, 38539, 38583, 38686).

Finally, on the 6th December, the Bufi government resigned, after the expulsion of its three Republican Party members and the withdrawal of the DP Ministers. The DP withdrawal was controversial among the party's leadership. Neritan Ceka, a distinguished archaeologist, who had been Deputy Chairman and Deputy Parliamentary Leader of the Party, objected to Berisha's criticisms of Bufi and resigned from his party posts in protest. On the 10th, Vilson Ahmeti, described as a non-party intellectual, was invited to form a new government. It was named on the 14th and consisted mainly of non-party technocrats. Later in December, Alia fixed a date in March for a further election (*Keesing*, 38686).

In what seem to have been the first such moves since the changes against leaders of the old regime, Manush Myftiu (a former Deputy Prime Minister), and also another former official from the PLA, were arrested on the 31st August; and Nexhmije Hoxha was arrested on the 4th December (*Keesing*, 38448, 38686).

Conditions had continued to worsen through 1991, when, according to accepted figures, the country suffered a 27% fall in output. In the succeeding winter, the system of production and supply very largely broke down. There was a wave of plundering and pointless destruction of public property and 'spontaneous privatizations' of land. Rubbish was scattered widely. People went severely short of food and many received little or no electricity and had difficulty obtaining water.

Ahmeti gave assurances in January that government wage-rates would be inflation-adjusted and he repeated assurances of financial help to the unemployed (*Keesing*, 38775-6). Employment had fallen drastically because of the end to restrictions on international trade and the general disruption.

Once again the only salvation seemed to lie in a further election. A new electoral law was passed on the 4th February, reducing the number of Deputies from 250 to 140 and providing that 100 seats should be filled by single-member constituencies and the remaining 40 used to approximate the proportions for various parties in the Assembly to the proportions of votes cast in the constituencies. Ethnic-minority parties were banned, which ruled out Omonia, represented in the previous Assembly. On the 11th the President signed a decree dissolving the existing Assembly and fixing the 22nd March for the first round of the election (*Keesing*, 38775-6).

In the weeks leading to the election, general disruption was probably

at its worst.   Food was looted.   Robbers held up cars.   Farmers claimed
land for their own without restraint.   Mines and bakeries were said to be
almost the only industrial establishments working (*Keesing*, 38829).

Full-Speed Reform and Turning the Corner, April 1992 to June 1993

According to official figures, 90% of those entitled to vote in the election
of March-April 1992 did so.   The Council of Europe monitored the election
to give reassurance that all was done fairly.   The DP had a candidate for
every seat except for one (unsuccessfully) contested by President Alia.

The election of March 1992 returned a clear majority of the
Democratic Party to the People's Assembly, 92 seats with 62% of the vote.
Though not obliged by the interim Constitution to do so, Ramiz Alia
resigned as President on the 3rd April, and on the 6th Sali Berisha, the DP's
Chairman, a medical specialist who had been Party Secretary in the
Medical Faculty and personal physician to Enver Hoxha, was elected by the
Assembly as President of Albania.   A government was formed under
Aleksandër Meksi, dominated by the DP but including 2 members of
smaller parties, (the Social-democratic Party and the Republican Party, with
7 seats and 1 respectively in the Assembly) and 2 independent members.
The Socialist Party, the successor to the former ruling PLA, received 25%
of the vote and 38 seats and became the main opposition.   In opposition
also was the Human Rights Union (EAD, PMDN), with 2 seats, which *de-
facto* represented mainly the Greek and Slav minorities (*Keesing*, 38829).
Pjetër Arbnori, a poet who had been a political prisoner, was elected
President of the Assembly (*Keesing*, 38878).

A certain enthusiasm and hope was generated by the Democratic Party
victory.   It is probably right to fix some time in mid-1992 as the lowest
point in the economic and social decline.   GDP fell by 9 to 10% from 1991
to 1992, but it is recorded as rising by 11% to 1993.   Inflation was also at
its maximum in 1992 and thereafter fell rapidly.   The new government
seemed to have determination and a clear vision.   Admittedly privatization
of shops and land had started under its predecessors; the liberalization of
foreign trade had been in large part accomplished; and the Law of the
Banking System (enacted 22nd April 1992, nine days after the Meksi
government was formed), which established a separate central bank, must
have been prepared under the previous administration.   Yet the effective
completion of internal liberalization, the essentials of the system of
stabilization, extension of the safety-net, and the framework legislation for
market-oriented business (company law, foreign-investment law, strong
budget-constraint on state enterprises) were largely the work of the
Democratic Party government.   It also carried through the privatization of

housing and began that of industrial and service enterprises other than the very smallest, and it was left to carry through most of the privatization of farmland.

The years 1992-94 represented the time of most intense reform. Governments dominated by the Democratic Party, all of them led by Meksi, were to remain in power for five years---until early March 1997. There were fairly frequent changes of Ministers, but beside Meksi three others remained and continued after the election of 1996 in essentially the same positions (as Foreign, Defence, and Mining Ministers) as they had held in 1992.

A week after the installation of the government it got approval from the Assembly for the essentials of its reform programme: completion of the privatization of farmland; privatization of state-owned enterprises and housing; removal of trade restrictions and of controls on retail and wholesale prices; the separation of the State Bank into a central bank and commercial banks (*Keesing*, 38878). Measures had fairly quickly to be taken to end the system whereby workers who were laid off because of lack of materials would receive 80% of their wages (*Keesing*, 38920). On the 1st July the exchange-rate for the lek was moved to a float, with an initial large devaluation to about 100 lekë to the US$. With the rate approximately targeted thereafter mainly by domestic monetary control, this initiated the stabilization regime that would last until the end of 1996.

In July and August, Ministers were obviously concerned about strikes and further attempts at migration to Italy (*Keesing*, 39014), but, comparatively speaking, Albania's domestic troubles increasingly slipped out of the world press (as reflected by *Keesing's Record of World Events*) from around the middle of 1992 until the end of 1996. On the principle that no news is good news, this is a further symptom of improvement. A high proportion of the continuing references to Albania concerned trouble with Greece. Over the first couple of years there was also a certain amount about the country's negotitions for aid.

Yet dissension within the Democratic Party was not long to surface. In the local elections of July 1992 the party seemed to have lost ground since March. The Socialist Party took 41% of the vote to the DP's 43%, but the effect of the distribution of votes was that the Socialists came to hold more Mayoralties of towns than the DP and to control more Councils in each category---District, Municipal, and Commune---though the DP gained control of the largest towns (*Keesing*, 39014). Given the differences that must have held between the circumstances of local and national elections, there is *prima-facie* no need to suppose that this represented a drastic drop in popularity for the DP over four months. However, some members of the ruling party in the Assembly criticized the leadership on this account. Six of them, including Pashko and Ceka who had been omitted from the new government, resigned from the party in November and formed the Democratic Alliance (DA), describing their new party as a 'liberal formation of the centre-right' and criticizing the government for 'diluting and altering the reform programme especially as regards privatization' (*Keesing*, 39191).

We end this period arbitrarily at the mid-point of 1993.   This is an artificial division which is used to highlight a political tendency discussed below.   But at the date we have chosen much was going well.   The exchange-rate had been fairly stable for a year.   The rate of inflation was to have fallen greatly over 1993.   Output was rising from its 1992 trough. The recorded rate of unemployment (for whatever it signified) had just begun to fall, as it would do *almost* uninterruptedly for three and a half years.   Within a few months the privatizations of farmland and housing, affecting the great majority of households in the country, would be virtually complete.

To summarize the mode of the change of regime to this point, we can say that Albania's political transformation was not as orderly and consensual as that of Hungary or Poland in 1989-90.   It was, however, despite the great importance of popular protest, more gradual and less revolutionary than in Czechoslovakia, Bulgaria or Romania.

Rapid Revival and Targeting the Opposition, July 1993 to April 1996

As has been mentioned, the arrest of high officials of the old regime had begun at least as early as August 1991---under the coalition government. But then, on the 12th September 1992, Ramiz Alia himself was put under house arrest---charged with misusing state funds and abuse of power---only six months after Berisha had in rather chivalrous terms explained his party's decision not to put up a candidate against Alia (*Keesing*, 39103-4, 38829). (Berisha's words then imply that he expected Alia to remain in office after the 1992 election.) Ramiz Alia was sentenced on 2nd July 1994 to nine years' imprisonment, though the term was reduced on successive appeals to eight, and then to five, years, and he was finally released by the Appeal Court on the 7th July 1995 (*Keesing*, 40012, 40198, 40328, 40659).

Nexhmije Hoxha was not so lucky and had her sentence increased on appeal from nine years to eleven, for allegedly misappropriating sums of money over the five years since her husband's death (*Keesing*, 39281, 39472).   What successor governments should do with people who have run oppressive regimes, or committed atrocities under them, is not an easy question morally or in political strategy.   South Africa, Argentina, Chile, the reunited Germany, South Korea, have handled it in different ways.   The dilemma is especially acute if the change of system has come by unilateral renunciation, as in South Africa, or by negotiation, as in Chile. If those at the top have done only what has at the time been been defended with reference to their ideology and has been widely praised---if those lower down have only obeyed orders or done what is expected of them by their superiors---there is a case for saying that they should not be regarded as criminals, even if the general judgment of mankind would be horrified by the acts that they have committed.

At all events, where the deposed rulers and their servants are punished, it is important that they should be punished under fairly clear law of some sort to which they can plausibly be held to have been bound. It is important that the usual rules about evidence and the accused's right to defend himself have been observed. And it is important that those selected to be prosecuted should be chosen according to the seriousness of what they have done rather than according to the convenience to their successors of having them put away, and that they should not be given long sentences for what appear to be technical failures without evidence of evil intent. (Once the precedent is established that a new government on coming to power finds ways of imprisoning its political opponents, the stakes in an election become unduly high. Those in government are then under very strong temptation to twist the democratic process to their advantage. Those in opposition are tempted to seek unconstitutional means. The departures from impartial justice and democratic fair play feed on themselves.)

We do not pretend to judge how far the criteria for just prosecution were fulfilled for the various leaders of the PLA regime who were sentenced from 1991 for crimes committed in their official positions. Yet we think that there is a strong presumption that a critical line had been crossed with the arrest (30th July 1993) of Fatos Nano and his subsequent trial and conviction (*Keesing*, 39606, 39971). For this reason, we take his arrest as a watershed. From this time, we suggest, if not earlier, the government's behaviour suggested that it was worried not about strikers and food-rioters and the like but about its political opponents.

Nano had joined the government only in late December 1990. No more than Berisha or many other latter-day reformers could he be held responsible for the abuses of the old regime. He was in fact accused of a specific misappropriation of funds. Yet an observer at his trial considered that no evidence had been given to show that he had benefited from the supposed misappropriation (*Economist*, 9th April 1994, p.39). And politically he had proved (as he has done since!) a very effective opponent of the Democratic Party. He was sentenced to twelve years and to make restitution of US$725,000, failure to pay which would entail imprisonment for a further 663 years, as the *Economist* (*ibid.*) observes.

There was to be a comic-opera ending. President Berisha pardoned Nano two days after he had been released through the opening of the prisons in the anarchy of March 1997 (*Keesing*, 41556-7).   Four months after that he was Prime Minister once again.

Early in August 1993 other former Ministers were arrested on similar charges, and on the 31st Vilson Ahmeti, the non-party person who had taken on the thankless job of Prime Minister in the three months before the election of 1992, was sentenced to two years' imprisonment for abuse of power (*Keesing*, 39606).   It was widely believed that the worst that could be said for his conduct in the matter with which he was charged was that he had put his signature to a document whose implications he had not understood.

Allegations of torture against the authorities were made in a case whose outcome, on 7th September 1994, was that five prominent members of the ethnic-Greek organization Omonia were sentenced to prison for treason.   Four of them had retracted their confessions and claimed to have been tortured.   The Greek government reacted by expelling between 45,000 and 50,000 Albanian guest-workers (*Keesing*, 40197-8).   Not long after, one of the five who had been convicted was pardoned and the other four had their sentences reduced.   Then, on 9th February 1995, the remaining four were released on appeal on the ground of 'procedural violations' (*Keesing*, 40228, 40419).   Whether this whole story should be seen as a good or as a bad sign of the state of the lawcourts is debatable.   Together with other successful appeals in what might be regarded as political cases, it does suggest, though not conclusively, that the judges were not entirely the pawns of government.   Judges might be independent, but those refusing to do what the President asked of them were likely to lose their posts.   It is in this light that we should probably see the Assembly's dismissal, on 21st September 1995, of Zef Brozi, the then Chairman of the Supreme Court, on the ground of failing to follow an order from the government and failing to recognize the Constitutional Court (*Keesing*, 40740).

Prosecutions against former Communist functionaries continued through the period we are considering.   At its end, on the 24th May 1996, three former officials (including a former President of the Supreme Court and a Procurator-General) were sentenced to death, and two more (Haxhi Lleshi, who had been head of state for 29 years from 1953 and was by this time very old, and the former Deputy Prime Minister Manush Myftiu, jailed earlier with Alia) were sentenced to life imprisonment.   In September 1997, 32 former Communist officials who had been convicted of crimes against humanity were to come on appeal before the Supreme Court, which released them on the ground that such a crime had not been part of the code when their supposed offences had been committed (*Keesing*, 41834-5).

These judicial decisions, and the actions of the government in prosecuting, *may have* been justified on a strict, impartial legal assessment, and if, as seems likely, some of them were not, it could be argued that they were minor compared with what would be routine under a genuinely totalitarian state, in which some of those convicted would not have hesitated to take part. Maybe. But for those governing a nation to make use of the system of criminal justice, even on rare occasions and within the letter of the law, for party-political ends, or in order to frighten potential critics, is to cross a significant divide. The governments of a number of countries today---and not only in Europe and the 'West'---are deterred from doing so by a network of institutions: public opinion, free press, the mores of judges and civil servants. To stray over the line is to foster a mistrust of governments. It also tends to silence criticism and so to hide (other) abuses: to keep out of the light what needs to be made public.

Court cases were not the only means adopted to make obstacles for the opposition. The new SHIK (National Information Service, *Sherbimi Informativ Kombëtar*) was popularly held to be a natural successor to the dreaded Sigurimi of Hoxha times. And there were unofficial agents too to punish anyone who said the wrong thing. A meeting of the Democratic Alliance in Shkodër on the 14th January 1994 ended in violence in which one person was killed, apparently because of an attack by DP activists, justified by the Interior Ministry on the improbable ground that pro-Serbian statements expressed at the meeting had provoked the attack (*Keesing*, 39829). A television presenter who had made fun of DP politicians appeared on his show next week badly beaten up.

There were also signs of a desire to restrict information and the expression of opinion. A press law of October 1993 is described as having 'restricted journalists' access to information' and as having 'provided for large fines to be imposed on editors deemed to have published "punishable material"' (*Keesing*, 39708, 41835). On 27th February 1994 two journalists on an opposition-sympathizing daily, *Koha Jonë*, were convicted of conspiracy to reveal state secrets and sentenced to four years and eighteen months in jail respectively. What they were accused of revealing was a quite trivial military order (a prohibition of the carrying of personal arms by off-duty troops) whose publication could hardly have enlightened Albania's enemies if any such existed (*Keesing*, 39883). Reception of B.B.C. Albanian Service broadcasts on medium wave was curtailed on the 1st March on the ground of their left-wing bias (*Keesing*, 39932). *Koha Jonë* was under attack again when police on 27th July seized its premises allegedly for non-payment of debt. Its editor complained that this was the result of a conspiracy between the government and the state banks (*Keesing*, 40012). From the 3rd to the 7th August, ten opposition papers halted publication in protest at taxes and tariffs on imports of their materials, though the President then hinted at concessions and *Koha Jonë* opened again (*Keesing*, 40154). All this is again trivial compared with what would go on under a totalitarian state, but it did suggest that the government, however uncertainly, was tempted to try frightening the independent information media into saying only what those in power wanted to hear.

A further test of the government's popularity, and (in some people's view) of its intentions, came with the attempt to have a new Constitution adopted by referendum. This would have given the President more powers than the 1992 Constitutional Law, and it was seen understandably as President Berisha's baby. Supporters of the change failed to gain the two-thirds majority in the Assembly that was needed for a draft change to be approved, but the President took the initiative of presenting it to the people by referendum (OECD, 1995, p.11; *Keesing*, 40466). The popular vote was held on the 6th November 1994 (*Keesing*, 40287). Of those eligible 84.4% voted, but 53.9% of those who did so voted against. So the interim Constitutional Law remained current. This could be seen either as a vote against President Berisha or as a vote against concentrating power. More dissension in the DP arose from a decision to have a further referendum. This time the Party Chairman, Eduard Selami, opposed the decision and was dismissed from his party post on 5th March 1995 (*Keesing*, 40466).

Politics in October 1995 was said to be dominated by the Law on Genocide that had been signed on 27th September. This had been opposed in the Assembly not only by the Socialists but also by the Social-democrats and the Democratic Alliance.   It had the effect of barring from public office until 2002 anyone who had been a member of the Central Committee or the Politburo of the former ruling party, and would by this means prevent a number of prominent politicians from standing in either of the next two Assembly elections.   Among those so excluded were Nano, the leader of the Socialists; Skënder Gjinushi, the leader of the Social-democrats (*Keesing*, 40740, 40786, 40893); and, according to Rama (1997), 'over 100 possible candidates for the SPA and other small Opposition parties'.

With the gradual mending of relations between Albania and Greece, with no further need for foreign aid, and with the Kosovo issue kept very low-key since 1992, Albania dropped even more out of world news through 1995 and also through 1996, except for the events surrounding the Assembly elections, to which we now turn.

The Democratic Party Unchallenged, May to December 1996

The issue of a readiness to play the democratic game came to a head in the Assembly elections of May-June 1996.   This was at the time of the 'funds' euphoria, and it is widely considered likely that the governing party could have won quite clearly without cheating. The Democratic Party had an overwhelming victory, but, as *Keesing* (41153) puts it, there were 'opposition and foreign allegations of widespread malpractice'. During the campaign too, television was said to have been effectively at the disposal of the ruling party only---though in spite of the pressures and fitful restrictions there was a fairly uninhibited press.

Two rounds were scheduled, for 26 th May and 2nd June. Of the 140 seats, 115 (as against 100 in 1992) were to be filled in single-member constituencies on those two dates, and the rest (reduced from 40 to 25) were to be distributed to parties---but not, it seems, as in 1992, to make the final *overall* distribution of seats more nearly *proportional to the parties' shares of votes:* rather *in proportion to the original numbers of seats won.* (This is our interpretation of Rama, 1997, and fits roughly with the numbers of the final 25 seats awarded to the DP. It would be, of course, much more favourable to the leading party than the 1992 system.) The President agreed to hold fresh elections on 16th June in 17 constituencies in which the Electoral Commission had noted irregularities.

In the first round on 26th May the main opposition parties 'pulled out' (which means that they ceased to monitor the process) several hours before polling had finished, 'alleging widespread ballot rigging, intimidation and violence' (*Keesing*, 41153). On the 2nd June voting in nine constituencies was boycotted by the Socialists (PSA, PSS) and four other parties. Then the opposition parties boycotted all the 17 re-run contests on the 16th June, with the result that the DP won them all. The upshot was that the DP (PDS) won 101 of the 115 constituency seats.

In the end, the DP, with an additional 21 seats out of the 25 distributed 'proportionately', had 122 of the 140 seats, the Socialists 10, Republicans 3, Human Rights (PMDN) 3, and National Front (PBK) 2. The OSCE, monitoring, 'detailed numerous instances of manipulation of poll and intimidation by police officers' (*Keesing*, 41153-4; the rest of the information is from these two pages of *Keesing*).

Peaceful demonstrations were held in Tirana against the electoral malpractices. These were suppressed fairly brutally, with protesters, including some prominent people, beaten by the police and imprisoned.

The local elections of 20th and 27th October 1996 also constituted an immense victory for the Democratic Party, but this time with the 'guarded approval of foreign observers' (*Keesing*, 41331). The Council of Europe coordinated the foreign monitors. It expressed satisfaction with the way the vote was carried out but regretted 'a few cases of irregularities'. The DP won 58 out of 64 Mayoralties of Municipalities (towns) and 268 out of 307 Chairmanships of Communes. If this was *mostly* achieved by the rules, it does support the view that the party could have won decisively in

May without foul play.

As has been mentioned, in some areas the DP is reported to have used a suggested association with some of the 'funds' as a selling-point before the May election.   The contrast between the result of the 1996 elections (especially the local ones, even with allowance for some manipulation) and the adverse vote on the Constitution at the end of 1994 suggests that events had swung in the government's favour.   It seems very likely that a sense of well-being partly generated by the funds was by this time politically important.   Whatever the funds and the organizations behind them may have done for the wealth of individual politicians, they were apparently doing wonders for the reputation of the ruling party.   With such a combination of a gift-horse and a golden-egg-laying goose, those in power were understandably cautious about asking too many questions.

No doubt it seemed that not only the DP's economic and social strategy but also its political tactics had worked.   The main economic indicators had been highly favourable for several years---after the country had seemed so near to chaos.   The international relations that mattered, even with Greece, were satisfactory.   And the party seemed to have nothing now to fear from its domestic opponents.   Even if some foreign journalists and official observers criticized the methods by which the election had been delivered, there seemed to be no real penalties following from their criticisms.   If the opposition took to the streets, the protests could be written off as organized by secret police from the former regime.

Those who were likely to have opinions on policy, especially if they were in state-funded posts, were once again conscious of the need to see who was listening before they expressed their views.   This was a long way from the atmosphere of the Hoxha regime, but there were reminiscences of it.   Also factual information held by the government was not always easy for potential analysts and critics to obtain.   Whether out of paranoia or sheer bueaucratic obtuseness, the very useful *Monthly Economic Statistics* of Albania prepared by the resident IMF Office was not supposed to be available to anyone in Albania other than certain specified officials.

One of the present editors as a foreigner was made aware at a seminar held in Tirana during December 1996 of the only-moderately-subtle pressure that could be exercised on 'intellectuals' not to utter what might be interpreted as criticism of the government.   A former Minister, still reputed to be a considerable power in the Democratic Party in the Assembly, was present and took an active part.   He vigorously attacked the views of all who took anything other than an extreme right-wing-liberal view on any policy question or expressed less than unqualified approval of policies in which he had been involved as Minister.   (He was, for example, against any urban land-use planning whatever, and against subsidizing health services for anyone.)   He was an able debater.   Albanian academics present saw him as a ruling-party agent, present to check for, or to silence, dissenting views. Some admitted that they were wary of taking positions of which he disapproved in case it put their jobs at risk. Certainly they kept their mouths shut in his presence and left him to the foreigners.

This, to put it mildly, was not an atmosphere conducive to ruthless probing and truth-telling about the events that were soon to drive much of the country to anarchy. Also, the position in which the Socialist Party and its leaders, and some of the other oppositionists, had been placed by the government was not one to encourage them to make common cause with their rivals against threatened collapse in the institutions of government.

Summary

Albania's change of regime was not as orderly and consensual as that of Hungary or Poland in 1989-90. It was, however, more gradual and less revolutionary than in Czechoslovakia, Bulgaria or Romania.

The Democratic Party, starting with democratic and liberal ideals, showed determination and clarity of purpose once it had a clear parliamentary mandate after the election of March 1992. Several important moves into transition that it continued, however, had been started by the Communist and Coalition governments of the previous year. The Democratic Party government retained the broad toleration, if not the continued enthusiasm, of the population through a series of very radical measures which by most tests soon seemed extraordinarily successful.

Having become the party in power, however, it was not immune to the temptations of bending the rules of justice and electoral fair-play to keep itself there. Eventually it appeared to have inactivated its most influential opponents through judicial and legislative proceedings, and it had intimidated to the necessary degree some who might have been effective critics or probed too deeply. The euphoria produced by the 'funds' in 1996 seemed at the time a political godsend for the governing party. This provided one reason why those peculiar institutions, and the very profitable activity behind some of them, would not be too closely scrutinized.

Politics had in this way become too much of a fight to the death for the advantages of liberal democracy to be realized. There could not be a full and open public debate about the dangers lurking in the informal financial system. The party protagonists could not be expected to pull together in an emergency. In retrospect, the elements of electoral foul-play, physical bullying, dubious justice, and concealment, increasingly practised by the Democratic Party---trivial though they might be by totalitarian standards--- did not turn out to be in the interest of the Party, as they were certainly not in the interest of the nation.

5 Liberalization

'Liberalization' refers to the process of progressively allowing prices and quantities to be determined in free markets.

Transition to a market economy is justified principally by the view that, with certain qualifications, freeing prices and quantities will allow individual and social choices to be satisfied more efficiently.

Particular measures of liberalization will be likely to add to the efficiency with which needs and wants are met *insofar as* they lead people, in their decisions as consumers and producers, to take greater account of the social costs of the goods and resources they are using and of the benefits (to others as well as themselves) of what they are producing.

This does not imply that *every* measure of liberalization necessarily adds to economic efficiency (in other words to potential material welfare). In particular, freeing prices and quantities is unlikely to have the full effects desired unless the resulting productive decisions are made *either* by private owners of assets and factors of production *or* by state organs constrained to act rather like private agents (through being subject to hard budget-constraints). From the starting-point of the Soviet-style economies, a large measure of privatization, and the abolition of automatic gap-filling subsidies for public enterprises, are essential accompaniments of liberalization if it is to achieve what is desired of it.

Liberalization can not be done all at once. So, it seems, all the transition-country governments have supposed. And surely they are right. The process may, and often does, leave wide classes of people without material support or at least much impoverished. It renders some assets and skills valueless. Liberalizing in stages avoids the need to deal with all the ill effects at the same time. But part-liberalization may lead to the *wrong* price-incentives for those who can now make the productive decisions.

There is now a fairly broad measure of agreement over the areas in which government intervention in allocation is and is not desirable. In this sense there is not a great deal of argument about the final goal. The difficult set of decisions that countries in transition have had to face is rather over the *pace* and *sequence* of liberalization and over how far simultaneous *privatization* is necessary to make the liberalization effective.

If the liberalization goes quickly, the disruption of existing activities is likely to be great. If it goes slowly, potential investors will know that the relative prices that they face now are probably different from those they will face in the future and they may postpone decisions until the ultimate position is clearer.

The sequence is also important. Crucial to any price system that accurately reflects the costs of inputs and the benefits of outputs is exposure to the outside world's relative prices. This consideration might dictate a quick opening to world trade and removal of any quantitative restrictions, and of any serious duties and subsidies, to which it has been subject. But a sudden opening to trade at anything near world prices, for tradable-goods industries that have grown up under very different conditions, may quickly put those industries out of operation. In some cases, certainly, they may be industries that do not in any circumstances represent an efficient use of the country's resources. In others, they may be industries that are quite suitable but need to change their techniques or equipment or employment policies in order to be viable under the new conditions. A rapid opening without other measures may well be equally devastating to both classes.

Agenda of Liberalization

Here is a list of the broad areas of liberalization. The order is not intended to represent a desirable sequence for them to be introduced.

First there is removal, from state enterprises, of subsidies that represent simply loose budget-constraints. (They are not given to reflect any social judgment other than that the enterprises so favoured must remain in operation.) Privatization is of course a way of reducing the temptation to this kind of subsidy. Without the removal of these subsidies, state enterprises feel no need to respond to the costs and values represented by the price system when they make their own pricing and output decisions.

Second is freeing the prices of goods and services that are industrial inputs. This may well be fairly unreservedly good in activities such as transport in which competition will be quick to develop. But, in cases in which a single state enterprise has a monopoly of some input, freeing prices might increase costs to users without increasing efficiency.

Third is freeing farm prices. Since the agricultural industries left to themselves tend to be highly competitive, the effect on efficiency---over which goods are produced, how they are produced, and how much effort and care is put into their production---is likely to be favourable, but of course the prices of certain products to consumers and other users may well rise, if, as is usual, they have been suppressed in the command economy. This will need to be accepted unless some compensation, such as subsidies on the consumer-prices of basic foods, is to be given.

Fourth is freeing prices of 'non-essential' consumer goods---a move not necessarily without its political penalties but otherwise probably unobjectionable, unless there are monopoly positions that are unchallengeable in some of the industries concerned.

Fifth, there is freeing of the prices of 'essential' consumer-goods such as food, public transport, water, fuel and power. This obviously has to be done cautiously and will often happen in stages. Freeing consumer-prices will generally involve *removing* the subsidies (explicit or implicit) that have made it possible to keep the consumer-prices down. While the utilities remain monopolies, upper limits on their prices are still likely to be maintained. Liberalization in these cases will go only so far as to relate these limiting prices to the costs of production.

Sixth is the freeing of international trade, with the necessary changes to the exchange-rate. As we have suggested, world prices provide a useful starting-point for an efficient system of domestic relative-prices. An efficient endpoint will necessarily involve some approach to market-directed international trade. Completely free trade has been rare, though apparently very successful in some of the cases, such as Hong Kong and (for practical purposes) Singapore, in which it has been practised. But each case of sustained rapid development in what used to be called the Third World has relied significantly on the international market, with fast and continuous increase in exports, mainly of manufactures. This requires exposure to the world market, even if the prices are distorted somewhat by duties and subsidies. The big move is from centrally 'managed' trade (the quantities of various goods determined without much regard to prices and costs) to decentralized trade (with numerous independent operators looking closely at costs and returns). Market-oriented trade has the further advantage, very important in an economy emerging from a command system, that it largely prevents the exercise of monopoly-power in any traded-good industry. This removes one potential source of abuse that might arise from the freeing of industrial-input prices. One view is that the sooner the whole economy is governed by world prices the better. The other is that, as mentioned above, a sudden opening may put much of industry out of operation, including much for which there is a long-term place.

Seventh is freeing of interest-rates and of the financial sector generally. There is fairly general agreement that market-determined interest-rates are desirable on certain conditions. Important among these conditions are that potential borrowers and lenders are in a position to know the rates on offer, and that measures are taken to overcome or compensate for the transaction-costs that lead financial institutions to discriminate unduly against small borrowers and certain others. There are also a number of qualifications necessary to make freeing of other aspects of the financial sector a reliably beneficial reform. These arise because of the asymmetries in information between financial institutions and many of their customers, and because of the strong externalities that exist for the players within a financial system: each acting in its own supposed interests may contribute to collapse of the system unless certain rules are observed.

Eighth is freeing of wages and labour markets. A number of mixed-market-economies in fact still have highly regulated wages and labour markets, the regulation having been introduced or permitted on the ground that it safeguards the welfare of vulnerable people or that it is the price of industrial peace. However, it is clear that there are also social costs of regulation, costs that are often reflected in unemployment. This has led to the view that it is better to protect wage-earners' incomes through social security or social insurance rather than by introducing rigid prices and restrictions into labour markets.

Ninth is liberalization of the foreign-exchange market. The mixed-market economies have differed considerably in the extent to which they maintain controls on foreign exchange. Controls have been often used to maintain a rate very different from what would operate in a free market. The fashion, however, especially since about 1980, has been toward dropping exchange controls; and doing so has generally enhanced the case for either a reserve-backed currency at one extreme or a floating rate at the other. Even if controls are maintained, transition to market is usually held to involve the abandonment of their use to support a *highly distorting* rate, that is one *very* different from a rate that would hold in a free currency-market. On the other hand, a floating rate may still be a fairly stable rate if the economy is managed to that end.

Tenth is opening to foreign investment. Worries in the past about this have been recognized as having little substance. Of all the changes it is likely to be the most immediately innocuous. But there has to be some legal framework for foreign investment.

This leads on to the question of *regulation and supervision*, which is inevitably bound up with liberalization. Precisely *because* the state is displaced as the prime mover by numerous independent actors, there must be rules to support the keeping of contracts among them, to tax them in ways that do not unduly 'distort' their behaviour and are accepted as fair, to safeguard funds that are lent for re-lending or are mobilized for common ventures, and to prevent the exercise of undue power by any of the players. However, we consider this in a separate chapter under 'Institution-building'.

The Timing of Liberalizing Measures in Albania

We shall deal with this topic not in chronological sequence but under the ten areas of liberalization in the order in which they are listed above.

1. In a move to subject state industry to market forces, a *hard-budgeting rule* was instituted late in 1992, making it difficult for them to be

subsidized except as a matter of a deliberate policy decision. Clearly there were industries such as banks and utilities that would not be allowed simply to fail. But the combination of this rule with the opening to the world market did apparently close down a number of tradable-goods enterprises.

2. Controls were removed from the prices charged by heavy industry and transport on the 1st November 1991 (*Keesing*, 38583), in effect freeing a large share of *domestic material-input prices* for industry, trade and services. This was in the time of the coalition government.

3. The freeing of *farm prices* began in January 1990, when surpluses (mostly fruit and vegetables, apparently) not required for delivery to the state were allowed to be sold without price restrictions (*Keesing*, 37195-6). The system of compulsory deliveries appears to have broken down in the general disruption that occurred between the riots of December 1990 and the election of 1992. By the time the realities of farm privatization were virtually complete at the end of 1993, farmers were producing what they chose to produce and selling what they chose to sell, at whatever prices they could obtain. Comparisons made for one of the studies on which this book is based (Karadeloglou & Stoforos, 1997) indicate that obstacles to foreign trade (presumably the continuing import duties), kept domestic prices of most of the main farm products above corresponding world prices, at least in 1995. The principal exceptions were wheat and beef. Wheat output prices were apparently *below* those that would apply under completely free trade. So there seems to have been some *negative* 'nominal' (that is output-price) protection for wheat, and *positive* nominal protection for most other farm goods, though we are not able to say how the negative protection was brought about. In fact, imports of wheat and flour were subject to zero rate of duty until the end of 1996, while imports of all other main farm products (including boneless meat) had positive rates (*AO*, 3, 1, January 1997, p.38), some as high as 40% . So, wheat seems to have been negatively protected then *in relation to* most other agricultural goods until that time. This suggests that the switch out of wheat production (a fall of 36%, according to one set of figures---more like 50% according to another---between 1990 and 1995 when the quantity of agrarian output in general was fast increasing) may have been excessive. At the start of 1997, however, the import-duty rate on grain and flour was raised from zero to 10%. Formally that is positive nominal protection, and the rate has since been the same as that of a number of other farm goods. Except for fresh fish (30%), all major foodstuffs from the start of 1997 were subject to duty rates of either 10% or 20% (*ibid.*). It is clear that, at the end of the period, there was not completely free *international* trade in farm products, though there was free domestic trade.

4. It appears that '*non-essential*' *consumer-goods prices* were completely free at least as early as August 1992, when, according to Muço

(1996, p.56), 75% of prices were officially liberalized.

5. *Essential-consumer-goods prices* were liberalized more gradually. There were two elements to be removed: the maximum sale price and the subsidy. With goods such as food, produced under potentially competitive conditions, the removal of any subsidy has naturally gone hand-in-hand with the abandonment of controlled prices. (Bread has been the exception, for which control continued after the removal of subsidy.) In the case of utilities, which have normally continued so far to be state monopolies, a price ceiling may be maintained after the subsidy is removed. 1990 and 1991 saw huge increases in the amounts paid out in subsidies: from 8.66% of GDP in 1989 to 20.30% in 1991. Thereafter there was an even more drastic fall: to 8.26% in 1992 and 2.64% in 1993, and the decline continued year by year, both as a proportion of GDP and absolutely in real terms, at least until 1996. These figures suggest how serious the change in fact was. The big fall between 1991 and 1993 seems to reflect mainly what was done by the Meksi government in its first year-to-eighteen-months. In summary, a series of moves, between August 1992 and July 1996, removed subsidies on food, utilities, fuels, and household essentials by stages, and allowed their prices to rise. In 1992 the prices of a number of consumer goods and basic intermediate goods (including meat, dairy products, chemical fertilizer, and cement) were freed, and others were raised (rice, electricity, public transport). Over 1993 to 1995, rice and cooking-oil, and subsequently firewood and coal, had their prices freed; there were successive rises in the prices of gas and electricity; and in 1995 there were rises in the prices of school books and public transport. (Details are from a paper privately communicated.) To mitigate the effect on consumers, there was, for a period from 1992 to 1995, 'compensation' paid to pensioners and low-wage public-sector workers to take account of the rises in prices of bread and electricity. At the end of this period the 'compensation' was incorporated into the minimum (public-sector) wage. In late 1994, 25 items were still subject to administrative price-fixing. By late 1995, the only food price controlled was that of bread, and it too, together with gas and kerosene, was freed in July 1996. The only goods and services (excluding health and education) that remained subsidized or price-controlled to the end of 1996 were rail and urban-bus transport, rural water, postal services, and electricity (EBRD, 1996, p.136). With these exceptions, the state enterprises remaining at the end of 1996 were expected to cover their costs, but might be subject to directions on the prices they could charge. Several of the utilities and the state oil company had in fact become significant contributors to government revenue through the taxes that they paid as corporations and as producers.

6. The state monopoly of *foreign trade* began to be removed by the PLA government in February 1991. Most quantitative restrictions on

import and export trade were removed on 14th September 1991 (*Keesing,* 38448).   At the same time duties on imports were introduced.   Freeing foreign trade was declared as part of the initial reform programme of the Meksi government in April 1992 (*Keesing,* 38878), though it seems that much of the job had already been done.   'Since 1992, there have been virtually no quantitative restrictions on imports and very few on exports' (EBRD, 1994, p.17).   By late 1994 there were no quantitative restrictions on imports and four rates of import tariff, together with a 5% import surcharge (EBRD, 1994, p.109).   The import duties were simplified in 1995 to 3 rates of 7%, 25%, and 40%.   A number of capital goods were exempt (EBRD, 1996, p.136).   From January 1997, there were 5 rates of 0%, 5%, 10%, 20%, and 30% (IMF, 1997, p.25).   At the start of 1997, Albania's application to join the World Trade Organization was said to be 'at a relatively early stage' (IMF, 1997, p.25).   On exports in late 1994 there were licence requirements for 8 product-groups and temporary export taxes on 6 unprocessed natural-resource-based products (EBRD, 1994, p.109).   There appear to have been no export duties and negligible restrictions on exports by late 1996 (EBRD, 1996, p.136).   Radical and sweeping liberalization of foreign trade was thought to be one of the striking (and controversial) features of Albanian policy.   However, it is not clear *by late 1994* that Albania was especially advanced among the *Central European* transition economies in its liberalization of foreign trade, though it was clearly more liberalized than a number of the *CIS* states (EBRD, 1994, p.109).   In 1996 Albania was given the second-highest of five ratings on the extent of liberalization of the trade and foreign-exchange system, but only 8 of the 25 transition economies (all of them bar Romania in the CIS) were rated *less* advanced (EBRD, 1996, p.11).

7. As a first step to transition within *the financial system*, the Law of the Banking System, passed on the 22nd April 1992, separated the central-banking functions of the State Bank of Albania from its other functions, creating the Bank of Albania as a central bank, with most of the usual responsibilities.   The rest of the state banking system was organized into three commercial banks.   Subsequent legislation tended to enhance the standing of the central bank, but the extent to which it can claim independence in fact, in view both of the rather limited action it can take to influence domestic credit and also of the events of early 1997, is debatable. (See chapter 13.)   Six partly or wholly foreign-owned banks have been operating in Albania as at the ends of 1996 and 1997.   There is legislation providing for insurance companies to compete with the existing state-owned operator.   There is also legislation for investment funds.   Law and a supervisory body to regulate the stock exchange have been established. Nevertheless, lack of regulation or of strict implementation of laws---acceptance of the argument that the informal 'funds' were not taking

'deposits'---left the hugely important informal sector without necessary controls.   Some regulation of *bank interest-rates* has been applied to the three state-owned commercial banks, which, subsequently reduced in number to two, have, remained into 1998 overwhelmingly dominant among banks except in foreign-exchange business.   A floor has been set by the Bank of Albania to their *deposit-rates* of various terms, but from early 1996 this was applied only to time-deposits (IMF, 1997, p.17).   The Bank's directives to them on *lending-rates*, though having no legal force, were nevertheless effective, but these instructions ceased to be given from July 1995.   From fairly early, there seems to have been nothing resembling 'financial repression': real interest rates on bank deposits and loans were both consistently positive from early 1993 into at least the latter half of 1996 (according to EBRD, 1996, p.136).   (Table 7.2, properly interpreted, is consistent with this assertion.)   Monetary controls have been maintained by the central bank from 1992 (i) through regulating (if rather passively) the quantity of base-money; (ii) through bank-by-bank credit ceilings; (iii) through a reserve requirement on the banks, with loans to them at penal rates if the requirement is not otherwise met; (iv) through interest-rate directives to banks; and (v) by absorbing excess bank liquidity through Treasury Bills (IMF, 1997, pp.14-18).   In its extent of interest-rate liberalization, Albania was not unusual among the transition economies by the mid-1990s, but earlier in the decade it probably moved away from financial repression earlier than some.

8. In the *labour-market*, residual regulation has been strongest in the state sector.   There has been throughout a minimum wage, which applies to both the public and the private sector.   By law there is some regulation of hours of work, and also some rather mild rules relating to dismissals, that apply to the private sector as well as the public, though their enforcement in the private sector has probably been weak.   Agreements with certain trade unions in 1996 indexed the minimum wage to the price of a basket of goods.   Estimates of *average* wages in both public and private sectors have consistently been well above the official minimum.   Until 1994, there was a ceiling on the wage-bill of each state enterprise, but this restriction was then removed.   A rule obliging employers to pay staff 80% of their salaries if they were laid-off because of shortage of materials was removed in the early days of the Meksi government.   Unemployment Benefit and Social Assistance moved in to fill the gap.   There has been quite a large employer contribution to social-security and medical insurance, amounting from March 1995 (at least until mid-1997) to 34.2% of wages between certain levels of wage (see chapter 8), but there has been little else in the way of non-wage costs of employment for private employers, and there seems to be extensive evasion by those private employers of the social-security obligation.   There has been negligible trade-union activity in the private

sector.

9. Albania had a pegged *exchange-rate* until the last day of June 1992. There had been several devaluations, with an attempt on the 1st September 1991 to peg the lek to the ECU at an initial rate of 1 ECU = 30 lekë. In the inflation and general disruption of the next few months further devaluations were necessary. The average over the first half of 1992 was about 50 lekë to the US dollar. From the 1st July 1992, the lek was *floated* at an initial rate of about 100 lekë to the US dollar. An *approximation* to this rate was maintained deliberately over the next four and a half years, but essentially through domestic monetary control. Why this was possible and far from disastrous will be examined in chapter 7. To judge from the EBRD *Transition Reports*, any exchange controls became progressively lightened. In late 1996 the *Reports* still talked of controls on some capital transactions (1996, p.186). To the person in the street, it appears (1996 and 1997) to be a completely free market. The IMF (1997, p.16) says that the kerb market in Tirana is 'the prime market in which the price of foreign currency is set'. It is difficult to see how effective controls could work in those conditions or why they might have seemed to be necessary. *De facto*, it does seem that the market in late 1996 was effectively free from controls.

10. Finally, *foreign investment*: by a law of 2nd November 1993 foreign direct investment was treated very similarly to investment by residents or nationals. Businesses involving foreign direct investment must, however, be incorporated; and foreign residents were not allowed to own land in Albania until a change of law in July 1995 permitted them to do so on condition of a certain amount of investment. A Foreign Investment Agency set up by the coalition government began its operations as early as the 1st October 1991. Its successor is the Albanian Centre for Foreign Investment Promotion. The EBRD (1996, p.14) classes Albania as in the most advanced of its five categories for the 'extensiveness of legal rules on investment', with only six others in the same category. However, on the 'effectiveness of legal rules on investment', Albania is included in the lowest category, rivalled only by Turkmenistan. (See chapter 9.)

It should be added that owners of privatized firms and assets of all sorts have been given a high degree of freedom in what they do with them. There was briefly to have been a restriction, over the first year, on what could be done with privatized farms (Hashi & Xhillari, 1996, p.10), but this seems to have been quite inoperative. From July 1995, farmland could by law be bought and sold freely, though rigidities, and possibly imprecision, in the law (with a lack of 'sublegal' acts---authorized administrative regulations---to clear the uncertainty) have made land sales difficult (IMF, 1997, p.16). There can be little doubt that the owners' freedom over use of farms and houses was a strength.

The speed of exposing industry to the world market will probably continue to be controversial.   As chapter 10 shows, industry dropped far more as a proportion of GDP than in any other transition country.   Without the safety-valve of emigration, it is plausible that unemployment would have risen to intolerable levels.   China's strategy of a much more gradual opening has a *prima-facie* appeal.   Yet it is extremely doubtful whether keeping most of the old industrial enterprises working and gradually modernizing them was a real option.   Industrial discipline in 1991 and 1992 had largely broken down.   Bureaucracy and management were not equipped for the task of technical and commercial modernization. Reconstruction of state industry would at best have been a long process, and the situation in early 1992 had come to seem desperate.   In the then-current state of world opinion, liberalization strengthened the case for international help.   Opening so radically to the world market was a gamble, but it is hard to see in retrospect that there was a clearly better alternative available.

Summary

The main acts of liberalization were complete by the end of 1993. Subsidies even in that year had fallen to about 13% in real value of what they had been two years earlier.   Outside agriculture the weight of the state sector was still considerable right through until 1997, but, with open (though not duty-free) foreign trade and hard budget-constraints, the remaining public-sector enterprises (apart from certain still-subsidized utilities) had to cover their costs---not precisely at world prices, but at least in some relationship to world prices for those in tradable goods.   Subsidies and price controls remained on a diminishing range of goods and services regarded as consumer-essentials, but these were *mostly* ended by July 1996.

After 1992, there was no significant financial repression; the private-sector labour-market was fairly free, even in law (aside from a minimum wage, substantial social-security obligations, rules on hours of work, and mild procedures on dismissals---none of these requirements likely to be consistently enforced); the exchange-rate was targeted indirectly through domestic monetary measures; foreign direct investment was treated almost on a par with domestic investment; and those who acquired privatized assets were for most practical purposes free to do with them as they chose. Paradoxically, a gap in *financial regulation* was to prove disastrous.

The main subject of possible controversy is whether Albania should have exposed its industry so rapidly to international competition.   Given the circumstances of the time and what we now know about the outcomes, it would be hard to argue that the policy was fundamentally mistaken.

6 Privatization

Privatization we shall take to mean simply 'the transfer of assets hitherto owned by the state into private hands' (Kornai, 1995).

There have been a number of different modes of privatization. We may describe:

* Spontaneous privatization (someone, usually workers or managers, simply takes over the enterprise);
* Special-claimant privatization (existing tenants of houses, or workers of land, or enterprise employees, or former owners, have preferential access, often either at reduced prices or free);
* Patronage privatization (certain people get assets on preferential terms, either to repay favours to, or to ensure support for, those in power);
* Cash auction of whole enterprises;
* Cash auction of shares;
* Voucher-bidding for whole enterprises;
* Voucher-bidding for shares.
* Negotiated deals with major investors.

Most of these methods have been applied in Albania, sometimes in combinations.

The method of privatization obviously has a bearing on who gains the assets. Reasonable objectives here are that the distribution should be *fair* and also *conducive to efficient use*.

Fairness may be taken to lead to two principles that are sometimes in conflict: first, that the value of national assets should be distributed equally to all or else in inverse relationship to other elements of material well-being; and second, that no one should as a result of the privatization be deprived of livelihood or housing or accustomed way of life. Pursuit of the first of these principles may inevitably have to be modified in deference to the second. Much of the special-claimant privatization follows in fact from the second. Voucher-privatization is an attempt to pursue the first.

Efficiency is a further consideration. It is important that management should be likely to improve under the new ownership. This means that the new owner must have the relevant experience either to run the enterprise competently himself or to find a competent manager. Negotiated deals with major investors may be the only efficient way of privatizing certain types of asset. Fairness in that case involves getting the best deal for the public finances consistent with attracting the investor and giving him incentives to behave efficiently.

Giving small shops and service units to their employees, and farmland to those who have been working it, also makes sense on grounds of efficiency: they are likely to have the right experience.   By contrast, there is a real problem about ensuring efficient management in the wake of voucher-privatization: those bidding with the vouchers may have no experience of the industry concerned or of market-oriented business in general.   So it is necessary to have support structures to guide the new owners toward suitable management resources.   Some countries using vouchers (such as the Czech Republic and later Romania and Bulgaria) have sought to overcome this problem by having intermediary institutions between the voucher-bidders and the enterprises.

Finance: an argument for privatizing state enterprises for *cash* rather than giving them away through *vouchers* is the additional funding this might provide for governments.   But a problem with this for ex-socialist economies is the limited capacity and willingness of the public to spend cash on equities.   In the early years, those in the best position to acquire a stake in a firm that was to be privatized for cash might well be drawn either from the leadership of the former regime or from organized crime.   With few bidders, such people might be able to acquire large accumulations of the assets at below reasonable estimates of their value.   So, with the best will in the world, the process might well turn out to be giving special favours to the gangsters and the nomenklatura.

Regulation of privatized enterprises is an unavoidable issue, principally when the enterprise is a monopoly, as is often the case with public utilities.   A monopoly may charge too high a price (*too high* not only in the sense that its owners benefit unduly at the expense of the rest of the public but also that there may as a result be too little use made of the services it provides).   It may also lack enough incentive to provide good service.   So, by law or by contract with the operator of the utility, the relevant government authority may need to be empowered to set *ceilings on the prices* charged or to require certain *standards of service*.   Alternatively it may be empowered to set rules that deal with the task another way through *making competition possible.*

There is another purpose for which regulation of utilities is likely to be required, especially in a situation such as Albania's.   This is to ensure that adequate investments are made *to restore and expand the infrastructure.* There may need to be commitments made on investment by any private operator, and machinery for seeing that the commitments are observed.

The Story of Albanian Privatization to 1996

Under the coalition government of 1991, the Law of Privatization was passed in August (Hashi and Xhillari, 1997, p.9; *Keesing*, 38448, attributes the announcement to the 1st September). This simply set out the general principles for privatization and established the National Agency for Privatization to implement the programme. A further law passed by the coalition government attempted to free enterprises from the influence of ministries under which they had been operating. The enterprises were expected to take the initiative and make the changes necessary for survival in a market economy. As this opened the way for 'spontaneous privatization' (with managers or members of the government establishment simply taking over the enterprises as their own property), the Democratic Party government, by a decree of June 1992, declared auctions as the only vehicale for privatization (Hashi and Xhillari, 1997, p.11), but then modified this rule in August to allow employee buy-outs in retail trade, services, and handicrafts (*ibid.*).

Even before this, the very first steps towards privatization were taken by the Communist (PLA) government in March 1991, when some employees in the **'small' trade and service sectors** were allowed by government decree to acquire their businesses. This led on to the rapid privatization of retail trade and small service establishments. Employees were encouraged to purchase the businesses in which they worked as long as all were prepared to participate. (If only a majority wished to proceed, the National Agency for Privatisation, NAP, established later in the year, adjudicated on the proposed basis of the privatization.) If employees were not interested in purchasing the business it was to be sold by auction to *outsiders*. By the start of 1992, 75% of retail-trade and small service establishments had been transferred. By 1994 over 15,000 units had been privatized in trade and services (generally sold to employees) and over 17,000 in other activities (including activities ancillary to agriculture but not farming itself) (Hashi and Xhillari, 1997, p.11).

The formal privatization of **agriculture** began under the Land Law of July 1991 (though as early as 1990 some peasants had simply seized cooperatives' land for themselves). The 1991 law allocated each cooperative's land to families according to the proportion of the size of each family unit on the civil register. By the end of 1993 some 94% of the land formerly belonging to *cooperatives* (73.5% of the total in 1989) had been divided up among members (who before had technically been its co-owners). *State farms* (23.8% of the total land in 1989) began their transformation under an Agency established in July 1992. Their land was leased to their former employees, who had a priority right to buy, with a provision that the land could be auctioned if the employees chose not to buy it. Since there were few sales under arrangement, former employees were later allowed to buy by deferred payment over a period of 10 years with no interest charged (Hashi and Xhillari, 1997, p.13). 90% of state-farm land was disposed of in this way. Agricultural equipment was sold to former users at low (pre-inflation) prices.   Vouchers could eventually be used to help pay off debts for state land (*ibid.*).   Former owners (from before collectivization) were eligible for compensation but could not reclaim the land itself.

Privatization of land had to be accompanied by the formalization and codification of legal ownership.   It took some time for all the farmers to be given formal title-deeds or even formal use-rights, but the granting of titles was expected to be completed by the end of 1996 (Kunkel, 1996).   About 450,000 peasant families became owners.

That there was a generally acceptable distribution of farm land depended on detailed work by local people in each former collective or state farm to apportion land area among families according to their numbers of members.   By the standards of most of the world the family holdings are tiny, and they have for the most part been divided into a number of plots each, in order that each household may get an appropriate share of land of different qualities.   The division of holdings in this way was regarded as unavoidable, but it was clearly desirable that there would be some consolidation of holdings through trading, and that later, as the urban sector grew and drew families out of farming, the average size of farms would increase.   Yet at the end of 1996 there appeared still to be inhibitions about buying and selling land: it was said that this was partly because of the claims on land by former owners, which, though they had not been given any legal basis, were sometimes aggressively asserted.   There were also difficulties in the legitimation of sales, partly because of the way the law was framed (IMF, 1997, pp.35-36).

Privatization of **urban housing** proceeded under a law of January 1993, and, as Hashi & Xhillari say, with great speed.   One-room flats built before 1970 were distributed free of charge to their tenants, as were two-room flats dating from before 1965.   Larger and more recently built flats were sold to the occupiers at very low prices.   Freehold of land under each apartment block was given to the occupiers collectively.   Small sums were given to help with repairs.   There was also a programme to provide finance on easy terms for victims of persecution and for tenants displaced by former owners, who could reclaim their property if they did so by a certain date.   Programmes of concessional loans to assist homeless families continue.   By November 1993, the privatization of 97% of urban apartments was complete, and 230,000 dwellings had been transferred to their residents (Hashi and Xhillari, 1997, pp.14-15).

Privatization of **small to medium state-owned enterprises** (SOEs), as distinct from the very small units that could often be run by a single family, inevitably took longer.   It was largely stalled through late 1992 and early 1993 because of the difficulty of finding buyers (other than members of the former leadership) with enough cash to provide a reasonable price at auction.   Accordingly in May 1993 various changes were introduced by government decree that were designed to speed up the privatization process. The role of the National Agency for Privatization was reduced and the process decentralized to the country's 36 Districts. In each of these a District *Privatization Board* was to be established, made up of representatives from local government, internal security, and municipal authorities. According to the regulations that were included as a part of the decree, all small and medium-sized enterprises, defined as those companies with asset book-values of less than US$0.5 million or employing fewer than 300 workers, were to be privatized through auctions or direct sales. It was planned that auctions would be the main form of sale, but very few cases were settled on this basis. Even when auctions occurred, employees were still to be given the option to acquire the company at a fraction (generally about one-third) of the highest bidder's offer, and the Boards had the right in certain coircumstances to reject successful bidders at auctions (Hashi and Xhillari, 1997, p.16).   Estimates of proportions of privatized enterprises transferred to employees over 1993 and 1994 range from 33% to 50% (Hashi and Xhillari,1997, p.18).   The same authors (*ibid.*) assert that, although the Boards

> were meant to act as overseers and monitors of the process, in many cases they exercised a preference for certain buyers, influenced the outcome of the process and selected people who were not the highest bidders at auctions.

If auctions were not held, assets were sold at prices related to their book value. High rates of inflation were said to have had led to book values below replacement costs, but then the outdated technology of much of the assets would often have pitched any real value they had in a market economy far below replacement costs too.   No method of fixing book-value could have been a suitable indicator of present value in use. Without intimate knowledge of each industry, it would be very difficult to judge whether or not the assets were properly valued. However, there was a very widespread *belief* that they were sold too cheaply.

The composition of the Privatization Boards made no attempt at depoliticization of the process, and the outcome was all too predictable. Thus it was not surprising that the role of these Boards became a key political issue in 1995-96 when criticism of the Government's handling of the economic reforms grew (*ibid.*).

This aspect of the privatization programme achieved the objective of transferring assets from public to private control, but did little to meet other objectives. It probably did not produce support for the process from any group other than the primary beneficiaries, who in this phase could not have been numerous. In particular, the transfer of assets to employees of state-owned firms at relatively low prices (below the auction price, for example), with indirect benefits sometimes accruing (or so it was suspected) to those involved in the decision-taking, hardly met equity objectives. Additionally, direct sales seem to have produced little in the form of revenues, although this could well have been a reflection more on the quality of the assets than on any fault in the privatization process.

It was decided by early 1995 that the privatization of **larger enterprises** should be undertaken through a voucher system---what was called **mass-privatization**. The vouchers would also be eligible for use instead of cash in future purchases of small and medium enterprises. A decree of early 1995 set out the arrangements.

Under the new provisions there would be two different kinds of sale. For small and medium enterprises, auctions of the normal kind would be held with the whole enterprise going to the individual or group who bid most. Biddding could be in cash, in privatization-lekë (vouchers with a lek face-value issued to victims of persecution), or in the new vouchers, to be called privatization-bonds (*bono privatizimi*). No less than 5% must be in cash. This is referred to (in the 1997 IMF report) as *Decree 203 privatization*. For the larger enterprises, the aim was to *spread* the ownership of each item sold. It appears to have been laid down that only privatization-lekë or privatization-bonds could be used in bidding, and, though this limitation was apparently not rigidly observed, only 14% of what was paid for larger enterprises over 1995-96 was in cash (Mema, 1997, p.49). (Confusingly, however, this proportion was *higher*, according to Table 6.1 below, than the 12% paid in cash for the *small and medium enterprises* over the same two years.) Shares in each enterprise would be divided among *all* who bid for it, in proportion to their bids. It was this method that was called *mass-privatization* (account as in IMF, 1997, pp.32-33).

What mass-privatization would ideally have accomplished would have been to neutralize the capacity of those already privileged to acquire state assets at knock-down prices and also to spread industrial-share ownership widely among the population. But it raised obvious problems of company governance and management.

Vouchers were to be allocated to eligible citizens according to their age. The first instalment would comprise 20% of the total to be issued. For that first instalment, those over the age of 55 were to be given vouchers with a face value of lekë 20,000; those between 35 and 55, vouchers worth lekë 15,000; and those between 17 and 35, vouchers worth lekë 10,000. It appears (IMF, 1997, p.32) that only those who had not received land free of charge under privatization or restitution would be eligible to receive vouchers. This left 1,067,446 potential recipients (Mema, 1997, p.41). A small charge of 50 lekë was made for the certificate representing the vouchers. It was decided to distribute the vouchers in three instalments. As there was no list of eligible recipients immediately available, the first instalment of voucher-distribution took several months to complete, and some vouchers were not distributed by the end of the first round of privatization offerings because those eligible were abroad or otherwise could not be traced. The first instalment began to be distributed in April 1995, and it was initially planned that the 20% of vouchers issued in the first instalment should be used by June 1996. As a result of various delays it was later decided to extend the expiry date of the first instalment of vouchers to 1999, and to combine the second and third instalments so that the remaining four-fifths of the vouchers could be used together. In November 1996, the remaining 80% of vouchers were made available to those who applied, but, probably because no further privatizations under the programme had been announced and the market-value of the vouchers had fallen quite low, many of those eligible did not apply for this second instalment (and had still not done so by early 1998).

Over the first period of mass-privatization in 1995 and 1996, shares in 97 companies were distributed, mainly through the voucher scheme (that is, exchanged for *privatization bonds*, issued widely to the general public, or for the *privatization lekë* that were distributed to victims of persecution). Hashi and Xhillari (1997, p.22) record that 72% of the value of these shares went in exchange for bonds or privatization lekë; 23% were retained by the state; and 5% went to former owners of land or productive assets. (Table 6.2 below would give the slightly different result that 19% had been retained by the state, and figures from Mema, 1997, already cited, are not apparently quite consistent with this account in that they indicate that 14% of what was paid was in cash.) The companies were offered for sale in five groups or 'rounds'. Voucher holders were given the option of subscribing to shares in one of the companies in the current list or waiting until a subsequent round; but no one without insider-knowledge---possibly no one at all---could know what would be offered in subsequent rounds and hence what opportunity would be lost by bidding in any particular round. Since some did not receive their first instalment of vouchers until the early rounds were past, they were at a disadvantage. There was no official information made public that might have helped purchasers to judge the prospects of particular enterprises. Potential purchasers of shares had thus to take decisions on the basis of very limited information. Furthermore each voucher-recipient received only one certificate which he had to bid as a single entity. He could not split it among bids for different firms. This added to the lottery-like character of the process.

Shares were allocated to those that had applied for them in proportion to the value of the vouchers submitted. The number of shares available depended on the estimated book-value of the company's assets. If a company turned out to be popular with investors, the number of shares acquired for each thousand lekë of nominal voucher value would be relatively small, and for the less popular companies the proportion acquired would be higher. This procedure invites potential bidders to consider the likely demand for shares rather than encouraging them to concentrate on the real value of the business. It has the merit of simplicity but at the cost of making share-acquisition an even more risky process than it normally is.

A secondary market in vouchers evolved quite quickly, but the value of the vouchers dropped steadily: in September 1995 the market value of a voucher was approximately 34% of its face value (Hashi and Xhillari, 1997, p.20 note). Calculations from figures recorded in the newspapers indicate that it averaged 25.6% in January 1996, 11.7% in September, 9.6% in November, 5.8% in December, 5.7% in January 1997, 1.6% in April, and 1.5% in May, but surprisingly it had then risen to about 6% at the end of August 1997, over which month the average had been 4.0%. The average over the last three months of 1997 and the first three of 1998 was about 2.9 to 3.0% (F.Mema, personal communication). (Probably the rapid fall-off in 1996 reflected in part the possibility apparent for much of the time that the vouchers would expire before they could be used, possibly also the increasing apparent attractiveness of the informal-sector 'funds'.) Some wealthy individual investors and companies are believed to have been able to accumulate large numbers of vouchers and to use them to bid for shares, with the benefit of at least some knowledge of the enterprises. They have thereby, it is alleged, been able to acquire large shareholdings in the more promising companies.

The effect of the new rules ('Decree 203') on the privatization of **small and medium enterprises** is evident in Table 6.1 below and a table (IMF, 1997, p.76) that presents similar data. There was a marked switch from 1994, when only 7% of sales were by auction, to 1995, when the proportion was 95%. Table 6.1 also shows that the proportion of the price paid in cash went from 84% in 1994 to 15% in 1995 and 9% in 1996.

The possibility of the government's setting up investment trusts to deal in shares, as in the Czech Republic, was considered but rejected. This meant that there was no likelihood, for the ordinary voucher-recipient, either of informed bidding on his behalf or of experienced oversight of his holdings after privatization. However, legislation was enacted (Law no. 7979 of 26th July 1995, 'On Investment Funds') to allow private investment funds to be set up. (The legislation sets out a regulatory framework: for example, funds are not allowed to allocate more than 10 per cent of their assets to any one company; banks are not allowed to invest in investment funds or to set them up). As at mid-1997, six investment funds had been licensed under this law, but only one, Anglo-Adriatika, had been operating, and, until that time, this fund had merely gathered vouchers, which it had been holding on behalf of their owners, and not invested at all.   Its aim seemed to be to take part, on behalf of its contributors, as a strategic investor in some of the big privatizations expected later.   A mid-1997 figure from the Ministry of Finance indicated that Anglo-Adriatika was holding privatization-lekë to the face-value of 2,239 million and privatization-bonds to the face-value of 7,776 million, on behalf of 41,182 people.   This suggests that, despite the current absence of statutory investment trusts, the evolution of private funds that will offer holdings (their own shares or 'units') to the general public on terms convenient to the small investor remains a possibility.

Under a decision of November 1996 a further method of privatization was authorized.   This was to offer up to 50% of the shares in any enterprise to a single buyer at auction---either for cash only or with allowance for vouchers.   Of the 14 companies in which a substantial share was offered in this way over the first three months of 1997, 10 had no difficulty in finding buyers at above (on average well above) the base price set, and some of the buyers were foreign firms (Hashi and Xhillari, 1997, p.23).

Privatization Outcomes and Impacts

In **farming,** there was a large, prompt, and continuing, rise in output that is readily attributed to privatization.   Estimates of the real value of agricultural output show it increasing at a high average rate (11.4% a year in one estimate) over the four years from 1991 to 1995.   This was accompanied by a large shift of the pattern of production within agriculture, principally from wheat, sugarbeet, and treecrops to livestock products, vegetables and fodder.   Much of the recorded growth in real GDP over the mid-1990s is attrributable to this revival in farming.   Farm output had begun to increase rapidly (in 1992) when overall GDP was still falling. After some movement of people out of farming with the disturbances of 1990 and 1991, there appears (according to one set of official figures) to have been quite a substantial movement in the reverse direction which would have helped to relieve overt unemployment.

It was probably a great advantage (in contrast to the position in Russia and Ukraine) that collectivization of farming had not been completed until 1967, only about 25 years before most land became private again.   In 1946 large landed estates had been confiscated from their owners and reallocated to peasants with the stipulation that they 'could not be sold, bought or rented' (Prifti, p.65).   Then collectivization was gradually pushed through between the mid-1950s and the mid-1960s.   So after 1993 the same land might have both pre-War and post-War former owners.   People who had been independent farmers clearly survived in full vigour into the present decade. Their potential for becoming very much more productive is suggested by the fact that the 4.2% of agricultural land in private plots just before privatization produced nearly five times that proportion of output: 20.9% (Kunkel, 1996), a story admittedly rather similar to that in the Soviet Union as well as in China under collectivization. As Aslund and Sjoberg note (1992), the same observation could be made about Albania as about China and Vietnam: 'it appears to be easier to revitalize a socialist economy if it is possible to resurrect family agriculture and small scale trade and services'.

Among the important effects of the **housing** transformation, according to Hashi and Xhillari (1997, p.15), were (i) the creation of a 'wealth effect', liberating further capital for business start-ups and small-scale entrepreneurial activity; (ii) the development of a genuine market in housing; and (iii) the opportunities of using one's apartment (or lettting it or selling it) for small-business. Private property rights are associated with the ability of individuals to use them as collateral for bank loans and financing, which is essential for new business investment; it is likely that the full potential of house-ownership for this purpose has yet to be realized.

The remainder of the privatization up to 1996, diverse though it has been, may be considered as a whole because the parts are difficult to separate clearly, either conceptually or in the statistics. This covers broadly **trade, services and manufacturing**. (Finance, most of mining and extraction, and most of the utilities, together with some manufacturing segments, remained in the state sector at the end of 1996 and through 1997.) Privatization within this wide field generally proceeded from smaller to larger. The general intention was to ensure that the change in ownership occurred as rapidly as possible. However, it became progressively more difficult to carry out the policies pursued as their requirements (concerned with items of an increasing scale) became ever more demanding, involving the auction of enterprises and the distribution of shares, rather than simple transfer of units to single households or direct sale to a small group of employees.

In June 1992, a decree declared auction as the only vehicle for the transfer of state property into private ownership. As Table 6.1 below suggests, this rule was not pursued rigorously through 1993 and later years, though auctions became far more common, as we have seen, with the issue of vouchers in 1995. Nonetheless, in spite of implementation problems, there has been a considerable boom in business activity within the SME sector. Despite four decades during which entrepreneurship had been totally suppressed, by 1994 there were 45,000 small businesses (other than farms) recorded as in operation, and this figure grew to over 55,000 by 1995, which amounts to nearly 2 per 100 of the population, or roughly 5 per 100 of the non-farm population. (Of course, some may have belonged to farm families.)

An Enterprise Restructuring Agency was set up in July 1993 to deal with 32 enterprises 'which required managerial and financial assistance prior to either privatization or closure' (IMF, 1997, p.33). This, according to the source, managed a large reduction in employment in these enterprises but succeeded in privatizing only 10 and liquidating 1. In July 1996, the Agency was terminated and its functions went to the National Privatization Agency. This Agency has been responsible not to the Ministry of Privatization but to the Council of Ministers collectively.

The exact number of privatized firms transferred, or still in being, is not easy to divine. The figures, all derived ultimately from the National Agency for Privatization, appear superficially to tell widely conflicting stories. The source of the confusion may depend partly on the different uses of the term *small and medium enterprises* (SMEs). There has been an upper limit defined for this class, but probably no similarly clear lower limit, and some within the upper limit may be treated as 'large' in other contexts. 'Enterprises' may sometimes mean units that had been operating separately *before* privatization or sometimes those that were operating separately *after* privatization. Hashi and Xhillari (1997, p.17) cite NAP figures to show that the number of SMEs privatized (apparently as whole units) from 1991 to 1995 was 482. One of the present editors was told by an authoritative government source in early April 1998 that by then 750 SMEs had been privatized, and 830 remained to be privatized. Taken with the previous figure this would imply that 268 had at that time been privatized since the start of 1996 (probably most of them *during* 1996).

Yet the figures cited in Table 6.1 above, also based on estimates derived ultimately from the NAP, show 5,596 SMEs privatized in 1994 and 1995 alone, nearly 12 times the 482 just mentioned as covering the whole of 1991-95.

Hashi & Xhillari (1997, p.11; 1996, p.15) cite two further estimates of the numbers of *units* or *objects* privatized, in one case from 1991 to 1994 and in the other from 1991 to 1995. These numbers are different, though not wildly different, from each other (the former giving 32,850 for 1991-94, and the latter 30,595 for 1991-94, 32,911 for 1991-95, and 5,091 for 1994-95); both show a much slower rate of privatization (by numbers of items) from 1994, but the figures for individual years in the two estimates do not fit together closely. These clearly include the many small bits and pieces of former state enterprises or of ministries' operations that were transferred separately.

It seems that the figures in Table 6.1 must also include the bits and pieces ('objects' or 'units')---those businesses that were separate only after

Table 6.1 Privatization of small and medium enterprises, 1994-1996

	1994	1995	1996
Auction and direct sale	1,776	2,336	1,707
Auction-exempted	980	473	534
Leased	19	12	7
Total number of SMEs privatized	**2,775**	**2,821**	**2,248**
Group workers	1.102	649	344
Albanian individuals	905	1,310	1,057
Foreign investors	6	1	2
Ex-owners	762	861	846
Total number of SMEs privatized	**2,775**	**2,821**	**2,249**
Book-value (million lekë)	2,148	3,757	3,184
Total privatization revenue (million lekë)	**2,182**	**3,953**	**3,302**
Cash revenue (million lekë)	1,838	576	293
Revenue in million privatization-lekë	344	2,630	773
Revenue in privatization-bonds (million lekë)	0	747	2,236

Source: Estimates based on National Agency for Privatization figures

Table 6.2 Information on enterprises privatized in the first rounds of mass-privatization, 1995-1996

	1995	1996	Total
Number of "packets" of enterprises for privatization	2	3	5
Number of privatized enterprises	50	46	96
Total book-value (capital value) of above (million lekë)	5,649	3,414	9,063
Part of book-value sold (privatized) (million lekë)	4,451	2,891	7,342
Part of book-value retained by state (m.lekë)	1,198	523	1,721
Number of privatized enterprises in which state retains a holding	6 (1 at 30%, 2 at 51%, 3 at 70%)	10 (9 at 51%, 1 at 60%)	16
Share of land in the total book-value (million lekë)	754 (13%)	511 (14%)	1,265 (14%)

Source: Estimates based on National Agency of Privatization figures

privatization---as well as enterprises that continued as single entities after privatization.   On that assumption, Table 6.1's total of 5,596 SMEs for

1994 and 1995 is reasonably close to the corresponding total of 'units' or 'objects' mentioned in the previous paragraph for those two years, 5,091. In fact, if we suppose (as an extreme case) that *all* of the 482 enterprises apparently transferred as single entities to 1995 were privatized *in 1994 or 1995* and are included in the former figure (5,596) but not in the latter (5,091), and that the remainder in the former are 'units' and 'objects', the two figures for 'units and objects' formed over 1994-95 come to 5,114 and 5,091 respectively, which must count as very close indeed.   But it is difficult on any terms to reconcile all of these figures closely.

If we accept the figure that something like 33,000 small businesses were formed through privatization over the five years from 1991 to 1995, *and suppose that virtually all continued in operation*, then the 55,000 small businesses mentioned above as existing in 1995 would appear to have been formed about 60% through privatization and 40% *de novo*.   Given that *not all* the 33,000 are likely in fact to have survived, the proportions might be closer to half and half.

What relationship did the face-value and the market-value of vouchers bear to the value of what was acquired?   The total face-value of privatization-lekë was 17.133 billion lekë.   The total value of privatization-bonds intended to be isssued was 72.383 billion lekë (Mema, 1997, pp.39-40).   Though it had been decided to distribute 20% of the bonds in the first instalment (which would be 14.456 billion), in fact only 85% of that amount (17% of the projected total) was distributed (according to a Savings Bank of Albania source), apparently because of difficulties in contacting some of those eligible.   In fact according to one source only 4.537 billion of bonds and privatization-lekë combined were *used* for bidding in mass-privatization over 1995-96 (Mema, 1997, pp.48-49; the author confirms this interpretation).

Table 6.2 indicates that *the book-value privatized* in the 1995 and 1996 rounds of *mass-privatization* was 7.342 billion lekë.   This is significantly greater than the face-value of bonds and privatization-lekë given up in mass-privatization over those two years (4.537 billion) or even the face-value with cash bids included (5.294 billion) (Mema, 1997, p.49).

When, moreover, account is taken of the fairly small fraction that the market-value of vouchers bore to their face-value, even during the actual months of mass-privatization (less than a quarter, during and after February 1996), the book-value of assets privatized seems likely to have been *immensely* greater than the *market-value* of the vouchers used.   We understand that the book-values had been at least updated to take account of inflation.   If this had not been the case the mis-match would have been even greater than these figures suggest.   We cannot of course rule out the possibility that real earning-power was much less than book-value.   But these were presumably operative enterprises, almost all of them presumably making their way (however precariously) without subsidy, as appears from chapter 5. If the book-values of the assets corresponded even roughly to their capitalized earning-power, or were even say twice as great, those who could *buy* vouchers and knew something about the assets privatized could clearly make very favourable deals.

The mass-privatization of 1995-96 accounted for only a small proportion of the value of what had been state enterprises: 6% according to an estimate by the (German) Agency for Technical Cooperation, while other methods of privatization to that time had accounted for 25%, and 70% remained in state hands (Hashi and Xhillari, 1997, p.22). By numbers of enterprises, the proportions are 5%, 56%, and 38% respectively. (We presume the figures do not include state farms.)

In retrospect the privatization of farmland, of urban housing, and of very small household establishments, appears to have been extremely successful in terms of production generated and to have justified the speed with which it was undertaken. Its probable *political* effect was mentioned in chapter 2, and events certainly seem to confirm it. Since those who became owners of dwellings were almost entirely different people from those who became owners of farmland, probably about 680,000 households came into one or other category---about one household for every five members of the population. Admittedly, after privatization of housing, 20,000 urban families were given special treatment as homeless (Hashi and Xhillari, 1997, p.15), and these could only have been a part of those without their own housing; but it is hard to see how all homelessness could have been avoided, and some action was taken to remedy it. The land-privatization is said (Preci, 1994, p.3) to have left 30,000 rural families landless, but the author who cites this figure does not make clear how this was brought about and what the circumstances of the families were; some landless families would of course have other means of support.

As we move up through larger enterprises and forward through time, *before the stage of mass-privatization*, there is perhaps not quite as much satisfaction with the outcomes, but no strong case appears for having gone more slowly, and there are no glaringly obvious ways of doing it better. There were dilemmas that lacked any ideal solution.

With mass-privatization, however---intrinsically a good idea---we believe that certain wrong moves have been made, and we put forward below what might be, or might have been, improvements.

The Remaining Agenda, End of 1997

The EBRD (1996, p.11) estimated that 75% of Albania's GDP was produced by the private sector in late 1996---the equal-highest proportion among the former Communist countries of Central and Eastern Europe. However, much of the privatized economy is in agriculture. While almost all farming, housing and retailing property has now been privatized, the relevant Ministry reported in late 1997 an estimate that 53% of 'state-owned enterprises' had been privatized 'totally', representing in value about 20% of the assets of the economy (Ministry of Public Economy, 1997, p.5). (It is not clear whether the 53% is by number or by value---presumably the former---and there is no corresponding figure given about the extent of part-privatizations.)

The sectors in which the state was still the owner of its former properties, wholly or largely, in late 1997, were banking and insurance; most of mining and energy; most of the utilities; the state tourist body; and some important but often ailing parts of manufacturing such as enterprises in wood-processing, glass and cement. These activities correspond on the whole to those in which substantial foreign investment is thought to be essential.   While there has been a certain amount of very small-scale foreign direct investment; some larger foreign investments in construction, food-and-drink processing, hotels and banking; and the beginnings of foreign participation in minerals and energy; there has been no great enthusiasm on the part of foreign investors for taking a controlling share in Albania's major state-run enterprises.

It is, however, important to mention that, at the end of 1995 and early 1996, the electricity-distribution systems of Elbasan, Shkodër and Vlorë were privatized. This was regarded as an experiment, but the regulatory mechanism and other conditions were held to be in place: under three laws ('On Electric Energy', 'On Privatization of the Electroenergetic Sector' and 'On Regulation of the Electric Energy Sector') passed in July 1995. The last of these set up what was designed to be 'an independent regulating entity' (REE).   Among other functions, the REE was to issue licences for generation, transmission and distribution; to approve tariffs within upper limits set by government; to impose an accounting system; and broadly to set standards of service. The outcome of the experiment is not yet clear. The legislation specified that the main form of privatization in the sector would be through joint-stock companies 'with controlling shares'.   This presumably meant that one firm would hold a controlling share in each case, but it is not immediately clear whether that was seen as meaning a majority share.   A further law, of 5th October 1995, however, was more specific on this matter and required that the initial holdings of shares in a transferred company in the sector should be no less than 30% to a *strategic investor* and no less than 30% 'by a mass-privatization plan'. It appears to have been envisaged then that the government might well retain a minority holding.

Electricity distribution is a tricky area for a private operator to take over in Albania because of the notorious 'stealing' of electricity through unauthorized connections. By the same token, however, any government would doubtless dearly like to be rid of responsibility for it. It seems likely that a private distributor would have to attempt the necessary corrective action, which might be politically too unpopular for the government.

There had also by the end of 1996 been some foreign investment in segments of copper and chromium production. Again there had been a law (9th November 1995) specifically on privatization 'of commercial companies that operate in the mineral sector'. This law also used the term *strategic investors*, which for this purpose was defined as meaning 'well known companies in the respective fields that have the necessary capital' and come to own no less than 30% of the shares. The law divides mining companies into big, medium and small, requiring each of the big ones to have a strategic investor, and allowing the medium to have one or not. For the big ones, no less than 20% of the shares, and for the medium no less than 30%, were to be sold through mass-privatization. For the small, the requirements were vaguer but suggest that most of the shares were intended to be sold for vouchers.

For petroleum, there was a set of laws and decrees of July 1993 and April 1994, allowing private firms to be given exclusive rights for periods of years for petroleum exploration and production, and also allowing the state oil company, AlbPetrol, to assign rights held by itself to local or foreign companies. Several foreign companies had been given exploration rights by the end of 1997. These included INA, a Croatian company, which had started exploring at two places not far to the southwest of Tirana before being halted by the troubles in early 1997, and Fountain Oil, which had a joint venture with Albpetrol and also suspended work early in 1997. (*AO*, 3, 3-4, March-April 1997, p.14). Early in 1998 it was announced that the Patos-Marinza field and associated block near Fier would be further jointly developed by a consortium of the state firm AlbPetrol, with Premier, Preussag, and the IFC, in what was said to be the biggest single foreign investment in Albania so far (*Albanian Daily News*, 31/3/1998, p.6) of US$ 275 million over 6 years (slightly more in dollar terms than the whole of new inward FDI---excluding that in trade and offshore exploration--- recorded over 1993-96). Other joint-ventures in oil or gas were arranged or under negotiation by late 1997 (Ministry of Public Economy, 1997, p.15).

In 1995 a law was passed to convert state-owned enterprises into commercial companies (while they remained state-owned). There was also a law (of 26th July), comparable to Britain's 'Private Finance Initiative', that would allow private firms to contract with the state to construct and operate items of infrastructure, and indeed to operate utilities. It provided for a number of variants of arrangements, as discussed and applied in recent years elsewhere in the world.

Feasibility studies have been conducted to assess the future strategy for telecommunications development, including the short-term possibility of partial privatization to permit joint-ventures with strategic investors, who would be encouraged to take a minority shareholding to help modernize and manage the network in return for an exclusive fixed-term operating licence, after which full privatization and competition could follow.   A draft telecom law has therefore been drawn up, which sets out the objective of privatization *in principle* and the licensing arrangements necessary for would-be competitors, which includes the possibility of interconnecting to the Public Switched Telephone Network (PSTN).   The draft telecommunication law also envisages the need to regulate prices and oversee the commercial activity of any privatized telecommunications operators, but the details remain sparse.

In the absence of privatization, the lack of prospects for investment in the Albanian utilities---electricity, water and telecoms---would be serious. Although AlbTelecom, for example, has spawned a new mobile-communications-service offshoot, AMC (which is already estimated to have 3000 subscribers as of mid-1997), the issue of providing a modern telecommunications service in rural locales remains largely unaddressed: for over 80% of rural dwellers, the nearest telephone is still over 20 km away.   Albania's 3.4 million population has the lowest rate of telephone density (1.7% *circa* 1994) in Europe (see EBRD, 1996, p.35), though it has been growing fast. A rate of 6% is the aim for 2002 (Ministry of Public Economy, 1997, p.11).   In relation to standards elsewhere, the situation is, if anything, even worse in the postal sector, where only about 35% of the population is said to receive a regular mail delivery, and that mainly in urban areas.

Another key element of Albania's privatization policy relates to its financial sector.   The central bank was separated from state commercial banking under the law of April 1992.   In addition, a number of private banks have been set up, though their role, except in foreign-exchange transactions, has been very limited.   In fact, despite the pivotal role that has to be played by lending institutions in a traditional market economy, the impact of commercial banks has been limited in Albania.   This is possibly attributable in part to a lack of precision in the original enabling legislation, which, it has been alleged, left issues such as collateral, movement of money between accounts, insider-dealing, and the regulation of savings organizations ill-defined.   Ambiguity in the law may have contributed to the financial disaster of 1997, while it has been argued that the passive behaviour of the banks left much of the need for intermediation unsatisfied.

The country's (originally three, by mid-1998 two) commercial banks are each held to need an equity partner to strengthen their financial reserves and hence their lending capability. Financial expertise is also at a premium and the absence of a modern and effective credit system has probably proved an obstacle to both attracting FDI and funding indigenous economic development. Unless promising investors appear, the full-scale privatization of Albania's financial sector cannot take place, and thus the scope for development elsewhere in the economy is restricted. However, it has to be said that determined efforts seemed to be under way at the end of 1997 and early 1998, under the aegis of the multilateral institutions, to prepare the state banks for privatization. In early 1998, the Rural Commercial Bank was closed and its liabilities and sound assets transferred to the Savings Bank. The privatization of the National Commercial Bank was targeted for the end of that year, and that of the Savings Bank for the end of 1999, but in early April 1998 a suitable strategic investor had not been found even for the National Commercial Bank. An institution had then been set up to take over the bad loans of the banks. A foreign bank had been engaged to administer the privatization of the Savings Bank, and a similar foreign administrator was being sought for the National Commercial Bank.

We can generalize to say that the great bulk by value of the complete enterprises still to be privatized as of early 1998 were held to require a *strategic investor*, a single participant with a large, though not necessarily a majority, shareholding, who would manage the enterprise. This strategy was designed to deal with the problem of management, which mass-privatization in itself certainly had not solved. Under the priorities set out in preparation for the legislation of early 1998, it is explicitly foreseen that normally there will be a share retained for the state. There may also be a share for voucher-holders in many cases, but mass-privatization seems to have a decidedly lower priority than in 1995-96.

For the utilities there will also be a regulator, as already for electricity. There are considerable technical difficulties in regulating utilities---difficulties most severe perhaps in telecommunications given the present possibilities in the industry. But the fundamental difficulty of privatization is that of finding the strategic investor who will consider the conditions attractive. The deal will probably require the private operator to be committed to extensive investment. Where there is to be a regulator, or any form of administrative control over prices charged or quality of service, there may need to be a prior agreement with the strategic investor, at least for a substantial initial period, limiting the discretion of the regulator or the government. Especially after 1997, potential foreign investors can hardly help regarding Albania as a somewhat risky arena. The art on the Albanian government side will be to give investors security without surrendering too much in the expected division of the spoils.

Policy for the Future

Principles for the Legislation of 1998

Legislation to implement the general privatization policy of the Socialist-led government was going through the Assembly at the time this chapter was under preparation in April 1998. However, what in Britain would be called a White Paper from the Ministry, issued in the previous December, outlines the thinking behind it (Ministry of Public Economy, 1997). This does not really signal any radical break with the past---at most some slight shift of emphasis and perhaps increased precision. At the same time, much is left for future decision, and some of what is ostensibly decided seems ambiguous.

A distinction is made between *strategic* and *non-strategic* sectors. The strategic comprise electricity, telecoms, water, ports, airports, railways, oil-gas, and mining. Remaining state holdings in tourism and in manufacturing are non-strategic. Banking and insurance are not mentioned.

Enterprises in the strategic sectors will require *strategic investors*, and it seems to be implied that they will also---normally or commonly, though possibly not in mining or transport---retain some state participation, even if only a 'golden share', which seems to be taken to mean a share carrying certain veto powers. With the non-strategic sectors, the aim seems generally to privatize wholly.

Telecoms and water will, like electricity, have regulators, and privatized ports will have a port authority fulfilling the same function.

Voucher-privatization is mentioned as a possibility for a number of the sectors, but with an upper limit to the proportion of shares to be distributed in this way. The upper limit specified in any of the strategic sectors is 15% or 20%, and it is clear in some cases, and a possible interpretation in others, that not all within this limit will necessarily go to those who have received privatization-bonds as members of the general public (or privatization-lekë). Some within the limit may go to employees or to local government. (A limit of 30%, out of which up to 5 of the 30 may go to employees, is mentioned for the non-strategic alcoholic drinks and by implication tobacco.)

The paper seems to denote some down-grading of mass-privatization, and at most a shade more clarity on the priority given to procuring a strategic investor and on the continuing role of state holdings. At certain points it is deliberately leaving open a range of possibilities.

What may be a step forward (though it is too vague for us to be certain) is a requirement on the government to publish a programme of the units to be privatized. There are also prospective dates mentioned, suggesting that much of the privatization still to be done should be accomplished, or at least under way, in 1998 or 1999. An extensive list of legislative changes, almost all to be accomplished by the end of 1998, is appended to the paper.

Getting Privatization Right: Efficiency, Equity, and Political Acceptance

We have seen that the commitment to having a *strategic investor* in many of the entities still to be privatized leaves scope for a continuing state shareholding and also for further sales of shares for vouchers, which, as we have seen, were actually required by legislation in certain cases. If a suitable strategic investor can be recruited, this is probably the best expedient for dealing with the problem of *management.* On the presumption that this will happen, most of the case for setting up statutory intermediaries on Czech lines would disappear.

Yet the other big issue of mass-privatization---*who benefits and how much from the distribution of assets*---is still of enormous importance, both for the economic welfare of the population and politically. Mass-privatization presented the opportunity of a potentially large and widely-spread distribution of claims on valuable assets, a big increase in fairly liquid personal wealth, to a population most of whom regard themselves as having suffered a huge loss of wealth in early 1997 through private chicanery and public mismanagement. This increase in wealth has the advantage that it does not entail any necessary increase in the lek money-supply or in any very close substitute. It is vital to keep the exchange-value of vouchers as high as possible, that is as near as possible to the real prospective value of the assets to which they will give claims. The higher this value is, the more absolutely and relatively valuable they will be to the ordinary citizens who receive them, as distinct from financiers and others with special knowledge.

There are also important questions of how to attract strategic investors while still safeguarding the interests of the public. Any entity, to be made attractive to a potential shareholder, must be relieved of undue liabilities and obligations resulting from past history. At the same time, there must be a framework of regulation making provision for imposing requirements on prices and standards of service. But there must also, in the case of the utilities (partly because of their monopoly position), be negotiated agreements between the state and the prospective bidder, committing the bidder to a certain amount of capital investment and maintenance, and limiting the extent to which the state will use its regulatory powers.

Pricing of Assets and of Vouchers

In order to increase the value of vouchers to ordinary members of the public it would be appropriate to reduce risk, uncertainty and ignorance. This could be done by increasing the certainty of the privatization programme, increasing the opportunities for relevant knowledge on the part of ordinary people who receive the vouchers, and elminating any unnecessary uncontrollable element from the share-allocation process. The provision of statutory intermediaries as discussed above might have been an effective way of allowing ordinary members of the public to make use of the knowledge of others and to spread their portfolios of underlying assets.   But, if these are ruled out now, as we guess they will be, other measures involving less radical change in the existing system might be adopted.   We suggest three.

   (i) If possible (consistently with other requirements), a realistic and credible timetable for future privatizations over say the next five years should be set out, with a clear statement about what proportion of shares in each enterprise (or on weighted average) is expected to be transferred by mass-privatization.   (This would allow rough calculations to be made of the value of assets that would be purchased on average by each 1,000 lekë of outstanding vouchers.)

   (ii) Sales of shares in an enterprise to a strategic investor should be arranged before any of its shares are offered to the public for vouchers. What proportion of shares are bought by the strategic investor, and for what price, should be widely publicized in order to make clear how an informed party values the assets of the enterprise that are to be offered for mass-privatization.   Government should undertake the publicity, drawing the simple arithmetical implications for the valuation of each block of shares, both absolutely and in relation to the expected value of a unit of outstanding vouchers.

   (iii) Something should be done to reduce the uncertainty for a bidder under the existing mass-privatization system over whether she will gain all, or only a tiny fraction, of the shares in an enterprise from the vouchers with which she bids.   This depends entirely on how many *other* people bid for the same firm, and she has no way of knowing this.   It is understandable that an ordinary system of auctioning to the highest bidder is not introduced.   But the present arrangements make the process into a lottery, even for a voucher-holder who is knowledgeable about the various enterprises.   There is a fairly simple way out.   Each bidder for an enterprise should be allowed to specify the lowest proportion of the total shares in it that she is prepared to accept.   If dividing the total number of shares in proportion to the face-value of vouchers bid would give her a smaller proportion than that, this bid would simply be withdrawn.   If there were any doubt about which of the various bidders who had set limits should have their bids withdrawn, some simple rule might be adopted (such as that one who had set higher limits should have her bid withdrawn ahead of one who had set lower limits, and that, if that did not suffice, priority should be determined by lot).

(iv) As a method of allowing risk to be reduced through spreading, a person should be allowed to divide his vouchers in bidding among several enterprises.

With the possible exception of the first, all these four changes would be simple to introduce. They would increase the value of vouchers by reducing the ignorance over how they could be usefully deployed to buy shares and also reducing the uncertainty and risk of any particular bid. This would be likely to raise their sale value in the market as well as their usefulness in bidding. It would consequently make their issue a more important addition to ordinary people's effective wealth. By disseminating relevant knowledge and allowing risks in the use of the individual voucher-allocation to be spread, it would reduce the relative advantage of those able to acquire special knowledge or to buy up large numbers of vouchers.

Regulation and Deals with Investors

The question of regulation arises particularly with the public utilities and in a somewhat different way with banks and insurance. We shall concentrate on the utilities.

On regulation of pricing, the basic model we suggest is the UK one: with prices limited under an *(RPI minus x)* formula and a regulator appointed for each utility industry. However, the application of this model would probably need to be considerably modified from British practice.

First, a limit or a fixed value for x in any utility industry would probably need to be agreed in advance for a substantial initial period, by negotiation with the prospective strategic investor. This would of course limit the regulator's discretion for that period. Such a negotiated limitation will very probably be essential to procuring any investor's commitment.

From the beginning the regulator would monitor compliance with the price formula and also with other requirements pre-agreed with the operator, such as extensions of the network, and would passively monitor quality stanndards. When the regulator came to the point of fixing a value for x, he would be obliged to set out his reasons in a public report.

After the initial period, he would proceed to active monitoring of quality and might have the discretion to trade-off quality improvements against reductions in prices charged. He might have more discretion than before over fixing x.

Attention should be given to ensuring that the regulators are and remain independent as well as being fully informed. The possibility of having some official of *ombudsman* type to scrutinize the regulators' decisions might be considered.

A key requirement in privatization of any utility should be to have an agreement with the prospective investor over how far the network should be extended, what investment there would be on repairs and upgrading, and what quality standards should be set.

Fiscal Rules for Natural Resources

In mining and oil-gas extraction, there is a strong case, in a country such as Albania, for having a fixed fiscal regime that is framed so that the state shares the private investor's risks but at the same time gets a large share of the returns when they are favourable---a system under which the investor knows exactly how he will stand under various financial outcomes, and one that the state will not be tempted to change when results are good. The rules should give the investor the opportunity to cover his costs at an acceptable minimum rate of return while, subject to that and other necessary constraints, giving the host-government, on behalf of its people, as big a share as possible in the realized value of the resources. There has been a certain amount of consideration (with a number of instances of practical application) of the best ways of doing this. (See Goss, 1986; Garnaut and Clunies-Ross, 1983.)

Summary

Like other transition countries, Albania has had to experiment widely with privatization. Virtually all the modes of orderly privatization that can be listed have been practised. Once the commitment had been made to a market economy, privatization of agriculture, and of urban housing, and of small shops and service establishments suitable for one-family enterprises, proceeded just about as fast and as thoroughly as was possible, and with little obvious ground for regret over the methods adopted. In these sectors at least the results seem to have been very satisfactory. At the end of 1996 there was not much still privatizable in the public sector, except banking and insurance, much of the mineral and energy industries, most of the public utilities, the state tourist body, and some enterprises and shares in enterprises scattered through manufacturing.

Much of the privatization occurred under favourable terms (free or at less than open-market prices) to people with special claims: collective-farm families, state-farm workers, tenants of urban housing, workers in very small separable units and in small establishments generally, former-owners of buildings and of non-agricultural land, and victims of persecution (who received allowances of *privatization-lekë*, which they could use almost like cash in auctions of state property).

Privatization in the urban productive sector moved generally from smaller to larger. Where cash auctions could not readily be used, favouritism was sometimes suspected. Medium and larger enterprises began from late 1995 to be sold on the most egalitarian principle: for *privatization-bonds* issued to all adult citizens who had not already obtained state or collective property free of charge (*mass-privatization*).

A number of the very largest will in future be sold, in part, by negotiation, to *strategic investors*: big players, mostly foreign, who are expected to take over management. This has happened already with some aspects of the mineral industries and with power distribution in three towns.

In retrospect, the main avoidable flaws in the process would seem to lie in some of the arrangements for *mass-privatization*, which in effect (i) made the vouchers less valuable than their potential command over resources justified and as a result greatly favoured those with access to finance and business information (who were likely to be buying vouchers) over the ordinary recipients (likely to be selling them), and (ii) had an inadequate bias toward ensuring sound management. As a result the distribution effects of the process were much less egalitarian than might have been hoped; and efficiency was almost certainly harmed by the lack of enforceable provisions to maintain continuity in management and to guarantee some element of expertise in direction under new and inexperienced owners.

These deficiencies might have been substantially remedied by channelling voucher-privatization through a handful of statutory intermediaries on some variant of the Czech model. Since this is very unlikely to be instituted now (though active use of the registered private investment funds is a possibility), and the main enterprises still to be privatized are planned to have management handed over in each case to an experienced *strategic investor*, the principal modifications now needed in the process are those that will make vouchers more valuable by reducing the ignorance, uncertainty, and risk asociated with their use.

Four specific proposals are made to this end: (i) that the published programme of privatizations be made as firm as possible; (ii) that relevant information bearing on the value of enterprises to be privatized, especially the terms on which strategic investors have bought in, should be published; (iii) that voucher-holders should be able, with any bid, to set a lower limit to the share in the enterprise that they are prepared to accept; and (iv) that it should be possible for any voucher-holder to split his bid over several enterprises.

Regulation of utilities after privatization needs to embody the monitoring of agreements on investment by the operator, and of rules and agreements on both price and quality. It is probably better if the price-regulation takes its starting-point from a British type *(RPI minus x)*, rather than an American-type (rate-of-return) model, but with provisos that (a) the mode of fixing the rate of real price-reduction *(x)* be set out as clearly as it can be in every instance, and that (b) there may be considerable restrictions on the value of *x* for each utility agreed in advance for a substantial initial period with the strategic investor. The regulator should in the initial period operate a light regime of ensuring that investment undertakings are observed, monitoring observance of the pricing rule, and passively monitoring quality of service; later extending standard-setting to quality of service and possibly exercising more discretion over the pricing rule. Undoubtedly there will be difficulties, in Albania as elsewhere, of ensuring that each regulator is both well enough informed and also completely independent if and when he or she is given a high degree of discretion.

A number of the utilities at the start of 1997 were self-supporting financially, and telecommunications was a substantial contributor to tax revenue. There are possibilities of competition in some aspects of their activities, such as mobile telephones. To be satisfactorily privatized, each needs a regime (with a regulatory body) to limit its prices, to see to the maintenance of quality and the fulfilment of undertakings made by the new owners, and to set up rules under which any feasible competition can operate. Each also needs a large and experienced (probably foreign) investor, who is prepared to take on the burden of considerable upgrading and expansion. These two needs are potentially in conflict. The way ahead unavoidably is (i) to proceed as quickly as possible to put the *framework* of a regulatory regime in place for each utility industry (as has been done for electricity distribution and is under way for telecoms); (ii) to negotiate the *detailed* rules and limits with potential investors along with their commitments to investment and service.

For mining and oil-gas extraction, there is a need for a clear and stable fiscal regime, which removes or reduces unnecessary risk and uncertainty for the investor while ensuring for the Albanian state a large share of returns when they are high.

7 Stabilization

The aspiration of Stalinist planned economies was that prices and quantities of everything should be centrally fixed. Stabilization becomes a completely different task once this aspiration is abandoned and it is accepted that prices and quantities may be determined through a huge number of autonomous transactions between individuals and associations, with the government only one of a large number of participants. An economy in transition has to develop a system for stabilizing the level of economic activity and the general price level in this changed environment. That is the first reason why stabilization has a critical role in transition.

There are also particular reasons why transition to the market should be initially destabilizing to the price level. Commonly command-economies have been run with a tendency to excess demand: there are many kinds of good of which consumers (a) would be glad to buy more and also (b) have the purchasing-power that would enable them to do so at current official prices if enough of the goods were available. Similar shortages often prevail with producer-inputs. There is excess purchasing-power at existing prices. To put it another way, prices are generally held below the levels that would equate supply and demand.

Removing price controls therefore leads to a rise in prices which, even without any other action, may be quite considerable. It is also likely to reduce personal saving or increase dis-saving as people reduce their cash holdings.

The initial rise in prices reduces the real value of wage and salary payments on existing schedules. It almost inevitably alters the distribution of real incomes. This may well lead to a demand for increased wages and salaries (in money terms). This will raise costs of production and the costs of government services. It is easy to see how a cycle of continuing inflation can be set up unless deliberate action is taken to stop it.

A further complication is the fact that the former methods of providing the government with purchasing-power may no longer be applicable. New forms of tax have to be introduced and effectively collected. Until that happens, the state may find its revenue in cash terms stagnant or falling while its expenses are rising. This means budgetary deficits which, in the absence of a domestic bond-market to finance them, have to rely on expansion of the money stock.

These problems of imbalance are aggravated if, as has invariably happened in the European and ex-Soviet transition economies, real national income has at first fallen. This means that (in the absence of sufficient inflow of capital and transfers from abroad) there are less goods and services available.   The rising stock of money and rising spending in money terms often meet a falling market supply.

In international trade, so long as an earlier (overvalued) exchange-rate is preserved, freeing transactions (removing implicit duties and subsidies that have hitherto made it possible to achieve a balance) is likely to lead to an excess of imports over exports.   Alternatively, allowing the exchange-rate to depreciate so as to equalize demand and supply for foreign-exchange would instead raise the domestic prices of both imports and exports. Further domestic inflation would in that case entail further exchange-rate depreciation, and so on.

The onset of inflation increases uncertainty; by so doing makes any form of budgeting more difficult; discourages commercial lending and borrowing; and creates an unfavourable climate for inward international investment.   It also redistributes real income on no equitable principle.   In its extreme form it reduces the useful functions of money.   Politically inflation is extremely unpopular. For all these reasons, controlling inflation is a prime requirement.

But it is important that inflation should be controlled with minimum loss of output.   Stabilization in normal conditions must ultimately be directed to stabilization of the level or growth-path of output and income or of expenditure.   During the transition period, however, as it has been experienced in Central Europe, this need is overshadowed by that of simply switching from falling to rising output.   Yet, at least in the short term, the measures taken to reduce inflation---reducing government spending, higher tax schedules, more effective tax collection, raising interest-rates, pegging the exchange-rate---may all tend to reduce output, which in itself will actually *increase the difficulties* of reducing inflation.   On the other hand, any prior rise in output makes it easier---less painful, less demanding on popular patience and government determination, less detrimental to subsequent growth---to control inflation.   Virtuous, as well as vicious, circles are possible.

Stabilization in Albania: Explaining the Virtuous Circle

From the middle of 1992, Albania seemed to move macroeconomically into a virtuous circle.   Its basic stabilization strategy from that time is easily set down.   What needs to be explained is why that strategy was relatively easy to implement, and why, from about the time it was introduced, the country moved fairly promptly to falling inflation and rapidly rising output.

The stabilization strategy from the 1st July 1992 was to float the currency, but to target, mainly by domestic monetary means, a fairly stable nominal rate against the US dollar. During the period from then to the end of 1996 there were, according to the IMF (1997, p.14) 'only occasional central bank interventions', that is direct interventions in the foreign-exchange market. The lek-dollar rate as reported varied thereafter from day to day, but it was never far from 100 to 1 over the four and a half years between the instigation of the float and the end of 1996. The IMF estimates (1997, p.16) that 'over the period 1993-96, the standard deviation of the exchange rate was only 7.5%; day-to-day volatility averaged just 0.5%, but rose during periods of political uncertainty'.

Pegging or targeting the exchange-rate to a fairly stable world currency or currency-basket is one possible discipline for achieving a low rate of inflation. Targeting it by domestic monetary policy implies that money supply is allowed to expand if the external value of the currency shows signs of rising above the target, and is contracted if that value seems to be falling below the target. Following a rule such as this also serves as a discipline for controlling the money supply. This will be the *right* monetary discipline considered solely as a means *for checking inflation* (keeping it down roughly to the rate in the targeted external currency)--- provided of course that the exchange-rate does act to tie the inflation rate in the domestic currency to that in the foreign currency.

A number of attempts to peg or target from a starting position of fairly high inflation, however, have entailed serious losses of output and employment, and some have been abandoned for this reason before achieving their anti-inflationary goals. The *first puzzle* is why this did not appear to have happened in Albania. Output and inflation improved at about the same time. By mid-1993, even the unemployment rate had begun to fall.

The *second puzzle* is how the Bank of Albania managed to maintain the exchange-rate with the rather feeble domestic monetary tools at its disposal. There were government budget deficits (after the receipt of counterpart funds), in excess of what was covered by foreign finance, amounting to 10.2%, 6.5%, 7.0% and 10.1% of GDP respectively in the four years from 1993 to 1996. There was no bond-market through which the authorities could borrow from 'the public' to finance these deficits. Hence they were covered in part directly by the Bank of Albania, in part by the sale of Treasury Bills, but the Treasury Bills were bought almost entirely by public-sector bodies and mainly by the state-owned commercial banks and insurance company. Rules were latterly introduced which ostensibly gave the Bank of Albania more control over financing the deficit, but it still seems to be the case that, once the deficit was set and foreign finance was exhausted, the central bank had a rather limited capacity for preventing the remaining 'domestic deficit' from constituting domestic-credit creation.

To examine this assertion it is necessary to know the means of monetary control available to the Bank of Albania. (It might seem, on the contrary, that the sale of Treasury Bills to meet the deficit would avoid an expansion of the the money-supply.) Monetary controls have been maintained by the central bank from 1992 through regulating (if rather passively) the quantity of base-money; through bank-by-bank credit ceilings adjusted quarterly (subject to penalties for infringement, which were not enforced); through a cash-reserve requirement on the banks (higher against deposits in foreign exchange), with loans to them at penal rates if the requirement is not otherwise met; through interest-rate directives to banks (after early 1996, only on time-deposit rates); and by absorbing excess bank liquidity through Treasury Bills (IMF, 1997, pp.14-18). Limiting the banks' net holdings of foreign-exchange, though subject to instructions with penalties attached, has in fact been effected by the Bank of Albania through purchase of the excess (*ibid.*).

It is true that, *if the starting-point was one in which the commercial banks had no excess liquidity*, and a certain part of the government deficit was then covered by the sale of additional Treasury Bills to the banks, those banks, in order to restore their cash-reserve ratios, would need to reduce their lending---to an extent even greater (because of the banking-multiplier) than the value of Treasury Bills bought. But in fact it seems likely that the banks would use *only their excess liquidity* to buy Treasury Bills. In that case the sale of Treasury Bills would *not* reduce bank lending and hence would have no effect on the money-supply, and there would be domestic-credit creation to the full amount of the domestically-covered government deficit.

Admittedly, the central bank could also in principle use its power to lower the ceilings on bank lending as an alternative means of reducing the monetary expansion arising from the government deficit. Yet the actual magnitudes suggest that, without making very large proportional reductions in bank lending, it could not have compensated for any large part of the government deficits of recent years. The domestically financed part of the deficit in 1996 would amount to 26.9 billion lekë (from figures in Table 11.1). The total claims outstanding of the banking institutions on the private sector at the end of October 1996 amounted to only 10.5 billion lekë, and on non-financial public enterprises to 3.5 billion; and over the preceding 10 months the *net* bank lending to the private sector had been only 2.1 billion lekë and to non-financial public enterprises 0.4 billion. (See Table 13.3.) So, without fairly drastic curtailment of bank lending, not much of the increase in domestic credit necessary to finance the deficit could have been offset by reduced bank credit to the private sector and public enterprises. Hence any need for domestic financing of a budget deficit *far out of line with the money-creation that could be accommodated by the exchange-rate-targeting policy* would have made it very difficult or disruptive for the Bank to maintain the monetary discipline.

We shall deal with the second puzzle first. We have to conclude that the money-creation entailed by the need to finance the large budget deficits (without a domestic capital-market from which to borrow) was not wildly excessive from 1993 *because the economy was growing so fast.* Either by good luck or by deliberate discipline on the part of those drawing up the government budget, the Bank of Albania was not set an impossible, or even a difficult, task. (It appears incidentally from Table 7.3 below that the readiness of the public to hold lekë in proportion to income was rising from around the end of 1994 for the next two years, as would not be surprising if confidence in the lek was growing.) Suppose, for the sake of illustration, money-creation over a year equal to 7% of national income, when the income-velocity of money was 3, real income was growing at 9% and the price-level rising at 11%. This increase in money supply would leave the ratio of money-supply to income at the same level as before. (Some of the actual magnitudes can be worked out from the tables below.)

It is true that, beside the money created as a result of the need to finance budgetary deficits, much additional money was also coming into the economy as remittances. But, because this money brought with it foreign exchange (it did not represent 'domestic-credit creation'), and foreign exchange on the whole was not accumulated by the public and non-financial institutions but spent on imports of goods and services, there was no particular reason to suppose a net addition to the money-supply in Albania as a result. The upshot of all this is that keeping to the stabilization policy did not seem to involve any significant monetary austerity. The authorities may have had limited *capacity* to restrain money and credit in any painful way. But as it turned out they also had little *need* to do so.

Yet this leads back to the first puzzle: why was income growing so fast from 1993 onward *in spite of the anti-inflationary discipline* of the targeted exchange-rate?

The first point to be made is that the policy was *introduced with a large depreciation* of the currency. The lek averaged 50 to the US dollar over the first half of 1992. Movement to the float involved something like an initial 50% devaluation of the lek against the dollar: from about 2 US cents per lek to 1. This would if anything have given an immediate boost to tradable-goods industries. From the starting-point on 1st July 1992 there was thus plenty of room for subsequent *real* appreciation (through domestic price rises)---which in fact went on for nearly two years---without putting these industries in any worse competitive position than that in which they had been during the first half of that year.

A second point is that probably *relative tradable- to nontradable-*

goods prices became less important to the level of economic activity once a number of the old state industries had ceased to function.   Exports of merchandise came to form quite a small proportion of GDP---about 7% in 1994 and 8% to 9% in 1995.   The upcoming clothing and footwear sector, which came to form an increasing share of exports, was probably in a very good position in its relative costs, so that the speed of its development depended mainly on other factors.   Similarly, for some of the emerging import-competing goods, notably livestock products and vegetables, the pace of growth seems likely to have depended far more on the provision of marketing facilities, and perhaps the accessibility of production inputs, than on relative price changes between competing imports and the industry's inputs.

Thirdly, as we have seen, a large part of the growth in output was borne by privatized *agriculture.   Internal trading, services and construction,* all directed to 'nontradable' (that is, not *internationally* competing) outputs and all largely or wholly in the private sector by the end of 1993, were also important.   Even if the stabilization policy *had* restricted bank credit, the effect on these sectors would probably have been small because on the whole *they did not depend on bank credit.*   (Some larger-scale construction was done by foreign firms, who probably got their finance from abroad.   Much of the building of apartment-blocks seems to have been financed by cash provided up-front by prospective occupants, no doubt largely from the proceeds of remittances.)   These elements of growth were likely to be largely unresponsive to financial and macroeconomic policies.   Here, what may be regarded as Albania's 'backwardness' has quite possibly contributed to its success in this particular.   The inadequacy of the country's banking and finance has meant that its real economy is not very sensitive to any financial restraint that there may be.   (But, as we have suggested, there is little evidence of such restraint in any case.)

Fourthly, as one of the studies on which this book is based has shown (Hallwood & MacDonald, 1997), there is evidence that the *real-exchange-rate* in Albania is *fairly strongly 'mean-reverting'*, that is to say that it tends to return to a previous equilibrium level if it has been disturbed, for example by a change in the nominal exchange-rate or in world prices. Casual inspection of the last two columns of Table 7.4 fits with this finding. Though there is a progressive real appreciation (against both the dollar and the mark) from the latter part of 1992 until early in 1994, thereafter, until the start of the disturbances of 1997, there is no obvious trend either up or down.   This seems consistent with the interpretation that the real-exchange-rate adjusted toward its equilibrium level over twenty months or so after the big nominal depreciation when the rate was freed in mid-1992, and thereafter hovered around that level.   From June 1994 to December 1996, the highest value of the real lek-dollar index (for the final months of the various quarters given in the table) is just about 10% above the lowest.

The real exchange-rate is an index in which the nominal exchange-rate (the exchange-rate in the ordinary sense, which we express for the present purpose so that an appreciation is a *rise*) is multiplied by a domestic price-index and divided by a world price-index.   It thus measures (inversely in this formulation) the impact of the changes in these three price-series taken together on the competitiveness of the country in world trade.   A *rise* in the real exchange-rate in itself tends to make the country's tradable goods *less* competitive.

Table 7.1 Growth rate of real GDP, and inflation, 1989-1996

Year	(1) GDP at current prices (m lekë)	(2) GDP-deflator (1990 =100)	(3) GDP at constant 1990 prices	(4) GDP growth from previous year (%)	(5) Increase of GDP-deflator from previous year-average (%)	(6) Increase of CPI (end-year) from previous year-end (%)
1989	18,681	100.0	18,681			
1990	16,813	100.0	16,813	-10.0	0.0	0.0
1991	16,473	135.5	12,156	-27.7	35.5	104.1
1992	50,700	449.4	11,282	-7.2	231.7	236.6
1993	114,200	923.7	12,363	9.6	105.5	30.9
1994	188,300	1,380.8	13,637	10.3	49.5	15.8
1995	225,060	1,507.2	14,932	9.5	9.2	6.0
1996	266,200	1,641.5	16,217	8.6	8.9	18.9

Source: Official figures

If the real-exchange-rate is mean-reverting, the implication is that, however the nominal rate and the world price-level change, the domestic price-level will fairly quickly adjust so that the real rate (reflecting the price-ratio between tradable and nontradable goods) returns to its previous level.   A fixed or steady nominal rate will in that case serve as an 'anchor' for the domestic price-level, keeping its rate of rise more or less in line with the rise of the price-level in the world currency to which the domestic currency is pegged or targeted.   By the same token the pegging or targeting will not (except initially after a sharp change of stance in which the value of the currency is forced or held *higher* than expected by the public) reduce the competitiveness of the country's own tradable goods.

Its domestic system of relative prices between tradable goods and nontradable inputs (such as wages and transport costs) will remain largely undisturbed.

Albania appears to be not unusual among the transition economies in having a tendency to mean-reversion in its real exchange-rate.   In their absence of rigidities, they contrast with the main economies of Western Europe, whose price-systems in this respect have become less 'market-driven'.   It is possible, however, that Albania's high degree of liberalization, especially of wages in the private sector, together with the fact that so much of its economy is small-scale agriculture with a low level of purchased inputs, makes its price-system *especially* flexible and responsive, and its real economy especially resilient to shocks involving initial changes in relative prices.

These four considerations, together with the observations made above in dealing with the 'second puzzle', seem between them to give a plausible enough explanation of the fact that targeting of the nominal exchange-rate against the dollar fairly quickly fulfilled *the one* objective of producing a reasonable degree of price stability, while not sacrificing *the other* objective of leaving the rate of growth unimpeded.   In fact, not all the explanations may be necessary.

Table 7.2 Nominal and real* bank lending rates, 1992-1996

Year	Average lending rate (%)	Inflation of CPI over year (%)	Implied real interest-rate (%)
1992	20.6	236.6	- 64.2
1993	29.6	30.9	- 1.0
1994	23.7	15.8	6.8
1995	19.7	6.0	12.9
1996	24.0	18.9	4.3

*   It is not to be inferred that the figures in the final column represent the most relevant estimates of real lending-rates for the relevant years.

Source: International Financial Statistics and official figures

Success in any one element of this complex task tended to make the rest easier.   The fact that the economy launched at the critical time into growth (while most of the relevant types of labour were probably still in abundant supply) conveniently reduced the severity that was needed in the monetary restraints.   In addition, we might expect that eventually the relative stability of the exchange-rate after mid-1992 and the continuing reduction in inflation would increase the tendency to hold money.   The evidence below in Table 7.3 suggests that this indeed began to happen from the third or fourth quarter of 1994 and continued at least until the middle of

1996. (A *fall* in the income-velocity of money is taken to signify that people are holding amounts of money in *increasing* proportion to their incomes.)

Table 7.3 Income-velocity of money, quarterly, end-1991 to mid-1996

Date	GDP/M1*	GDP/M2*	GDP/M3*
31/12/1991	3.4	3.0	3.0
30/06/1992	3.7	3.3	2.9
30/09/1992	4.6	3.7	2.9
31/12/1992	4.8	3.8	2.9
31/03/1993	5.2	3.9	2.9
30/06/1993	5.3	3.8	2.9
30/09/1993	5.4	3.8	3.0
31/12/1993	5.4	3.8	3.1
31/03/1994	6.1	4.0	3.2
30/06/1994	6.3	4.1	3.3
30/09/1994	6.3	4.0	3.2
31/12/1994	5.5	3.7	3.0
31/03/1995	5.4	3.5	2.9
30/06/1995	5.2	3.4	2.8
30/09/1995	4.8	3.2	2.6
31/12/1995	4.1	2.8	2.3
31/03/1996	4.2	2.8	2.3
30/06/1996	3.9	2.7	2.2

*   1. GDP figures used are linearly intrapolated from nominal GDP values as they
     appear in Table 7A, column (1), with the annual figure applied to the 30th June.
   2. M1 = currency held outside banks + demand-deposits
      M2 = M1 + time-deposits
      M3 = M2 + foreign-currency deposits
Source: Official figures

This shift in behaviour would tend to reduce the inflationary effect of a given increase in the money stock.

So the vicious circle---in which monetary contraction reduces output, which requires further monetary contraction---was replaced by a virtuous circle---in which output growth allows prices to stabilize *without* monetary contraction or tightness, and eventually the stabilized prices increase the demand-function for money, which further contributes to stabilizing prices.

Table 7.4 Nominal and real exchange-rates of the lek, 1992-1997

Month	(1) Nominal rate lekë per US$	(2) Nominal rate lekë per DM	(3) Real rate: lek to US$* (12/93=100)	(4) Real rate: lek to DM* (12/93=100)
12/92	102.9	63.8	73.4	68.0
12/93	98.9	57.3	100.0	100.0
03/94	100.5	60.1	102.5	99.1
06/94	93.3	58.5	123.2	114.5
09/94	84.7	54.7	127.1	115.9
12/94	95.6	61.7	120.8	105.8
03/95	93.3	67.4	121.7	100.1
06/95	91.7	66.3	120.8	101.4
09/95	93.3	65.8	117.0	100.7
12/95	94.2	65.7	120.3	104.8
03/96	100.5	68.1	118.4	106.0
06/96	111.7	73.4	107.9	100.0
09/96	107.8	70.6	118.3	109.7
12/96	103.1	66.3	128.5	120.5
03/97	148.5	88.5	99.0	98.6
06/97	178.7	102.5	93.4	94.7
09/97	147.4	83.5	114.4	116.7
12/97	149.8	83.8	n.a.	n.a.

*   Real exchange-rates are expressed in such a way that a *rise* represents a real *appreciation.* Thus columns (3) and (4) are based on the *reciprocals* of columns (1) and (2), multiplied in each case by the Albanian consumer price index for the month and divided by an index of dollar and mark prices respectively. The index of dollar prices is the mean of US indices for export and import prices, and the index of mark prices is the corresponding mean for Germany.

Source: Official figures and *International Financial Statistics*

However, there were signs by 1996 that the capacity to stabilize might well be slipping because of failings in the revenue system. Between 1993 and 1996, government revenue fell each year as a proportion of GDP, and in real absolute terms it was 6% lower in 1996 than in 1993. This in spite of the fact that income was rising fast over the four-year period. Enforcement of a number of taxes was clearly deteriorating. This will be discussed in chapter 11. The most recent estimates for CPI inflation over 1996 put it at 18.9%, well up on the 6.0% of 1995. Even if the disasters of 1997 had not occurred, Albania's achievements in stabilization might well have been at risk unless there were rigorous collection of taxes and a continuing fiscal discipline.

The Balance of Payments: the Key Role of Remittances

Albania's balance of payments over the eight years ending in 1996 is shown in Table 7.5. One of its most striking features is the big proportional disparity between exports and imports of merchandise (rows 2, 3). In 1992, imports were well over 7 times as high as exports. However, thereafter exports grew faster proportionately: at an average rate of 36.6% a year, as against 14.3% for imports. The balance of goods, services, and (factor-) income account (row 8, the first one in bold) was strongly negative in every year of the table but especially from 1992, to the value (in 1995, the year in which it was at its lowest of the last five in the table) of about 20% of GDP. But a positive net transfer figure of the same order (row 9 *minus* row 10) made the balance on current account (row 11) much closer to zero or sometimes even positive. Net inward capital transactions had the effect that the 'total balance' was positive in each of the years 1993 to 1996, and even in the first half of 1997 (Table 7.6). In fact, over the whole of 1997, reserves rose by US$44 million (Bank of Albania source), after having risen in each of the previous five years.

Inward transfers---partly public and NGO aid, but from 1994 or earlier principally remittances from emigrant workers---have performed the valuable role of taking the place of exports, allowing residents of Albania to import much more than they are exporting, to consume and invest much more than they are producing within the borders of Albania. To regard them as in any sense malign, as some commentators have done, seems perverse.

One such objection sometimes raised against the transfers is that they have held the exchange-rate unduly high and consequently discouraged exports or more broadly tradable goods. But it is the authorities who have chosen to hold the exchange-rate near the 100 to 1 level. To do so in the first instance involved a big real-depreciation. If it is true, as the evidence cited above suggests, that the the real exchange-rate tends to revert to a stable equilibrium wherever the nominal rate is set, it is hard to see how a nominal rate that is stable on a float for a considerable period (without any apparent need for a growth-restricting monetary stance to keep it there) can be held to make domestic tradable goods *unduly* uncompetitive. As a matter of practical judgment it would be hard to maintain that arrangements which allow merchandise exports to expand at 36.6% in dollar terms (well over 30% in real terms) on average each year for four years are unduly discouraging to exports. The more capacity a country has to import, the higher the real domestic expenditure (consumption and investment) it can sustain, and hence indirectly (in an important sense) the higher its real income can be.

Table 7.5 Albania's balance of payments[b], 1989-1996 (US$ million)

	1989	1990	1991	1992	1993	1994	1995	1996
Export goods	393.7	322.1	73.0	70.0	111.6	141.3	204.9	243.7
Import goods	*455.8*	*455.9*	*281.0*	*540.5*	*601.5*	*601.0*	*679.7*	*922.0*
Serv's credit	40.2	31.5	9.2	20.3	77.6	79.1	98.8	129.2
Serv's debit	*27.9*	*29.1*	*33.4*	*89.1*	*161.9*	*132.5*	*156.5*	*189.4*
Income credit	0.4	..	0.8	2.6	64.9	55.1	72.0	83.7
Income debit	*0.5*	*1.9*	*25.9*	*37.7*	*31.0*	*41.3*	*28.4*	*11.9*
Bal. g.,s.& income	***49.9***	***133.3***	***257.3***	***574.4***	***540.3***	***499.3***	***488.9***	***666.7***
Tr'fers credit	10.6	15.0	89.3	524.0	556.9	347.5	521.2	595.9
Tr'fers debit	..	..	..	*0.3*	*1.7*	*5.5*	*43.8*	*36.5*
Bal. curr't acc't	***39.3***	***118.3***	***168.0***	***50.7***	***14.9***	***157.3***	***11.5***	***107.3***
Fin'l acc't n.e.i.	359.4	*117.7*	*181.2*	32.2 (22.0)[a]	44.1 (58.0)[a]	40.2 (53.0)[a]	*411.0* (70.0)[a]	61.5 (90.1)[a]
Cap'l acc't n.e.i.	..	..	..	..	..	..	389.4	4.8
Errors & omis'ns	4.8	2.0	125.2	47.4	*10.3*	123.9	53.7	96.9
Total bal.	**324.9**	**238.0**	**224.0**	*35.5*	*48.7*	*6.8*	*20.6*	*55.9*
	324.9[c]	32.0[c]	28.0[c]	27.4[c]	114.9[c]	55.2[c]	30.5[c]	47.6[c]

a   Figures in round brackets represent new foreign direct investment in Albania.

b   Items that entail cash flows out are given in italics, as are negative balances in the aggregates given in bold.   Of these aggregate rows, row 8 is the sum of rows 2 to 7. Row 10 is the sum of rows 7 to 9. Row 14 is the sum of rows 10 to 13.

c   The figures so marked are changes in reserve assets, those in italics being falls.   The differences between these figures and 'total balances' are made up of transactions with the IMF and 'exceptional financing'.

Source: International Financial Statistics

We can see the transfers as carrying Albania over a potentially difficult period when its traditional exports almost disappeared in the face of liberalization and other events.   It takes time for substitutes to emerge. They were clearly doing so in the years to 1996.   In the meantime it is convenient if people can eat---and enjoy some other amenities that depend on imports.   However exports expand, imports are likely to continue far exceeding exports so long as net inward transfers and capital movements remain at high levels.   But the additional imports are a boon, not a burden. Unless there is a serious risk that the transfers will be suddenly cut off through political action, they are in themselves an unmitigated advantage.

Private inward remittances over 1997 were judged to be lower than their annual average over 1993-95 (Bank of Albania source).

Table 7.6 Albania's balance of payments[b], 1995 to June 1997 (US$ million)

	1995	1996	1997 first half
Export of goods	204.9	243.7	76.5
Import of goods	*679.7*	*922.0*	*258.5*
Services credit	98.8	129.2	28.0
Services debit	*156.5*	*189.4*	*44.7*
Income credit	72.0	83.7	23.5
Income debit	*28.4*	*11.9*	*5.0*
Balance of goods, services & income	**488.9**	**666.7**	**180.3**
Transfers credit	521.2	595.9	161.1
Transfers debit	*43.8*	*36.5*	27.5
Balance on current account	**11.5**	**107.3**	**56.7**
Finamcial account n.e.i.	*411.0* (70.0)[a]	61.5 (90.1)[a]	65.5
Capital account n.e.i.	389.4	4.8	1.0
Errors & omissions	53.7	96.9	*8.4*
Total balance	**20.6**	**55.9**	**1.5**
Reserve change	30.5[c]	47.6[c]	1.5[c]

a Figures in round brackets represent new foreign direct investment in Albania.
b Items that entail cash flows out are given in italics, as are negative balances in the aggregates given in bold. Of these aggregate rows, row 8 is the sum of rows 2 to 7. Row 10 is the sum of rows 7 to 9. Row 14 is the sum of rows 10 to 13.
c The figures so marked are changes in reserve assets, those in italics being falls. The differences between these figures and 'total balances' are made up of transactions with the IMF and 'exceptional financing'.
Source: International Financial Statistics

Lines of Stabilization after 1997

There would appear to be several priorities for stabilization in the aftermath of the disasters of 1997.

1. There should be a return, as explicit as possible, to a stable targeted exchange-rate. Educated opinion in early 1998 seemed to be that in fact a range of either 150 to 160 or 160 to 170 lekë to the dollar was being deliberately targeted by the authorities.

2. Tax administration should be greatly strengthened both to allow for

higher government spending (especially capital spending on schools, hospitals and roads) and also to give the government some choice over the level of its deficit without the risk of damaging or politically dangerous cuts in expenditure. (As chapter 11 suggests, there were signs of apparent improvement over 1996 performance in at least customs collection during the second half of 1997.)

3. A negotiable government bond, of a kind that would suit the needs of the mass of the public (probably indexed for inflation), should be introduced. This is principally to channel private savings in the immediate future for public-investment purposes; but also to start a process so that, as a bond-market develops over the years, it becomes increasingly easy for government deficits to be financed without equal increases in money supply.

Summary

Albania's stabilization discipline, introduced from mid-1992, was remarkably successful in curbing inflation fairly promptly while allowing very rapid growth to proceed. We have suggested that the success was due partly to good management and partly to good luck, though a large part of the good luck in this department depended on good management in other spheres.

For various reasons connected with the structure of the economy, measures could be taken to stabilize prices without disturbing the growth of output. The fact that growth 'took-off' after 1992 greatly facilitated stabilization by making it consistent with greater monetary expansion than would otherwise have been possible, and so removing the necessity for blatantly painful monetary restraints. Stabilizing the exchange-rate and the domestic price-level seems to have eventually increased the tendency to hold money. This again tended to facilitate the reduction of inflation without tears. Albania thus found itself in a virtuous circle of relative price-stability with rapid growth.

The main macroeconomic measures taken, in particular the targeting of the exchange-rate by domestic monetary means, seem to have been well-conceived for the circumstances in which Albania found itself. The success also rested largely on fast growth, which depended in part on measures outside the macroeconomic field, such as the prompt privatization of farms, shops, and housing.

Yet there were signs by the end of 1996 that poor collection of tax revenue might not only limit urgently needed public investment but also hazard the virtuous combination of stability with growth.

Albania's external position over 1993 to 1996 was one in which remittances and other inward transfers largely took the place of exports, allowing a comfortable rate of rise of merchandise imports to coexist, in spite of a huge trade deficit and only modest net capital inflows, with steadily rising international reserves.   At the same time merchandise exports showed no sign of being suppressed by macroeconomic conditions and were rising proportionately very much faster than merchandise imports

In the aftermath of the events of 1997, there was a need to return to a targeted exchange-rate; to improve tax collection and administration radically; and to issue readily negotiable (indexed) bonds that ordinary members of the public might be willing to hold.

8 Safety-Nets and Social Security

Albania has had the task of changing its social-security system to deal with the possibility of unemployment and the existence of a private sector. The main changes necessary were the introduction of two new forms of safety-. net: Unemployment Benefit and a last-resort Social Assistance. *Among transition economies*, Albania's response has not been particularly distinctive, though in one respect (the size of the employee contribution to social security, mentioned below) it has been *unusual*.

Where Albania is possibly unique is that, *as a low-income country with the majority of its workforce in agriculture*, it has attempted to run a comprehensive national social-security system and safety-net of a kind typical of industrialized societies. It is not surprising that there are anomalies, and that the system in practice is not quite what it aspires to be.

Transforming and Supplementing an Existing System

Provisions for retirement pensions and certain other benefits formerly applying to state employees were carried over from the command-economy period and now apply to employees in both public and private sectors, and, with variations, to farmers, other self-employed people, and employers. The Social Security Institute manages the transactions.

The old system was formally contributory, with 11-13% of the wage being deducted. The new system is also contributory (though over 1993 the employee paid nothing) and, like the old, applies to maternity, accident, and sickness benefits as well as to retirement and invalidity pensions. A big addition, however, has been unemployment benefits, which started, like Social Assistance, to be paid in 1992. At first they were recorded in the budget figures independently of the other payments coming under the Social Security Institute.

In late 1996, the total rate of contribution for *employees* (exclusive of obligatory medical insurance, which was introduced in March 1995) was 32.5% of pay from the employer and 10% from the employee. The employee share had risen by a step each year from zero in 1993. These proportions applied to pay within a certain wide range: from very roughly 50% to 150% of the average wage in 1995. In principle, farmers, and the other self-employed paid 34.5%, though it was 34.5% not of their actual incomes but of a certain standard amount, namely the state-sector minimum wage, so that their contribution was in some respects like a poll tax: it was independent of what they actually earned.   Farmers, however, were allowed a further reduction (at least until the end of 1996).   Depending on the District in which they lived, they paid either 9% or 15% of the amount laid down.   This means that those in the Districts judged as most deprived paid in a year little more than the urban self-employed paid in a month.

An employee contribution is in effect an income tax, usually *proportional* at least over a certain range, but distinguished for being especially easy to collect.   The fact that there is an upper limit to the range of wages over which the contribution is proportional to the wage, however, and that for higher wages it is simply a fixed amount each month, means that, for ranges of wages above that limit, the contribution is in effect a *regressive* tax; that is, it takes a *lower proportion* of income as income rises.

The 10% employee contribution in Albania has to be seen beside the very low impact on the employees of personal-income tax itself.   This has had marginal rates from 5% to 40%, but it realized only 605 lekë per 'employed' (in the sense of gainfully occupied) person over the whole twelve months of 1995, about 0.8% of the average wage reported for that year. It must of course be remembered that personal-income tax is paid only by employees (people receiving wages and salaries), who are a minority, probably 30-35%, of 'employed' (gainfully occupied) people. So for each wage-employee, the personal-income tax in 1995 would have taken about 2.7% of the average wage.   It is clear that, for this part of the active labourforce (even when we take account of the fact that, as explained below, quite a large number of those wage-workers who should pay the contribution do not do so), the social-security contribution has been a much more important direct tax than the personal-income tax.

In March 1995, an obligatory medical-insurance contribution of 3.4% of 'income' (as assessed for the social-security contribution) was added. For employees, this was paid half by their employers and half by themselves.   The two sets of contributions together amounted in August 1997 to 34.2% for employers and 11.7% for employees, a total of 45.9% of the employee's 'income'.   Medical insurance was intended to help cover the cost of general-practitioner services and certain medicines, not hospitals or specialist services.   At that time, it seemed quite possible that both the medical contributions and also the employer and employee contributions to general social insurance would before long be raised.

The employer contribution can be regarded as a *payroll tax*, and of course it adds quite considerably to the cost of employing workers.   It is part of what are called *non-wage costs* of employment.   It seems to be typical of the transitional economies to have a much higher employer than employee contribution (see EBRD, 1996, pp.137-84, which, however, reverses the two figures for Albania and gives the lower at 6% rather than

10%). The EBRD notes on social security (pages just cited, *passim*) seem to indicate that employee contributions, other than very small ones, are the exception rather than the rule in the transition economies. They seem to imply that, beside Albania, only three (Hungary and the Czech and Slovak Republics) had in 1996 employee contributions at rates other than 1% of gross wages; four more had contributions at 1%. This is the respect in which, as we have said, Albania is *unusual* among the transition economies.

Yet, like those of other transition countries, its *employers* have had what seem by Western standards quite large burdens in their contributions to the social-security funds. To get these non-wage costs into perspective, however, we must remember that in the private sector there are only very weak (probably inoperative) obstacles to dismissing workers, and that, except in a few of the state enterprises, no payment has to be made to workers on dismissal. In these respects no further employment costs are added. Moreover, many private employers do not in fact pay the social-security contributions due under the law.

The social-security contribution of employer and employee combined, when it was reformed in the early 1990s, was supposed to cover the various social-security needs in the following proportions of the wage-bill used for assessing it.

Pensions (retirement, invalidity and other)	31.7%
Illness	1.5%
Maternity	2.8%
Unemployment	6.0%
Accidents	0.5%
Total	42.5%

However, the accident share of the contribution given here is an average. The percentage actually charged varies from industry to industry in relation to their proneness to accidents (Mima, 1994). The self-employed and farmers, who in principle paid only 34.5% of the sum imputed as their income (the minimum wage), were accordingly entitled only to pensions and maternity benefits. Moreover basic farmers' pensions are much lower than basic urban pensions.

The Social Security Institute (SSI) manages the system, but legally its inflows and outflows are not separate from state revenue and expenditure.

How Far Self-Funding?

The EBRD by 1996 regarded the system as being 'on an actuarially sound basis' (1996, p.137). This is perhaps premature. Koliadina (1996) said that, with World Bank help, the SSI had *started to develop* actuarial methods for assessment of contributions. But up till the time of writing the system has certainly not been 'funded' (which would involve holding or building up accumulated assets). Its principle is 'pay-as-you-go'. Yet at the same time inflows have been very far from covering outflows, and it is difficult to see in what sense the judgment of actuarial soundness can be right. Even aside from Unemployment Benefits (which, in the fiscal accounts until 1996 inclusive, had not been recorded along with payments coming under the SSI), the government has had in the last few years to cover a large proportion of social-security payments from other resources. This 'budgetary transfer' to social security, 4.913 billion lekë in 1994 and 4.975 billion in the first nine months of 1996, represented 35.5% and 36.4% respectively of social-security expenditure (again excluding Unemployment Benefit and Social Assistance). In 1996 and before, the government also made some of the payments *into* the SSI funds (that is our interpretation of what is reported, and it is true in effect even if not in terms of the actual accounting procedures): not only (a) the employer's contribution for the administrative departments ('budgetary institutions'), but also (b) the difference between the total contribution nominally due from the farmers and the 15% or 9% actually paid, and in addition (c) the continuing employer and employee contributions for insured workers currently in their first year of unemployment and receiving unemployment benefit. These three items, as far as we can tell, were separate from the 'budgetary contribution' just mentioned

In 1993, when the unemployment rate was at its highest, the ratio of social-security contributors to pensioners in Albania was 1.0 (*WDR 1996*, p.79), the lowest of the ratios quoted for a number of transitional economies in that year, against an OECD average in a recent year of 2.6. This was despite the fact that the age-distribution recorded for Albania (according to the same source, 7.9 people of working age for every person over 60) was easily the most favourable of those examined.

According to Koliadina (1996, p.14), the ratio of contributors to pensioners in 1994 was even lower than in 1993, at 0.86. She argues that the low level of the figure was due in considerable degree to *non-compliance*, because in the same year the ratio of *workers* to pensioners was 2.27. But non-compliance was not the whole reason for the fall of course: the ratio of workers to pensioners had then already fallen from the higher figure of 3.70 in 1991. The low ratio of contributors to pensioners illustrates not only the seriousness of non-compliance but also the difficulties of financing a contributory pension system when many of what would have been the working-age population have gone abroad or become unemployed or self-employed, while the elderly and invalids remain at home.

If the wage and salary structure had remained constant in real terms, and pensions preserved in real value at an average of say 65% of income, a contribution of 31.7% (the share allocated to pensions) on all contributors' incomes would just serve (after allowance of 5% for administrative costs) to finance pensions (old-age, invalidity and other) by pay-as-you-go if the number of contributors was 2.16 times the number of pensioners.   This calculation, needless to say, oversimplifies the actual relationships of both contributions and benefits to income, but (in view of the figure cited above, that the ratio of active *workers* to pensioners in 1994 was 2.27 in spite of emigration and unemployment) it suggests that, if there were full compliance, covering pension costs on pay-as-you-go with the current rates of contribution and benefit is not out of the question.

Compliance

Non-compliance is clearly a large part of the problem.   In spite of the fact that social-security contributions were by far the most buoyant part of government revenue during the period of rapid economic growth in 1994-96 (see chapter 11), the rate of compliance was not even moderately good except in the public sector.   For state enterprises, an estimated 96.4% of contributions were up to date in 1994 (Koliadina, 1996, p.8), while for administrative departments (the main contributors to the SSI in recent years) compliance was said in 1996 to be less than 95% (*ibid.*, p.9). However (*ibid.*, pp.6-7), the private sector in total, which accounted in 1994 for 70% of workers (including farmers, urban self-employed, and employers), provided only 16% of contributions, and from this the source made a rough estimate that compliance in the private sector (relating presumably to wage-employees only) was 21 percentage points lower than that in the public sector.   Worse still, only 10% of farmers were registered to contribute in 1994 (*ibid.*, p.8).

Two of the commercial banks receive the SSI contributions. From employers who do not keep up their contributions, these banks are said to withhold funds for paying wages, but this presumably is not much help with the many private enterprises that have not registered with the SSI as they should, or with those that do not deal with banks.

It has been suggested, nonetheless, that one reason that the social-security contributions held up so well in 1994-96 was that employees in the private sector often put pressure on their employers to register.

Elements in the System

Old-Age Pensions

Retired urban people in the contributory system receive as a pension 70% of salary if they retire no earlier than the age of 65 for men and 60 for women and have given no less than 25 years' service. They receive 60% of salary if they retire no earlier than the age of 60 for men and 55 for women and have given no less than 18 years' service. There are further maximum and minimum restrictions on the amounts paid. This represents only a slight modification of the pre-transition rules.

Rural-urban disparity Presumably (in part at least) because incomes as assessed are much lower generally in rural than in urban areas, the average monthly rural retired pension has also been much lower---less than a third as high in 1994, and, at 700 lekë a month (roughly $7 at the then-current exchange-rate), an amount hardly designed for survival without other means of support. The rural minimum and average pension were then the same (INSTAT, 1995a, Tables 40, 41). This fits with what might be guessed from the details given above about contributions: farmers' pensions appear to be paid at a flat rate or something close to it (Koliadina, 1996, p.12), while urban employees' pensions are related to past earnings. Officially, however (INSTAT, 1997, p.19), the maximum rural pension is cited each year as at least slightly above the minimum: 750 as against 700 lekë at the ends of 1994 and 1995. This cited rural maximum of 750 lekë remained constant *in cash terms* from end-1993 to end-1995, when it was 22.7% of the official minimum wage. It was 1,138 lekë a month at the end of 1996, 25.9% of the then minimum wage.

If there is any rationale at all in these almost-negligible rural pensions, it must be the belief that elderly rural people will be supported by their children. But what of those who have no children or close relatives? There will certainly be people so situated.

By contrast with rural pensions, urban pensions rose over the same period not only in cash value but in real value. Without indexation for inflation or repeated upgrading, the real value of urban pensions would fairly quickly fall. Yet there does seem to be some adjustment of cash values which, at least with urban pensions, has exceeded the rate of inflation in some years; for over 1994 the average (per-recipient) real value of pensions overall increased by 20% and over 1995 the average real value of urban pensions grew by 9% (Koliadina, 1996, p.12).

Another manifestation of the extraordinary difference in treatment between rural and urban areas (presumably reflecting a difference in treatment between farmers and others) is that in 1994 the absolute number of urban people receiving pensions was nearly twice as high as that of rural people (INSTAT, 1995a, Table 42), despite the fact that the ratio of urban to rural population has been about 1:2, or even according to some estimates 1:3.   The result of such discrepancies in 1995 was that total outlays for urban retirement pensions were about eight times as high as for rural.

In spite of all the reasonable pretexts that there can be for these rural-urban differences, it is hard to be convinced that farmers are getting a fair deal.   It is not surprising that now, when they appear to have (*de facto* though not *de jure*) a choice, most of them do not choose to contribute, but many of the present pensioners must be people who spent all or most of their working lives under the old regime, when presumably they had no choice.   The fact that farmers are largely not contributing *now* can not, it would seem, be a full explanation of why there are so *few* rural pensioners *now*.

But we must consider the intrinsic difficulties of the task Albania is attempting.   Farmers with very low real incomes, drawing what income they have to a significant extent from consumption of their own produce, and forming about two-thirds of the workforce, are an inevitable problem for the kind of social-security system, devised for an industialized economy, on which the country has launched itself.   Albania's social-security system is based closely on West European models.   Probably no other market economy with comparable average-income levels, and such a high proportion of the workforce in farming, has tried this.   The attempt is daring, and it is not surprising that there are apparent flaws and inequities.

Unemployment

Those who lose paid employment and have been contributors in the social-security system for at least a year are given a basic sum for the first year of unemployment.   At end-1994, this sum was 80% of the minimum wage, which made it 1,920 lekë a month.   The proportion to the minimum wage, however, was allowed to fall to 65.2% at end-1995 and 48.9% at end 1996. In real terms (deflated by the CPI), the amount was 3.9% higher at end-1995, and 4.3% lower at end-1996, than at end-1994 (INSTAT, 1997, pp.16-17).   There are extra allowances for family members, more per child if both parents are unemployed than if one is at work.   This is paid by the state, though apparently it is in future to be treated as covered by the social-security contribution.   Registered unemployment was 301,289 at the end of 1993 and 261,850 at the end of 1994.   Numbers receiving Unemployment Benefit, however, fell between these two dates by about half: from 106,783 to 50,776.   The reason is that an increasingly large proportion of the unemployed came to be long-term (a rise from 65% to 81% between these two dates according to INSTAT) and hence had to rely on Social

Assistance. The numbers unemployed for over a year in fact rose slightly between end-1993 and end-1994, though the total number of registered unemployed fell. These tendencies continued, with the proportions of the unemployed who were long-term generally rising even when the total number of unemployed was falling (see Table 12.1). See chapter 12 for the very small proportion of the unemployed who move out of unemployment into jobs each month.

Maternity Provisions

This is one of the elements covered by contributory social security. Maternity-leave arrangements apply to any woman who has been employed for over 12 months, has been enrolled in the social-security system, and has continued in employment, even for only a few days, after the start of the pregnancy. Such women are allowed maternity leave at 80% of salary for six months, and then at 50% of salary for a further six months. There is also a 'birth reward', a fixed sum (recently of 1,500 lekë) paid on birth if either father or mother has been a contributor to social security for more a full year beforehand. In 1995, urban expenditure for maternity benefits (excluding 'birth reward') was 3.5 times as high as rural expenditure: a somewhat similar picture to that for retirement pensions.

Social Assistance or Family Protection

Those without any other adequate means of support receive a sum that depends on size of family. An attempt is made to keep this slightly less attractive than unemployment benefit by limiting the total amount that a family may receive to the value of Unemployment Benefits for two people, which at the end of 1994 would have amounted to 3,840 lekë (INSTAT, 1995a, p.42). The norm assumed for a family appears to be to have two potential earners.

At the end of 1994, 145,002 families were reported as receiving Social Assistance. Added to the roughly 50,000 people receiving Unemployment Benefit they come to a little under 200,000, about 75% of the number of registered unemployed. (A family receiving Social Assistance might of course have more than one member registered as unemployed.) Of the recipient families about 44% received the full allowable amount and the rest somewhat less. 42% of the recipient families were in the Municipalities (urban areas) and the rest in the rural Communes. This would mean that, in relation to their total numbers, rural people were much less heavily represented among the recipients than urban people.

In principle any means of support is taken into account in the assessment of eligibility for social assistance. But it must be very difficult to keep a check on disposable income received irregularly, as with emigrants' remittances or farm income or streetstall income. People may receive the full allowable amount or some part of it according to how their needs are assessed. Social assistance is administered by the Municipal (urban) or Commune (rural) authorities. It must be hard to avoid arbitrariness in judgment of need.

Minimum and Actual Wage-Levels

There is a legal minimum wage, which also serves as an indicator of the poverty level for the purpose of certain pensions and benefits. Though many informed Albanians sem to think that the minimum wage does not apply in the private sector, ACFIP (1997), in its advice to foreign investors, clearly implies that it does. After a period in which government set wage ceilings, at least for public enterprises, there are now no upper limits. Government wages are now indexed, under an agreement with a trade union, to the prices of 24 commodities, and the minimum stood at 4,744 lekë a month in mid-1996 (EBRD, 1996, p.136). If that figure is correct, the minimum had risen by 74% in real terms over 18 months.

It appears that over 1994-96 private-sector wage-rates on average were higher than public-sector wage-rates (though it does not follow that the rate for the same job is likely to be higher; this depends also on the pattern of types of job). At the end of 1994, when the official minimum basic rate was 2,400 lekë a month, the average wage paid is given as 4,955 lekë, with that in 'state enterprises' 4,222 lekë, and that in the private sector 6,342 lekë. Informants guessed too that the *effective* minimum, at least in Tirana, would be higher in the private sector than in the public. By the end of 1995, the overall average had risen to 6,406 lekë, an increase in real terms of 22% from a year earlier (INSTAT, 1996b, pp.3, 4), and by end-1996 it was 8,638 lekë, 49% higher in real terms than two years earlier.

How may these wage-relationships be interpreted? Why do the higher rates in the private sector not attract people out of public employment so that rates in the sectors are equalized? It is plausible that public-sector workers are accepting some immediate sacrifices for security. It may also be that many public-sector workers lack the skills or other qualities typically wanted for the larger foreign enterprises and joint-ventures on the one hand (asking often perhaps for a high level of education or special skills), and for the very small locally-owned establishments on the other (which may require long hours, adaptability, and physical endurance). It does seem plausible that real private-sector wages, though extremely low in external purchasing-power by European standards, were being driven up by market forces at the same time as the unemployment rate was falling---and that market forces were setting the effective private-sector minimum. The apparently market-led rise in real wages until 1996 is *prima-facie* an encouraging sign, suggesting that Albania's fast development was increasing the demand for low-level labour.   Yet the fact as recorded (Table 12.1) that numbers in employment, actually fell slightly over 1995 and over 1996, even though the pool of unemployed also fell, raises doubts about this optimistic interpretation.

Social Transfer Payments and the State Budget

We first follow the fiction that regular budgetary funds are one thing, and the SSI fund another (its expenses in 1995 supplied to the extent of 35.5% by a transfer from the former).   Payments for 'Unemployment' until 1996, and for 'Social Assistance', have been recorded as out of regular Budget funds, not the SSI fund.   Together with the transfer to the Social Security account from other revenue, these (15.190 bn. lekë) constituted for 1995 32.9% of expenditure from that budget (46.143 bn. lekë).   What appear to be the contributions of the government as employer to social security for its on-budget employees (3.776 bn. lekë) would add an additional 8.2%.

If more realistically we consider a figure roughly covering simply all social transfers to persons (social-security outlays, unemployment and social assistance, 24.121 bn. lekë all told) against total 'current expenditure' (59.987 bn. lekë), the proportion is 40.2%.   On any basis, the social transfers constitute a large share of public outlays.

In the years 1992 and 1993, government outlays on pensions and cash benefits on one calculation ranged between about 10% and 12% of GDP. Over 1994 to 1996, they were equal to about 8% of GDP.   (See Table 11.1.)   These percentages are rather lower than we might expect from the proportion to total public outlays given at the end of the previous paragraph.

Adequacy of the Safety-Net

The Tirana Household Expenditure Survey of 1993 (conducted for the period August-October 1993), the only one of its kind,   indicates that average expenditure per head per month was 2,940 lekë.   Inflated in proportion to the cost-of-living index from December 1993 to April 1995, this becomes 3,610 lekë.   Corresponding figures *per consumption unit* (which will probably approximate closely to figures per head) *for the lowest quintile* are 1,370 lekë in current prices, and 1,690 lekë inflated to bring the figure close to 1995 prices.   This may be compared with the 1,920 lekë *per worker* per month paid in Unemployment Benefit at the end of 1994, to which would be added allowances for child-dependants, and with the 3,840 lekë per month, which is the *maximum per household* receivable as Social Assistance.

So, at a rough approximation, we can say that Unemployment Benefit, or the maximum rate of Social Assistance, as of late 1994 and early 1995 would have given a household support of the same order as that required to cover the average late-1993 consumption of the lowest quintile of households in Tirana. This is not surprising because it seems likely that most of this lowest quintile (in terms of expenditure per head) of households in Tirana were receiving one or other of these benefits.

A further comparison may be made with the price of bread and expenditure on bread. At the time of the Survey, Tirana households spent on average 382 lekë per month per person on bread, which was still the main household food: 13% of total expenditure. If the regulated price of bread was then, as it was in May 1995, 40 lekë a loaf (and the CPI gives bread as just slightly lower in price in April 1995 than in December 1993), this would mean that the average person ate 9.6 loaves a month, roughly one every three days. Another table gave the average consumption of bread per month as 15 Kg. This would mean 0.5 Kg per day. If the standard loaf (priced at 40 lekë when still controlled in May 1995) weighs 1.5 Kg, these figures fit together.

If these inferences are right, the maximum per-household Social Assistance of 3,840 lekë per month at the end of 1994, if required to support a household of four with an average per-head consumption of bread, would find bread taking 40% of its disposable income. A single person on Unemployment Benefit, who, being an adult, might consume somewhat more than the per-head average of bread (say 25% more), and would receive at end-1994 1,920 lekë a month, would find expenditure on bread taking 25% of his or her benefit.   On the assumption that a household would set a high priority on satisfying its members' desire for bread, these comparisons are perhaps significant. A household that has to spend 40% of its disposable income to satisfy normal requirements for one staple food may escape starvation and, with good management, undernourishment, but it is likely to be barely able to live a dignified urban existence. In 1994 it could have been said that making the level of support any higher would bring it close to the official minimum wage. Unemployment Benefit per worker was initially fixed at 80% of the official minimum wage.   At the end of 1994, it was 39% of the recorded average wage.   Social Assistance is of the same order as Unemployment Benefit but designed never to exceed it, and, for certain sizes of family, to be slightly lower.   Yet, as we have seen, the proportional gap between these benefits and the minimum wage has grown since 1994.

In fact it seems very likely that many or most people on very low wages, like many or most of those receiving social assistance, are receiving payments from other sources as well: principally emigrant remittances.

This emphasizes the problem of trying to run a Western-style social-security system in the present extraordinary state of the Albanian economy. Albania depends, far more than any other country in Europe, on emigrant remittances. These probably take for the most part a form under which there is no direct official cognisance of them. They are estimated by inference from what would otherwise be a gap in the balance of payments and by other disparities between official figures and apparent realities. The remittances to any particular household may not be regular like a wage. It will be almost impossible to take them fully into account when an official is deciding whether any person is eligible for Social Assistance, and, because of their irregularity, it might in addition seem at times very unjust to do so. All this applies even more to other, legally dubious but perhaps quite important, sources of income.

Farm income too, inevitably irregular and much of it in kind rather than cash, must also pose considerable problems for the fair application of a means test by administering officials. We have already noted that rural Social Assistance dispensed is much lower *per recipient* than urban, and the discrepancy *per member of the population* between rural and urban is even greater because a smaller proportion of rural households are recipients.

The difficulty of administering fairly an adequate living-standard floor by central-government means-tested transfers leads to the question of whether a locally-based, informal approach to social security would serve as a substitute or supplement.

Alternative Approaches to Social Security

There are three main approaches to social security: contributory (insurance-type), non-contributory government transfer, and informal. It appears that Albania uses the contributory principle for pensions, maternity benefit, sickness benefit, and accident and occupational-illness compensation, and (in principle) for short-to-medium-term unemployment. It gives direct government transfers for social assistance (government payments to those otherwise destitute, including the longer-term unemployed), which are means-tested. The informal approach possibly plays a part within rural areas in helping to determine eligibility for means-tested social assistance.

An Informal Approach

Twentieth-century West European and Australasian approaches to social security have depended heavily on cash payments by the state. These require a substantial and highly effective bureaucracy and an environment which makes that bureaucracy able with reasonable accuracy to judge the means, or the employment or the health status, of applicants. They also involve fiscal payments amounting to quite a large proportion of national income. In lowish-income countries, much of output (measured in real-value terms) may be non-marketed, constituting so-called *subsistence income*. Some of the rest of output/income may well escape the tax net. In real purchasing-power terms, the government budget may command a rather smaller proportion of national income than in most affluent countries. The bureaucracy is often less reliable and effective. In addition the tests commonly applied in affluent countries to determine eligibility for income-supporting payments (evidence of current income levels, of hours of employment, of age) are often difficult to apply, either because the information is less well recorded or because the categories used are simply inappropriate.

Whether for these reasons or for others, *universal* systems of *bureaucratically administered* social payments scarcely exist (within basically market-oriented economies) except in high-income countries. Elsewhere, there may be contributory social insurance in the state and capitalist sectors, but this generally covers only a minority of the workforce and population.

Albania will be susceptible to unemployment and other sources of gross fluctuation in personal disposable incomes, and in present circumstances it has various features that make Western bureaucratic ways of providing a safety-net difficult to apply effectively in a universal fashion.

One of the localized 'informal' models that might be worth considering is the English Elizabethan Poor Law definitively laid down in the Act of 1601 (the 'Forty-third of Elizabeth') which was in effect for over two centuries. (It must not be discredited by confusion with its replacement, the utilitarians' Poor Law of 1834, the Poor Law of *Oliver Twist*.) This laid on the local community, under defined procedures, the responsibility of providing paid work for the able-bodied unemployed and support for the non-able-bodied destitute. The Justices of the Peace, local unpaid magistrates, were obliged to impose a local tax in order to pay for these provisions.

A second model is the Commune-Brigade-Team system as it operated in China's countryside from 1962 until about 1978 and according to local studies has left a legacy of flourishing local social-security systems in being in at least some rural areas today. In its original form, this was bound up with collectivized agriculture, and unfortunately foreign academic studies of it on the ground were not easy to arrange until a time when it was already beginning to be broken down. But essentially it laid on the Team (a local unit of 20-50 households) the responsibility of providing rewarded work for the able-bodied and a level of support for households without able-bodied members.   The larger units, the Brigade and Commune, provided certain common services and may themselves have offered a safety-net for the Teams within them.   There is no obvious reason why the local safety-net responsibility should disappear with collective agriculture, and in some villages in China it has not done so, though the transition to household agriculture during the early 1980s clearly meant that the arrangements for support of the destitute and unemployed would have to alter.   Unlike China's farmers, Albania's are technically within a national social-insurance system, but the provisions for them, and their contributions, are so meagre that substitutes or supplements in rural areas may well be sought.

The advantage in principle of local (village- or hamlet-level) provision out of local resources is that it relieves the state budget and the state bureaucracy of the task (it may even be administered by volunteers); that it provides access to local knowledge about the individuals and households concerned; that it introduces a direct interest in economizing on the part of those who are close to the administration of the relief; and that for the beneficiaries it does not depend on a capacity to handle dealings with the bureaucracy.

Possible disadvantages or sources of abuse are: that eligibility may be determined somewhat arbitrarily with opportunities for prejudice and favouritism; that local administrators, especially if they are volunteers, may lack the elementary financial and book-keeping skills necessary; and that in itself it offers no remedy for the plight of a whole village that may be generally affected say by a crop failure.   This suggests that there must be opportunities for individuals to appeal to external authority against their treatment by local safety-net administrators; that there needs to be training for the administrators, whether volunteers or not; and that higher levels of authority, maybe in Albania's case the central government, must have the responsibility of using their resources as a safety-net to help especially disadvantaged villages or other lower-level units within them.

In fact eligibility for social assistance seems to be determined in Albania by the Municipal (urban) or Commune (rural) authorities.   In the Communes, some of them with quite small populations spread over three or four villages, it may be possible to make use of local knowledge of the individuals concerned.   One possibility is that the lowest level of such government, at least in rural areas, might universally be in units small enough for face-to-face acquaintance; that it might be given a broad brief for pursuing matters of interest to the local community; and that it might have the specific task of providing for the destitute by means of a levy imposed by local decision on its members.

We need not suppose that such an arrangement could be anything like a complete replacement for a bureaucratic safety-net in a modern European society, even in small and remote villages, but it might be used as a check, to make more certain that those who were not in real need did not receive national support, and that those who *were* in real need did so. And it might make feasible the adding of a supplement to the very meagre national provisions. If, partly for other reasons, the modern world may be driven back to recognizing and supporting institutions at this very small-scale local level, their use as a supplement in the administration of social safety-nets will have all the more claim to be considered.

Extending the Contributory Principle

Albania's fiscal revenues have fallen in real terms faster than its fiscal expenditures (see chapter 11 on the public finances).   As a proportion of GDP, the fiscal deficit, after having fallen from a peak level to 1994, rose in real terms (and was more or less static as a proportion of GDP) over the next two years of rapid growth.   There is an urgent need for new or enhanced sources of revenue or improved collection.   Direct taxes (which include income, profit and property taxes) seem to offer particular difficulties.   No doubt the obstacles are political and administrative, added to the fact that the number of wage- and salary-earners in Albania has been greatly reduced.

The advantage of contributory social insurance over taxes as a means of financing retirement, where retirement pensions are related to contributions, is that earners who are not regular wage-earners (farm-family members, or employers, or non-farming self-employed), and whose incomes might be hard to assess independently, may enter the schemes if they choose to do so and receive pensions based on the contributions on which they assess themselves; they do not need to have their incomes assessed by officials, as is in principle necessary for income tax.   (As we have seen, *in practice* though not in law, something like a *voluntary* contributory system applies to farmers in Albania.)   Also, if there is a plausible approximation to the financing of people's pensions by their own contributions, the introduction of a contributory scheme, voluntary or not, does not encounter the same political objections as a tax rise.

In Albania during the course of transition the contributory principle has been extended to Unemployment Benefit, and in March 1995 to help pay for certain medical expenses.   Several difficulties may arise here, however, over reaping the full fiscal advantages supposed above for a contributory system.   Unemployment Benefit in Albania is not much better for the recipients than Social Assistance, which those unemployed who are not in the contributory scheme would receive.   Hence people (farmers, self-employed, all whose incomes are hard to assess) would not be very likely to make the extra contributions voluntarily.   Similarly, if people receive medical treatment regardless of whether they have contributed to government health insurance, those who are not *obliged* to pay the health insurance may not choose to do so of their own accord.   As has been mentioned, even the financing of retirement pensions has been deficient over the last few years, partly because of non-compliance but also partly because the resident wage-earners who would have been contributors have declined in number, while the recipients are as numerous as ever.   This last problem will gradually tend to right itself if and when fairly rapid growth of income is resumed after the crisis of early 1997.

Yet the results in Albania over the mid-1990s told strongly in favour of the use of social-security contributions. As Table 11.2 shows, they were the only major source of revenue that increased as a proportion of GDP, both overall and in each of the three years from 1993 to 1996.   (This assessment excludes medical-insurance contributions.)   Moreover, the *increase in the proportion* which the contributions bore to the (fast-rising) GDP over the three years was more than 50%.

Despite the manifest difficulties, the point remains that it is worthwhile considering contributory social insurance as an alternative to tax wherever it can fairly and acceptably be applied.   At present the main opportunity for further application of the contributory principle is probably extension of obligatory medical insurance to cover hospital and specialist services.

Summary

Among market-oriented low-income countries, Albania is probably unique in attempting to run by bureaucratic means a universal and comprehensive social-security system, with a catch-all safety-net.

Albania took the main steps of adapting its social-security system in 1992 when it introduced Unemployment Benefit and the last-resort safety-net of Social Assistance.   The idea is that the former will be incorporated in the contributory system.

The contributory system itself has been modified too by increasing the total percentage payroll contribution, with the larger part of the contribution paid by the employer but (in contrast with most other transition economies) a substantial employee levy as well.   This latter constitutes in practice a much more important wage-and-salary tax than the Income Tax. Special arrangements are made for farmers and for other self-employed people and employers.

A payroll contribution for medical insurance was added in 1995, that for employees was split equally between their employers and themselves.

Compliance with contribution requirements has been less than perfect in the public sector, but far worse in the private, especially among farmers. Nevertheless social-security contributions proved a buoyant source of revenue over the years of rapid income growth from 1994 to 1996, when yields of a number of taxes fell as a proportion of income or even absolutely.

There are apparently anomalous differences between the pensions and benefits received by farm families and those received by the rest of the population. These reflect partly differences in contributions and probably also in part the intrinsic difficulties of applying a bureaucratically administered safety-net to very poor self-employed sector in which much of the income is constituted by direct consumption of the household's own production. The large reliance on remittances is another element that must help to make the fair administration of the means test on Social Assistance extremely difficult.

Unemployment Benefit, and Social Assistance at its full rate, seem generous enough to protect people from starvation, but it is quite likely that in 1995 about 25% to 40% of these benefits that would be received by a family with no other means of support would be spent on bread alone.

The contributory part of the social-security system has recently been far from self-supporting. A transfer from the regular budget has been needed over and above what is paid out for Unemployment Benefit and Social Assistance. Total payments of state pensions and benefits in 1995 were reckoned to constitute about 40% of public outlays. On another (apparently more conservative) interpretation of the figures, pensions and benefits paid out equalled over 1994 to 1996 about 8% of GDP.

There may be some scope for greater reliance on informal methods for determining a household's eligibility for the safety-net benefit. The possibility exists in principle of a largely locally-funded and locally-administered system of relief in rural areas to supplement the very meagre national provision now applying to farm families. There may also be scope for extending the contributory principle, probably to cover further medical expenses.

9 Institution-Building

Institution-building does not lend itself to precise objective reports as do some of the developments discussed in the previous four chapters. What we shall do is to mention some fields in which institution-building in transition is likely to be important and to raise questions that they suggest for the Albanian economy.

The seminal changes in the constitution occurred from 11th December 1990 to the adoption of the Law on Major Constitutional Provisions on 29th April 1991. Then Albania's reforming governments of 1991 and 1992 fairly quickly passed laws that allowed a market economy to operate. This activity, including the creation of new supervisory organizations, continued through into 1996.

The more difficult part, that cannot be brought about by any decree, is the creation of the attitudes and expectations that enable a market economy and a free society to work effectively. This covers a spirit of **enterprise**, a readiness to trade and adapt to changed conditions and take risks, which the Albanian people have displayed perhaps more widely and strikingly than most other peoples of transitional countries.

It entails also a considerable measure of **trust**: a general trust in traders and business-partners, in the courts, in the police, in the information media, and in politicians. This does not mean blind or undiscriminating trust--- merely a presumption that most of the time these actors will play their parts benevolently and in accord with accepted social roles and rules. In order to create trust, the actors must of course on the whole be trustworthy.

There is a further characteristic of behaviour (within certain spheres of activity) on which the market economy and the free society rest. This is **impartiality.** The courts and the police must be impartial in order to generate trust. Lending institutions too need a large measure of impartiality. It has been recognized that, if the financial institutions favour the friends of their owners, or those commended to them by politicians, they can easily find themselves with bad loans. The Southeast Asian financial collapse of late 1997 has been attributed in large degree to favouritism on the part of banks. Elected politicians in some respects will be partial, but there are limits that need to be observed if they are to be trusted. They must submit themselves to a free and genuine choice on the part of the public. The information media must also to a point be impartial. Journalists and broadcasters may have opinions and commitments. Presentations of facts will inevitably be coloured by the presuppositions and prejudices of those who present them. But beyond a certain point interpretation shades into distortion and misrepresentation. The public needs to be reasonably well assured that it is not being told *deliberate falsehoods,* even by advertisers. It also needs to be reasonably well assured that journalists are not slanting the news *because they have been told to do so.* These may seem subtle distinctions. Making them is a matter of habit and practice.

Linked with trustworthiness and impartiality is a further requirement: the exercise of **personal responsibility**. In a totalitarian state those in power are identified with what is wise and right. In the Communist states they were the infallible interpreters of infallible texts. If that is the case, there is no call for impartiality or personal responsibility. The courts and the police and the press and broadcasting should simply do what they are told and act so as to maintain the existing structure of power. But the market economy and the open society stand on the supposition that there is no infallible human source of wisdom and right. They require the many individuals to decide for themselves. Therefore it is important that they should not be misinformed. But equally the journalists, like the judges and the police, have no special source of authority to tell them what is true and just. They too have to decide for themselves. Hence the importance of the traditions by which they decide responsibly, in such a way as to create trust.

No society scores 100% on these tests. A failing in any one may suddenly assume great importance. The ex-Communist countries may well face special difficulties because of the high degree of regimentation under their old regimes and the consequently small area for the exercise of personal responsibility. Much has been made of the weakness of what is called *civil society* under these regimes. This term seems to cover at least two related phenomena. One is the free and voluntary associations that people form for particular purposes. Such associations must depend largely on trust, reinforced by moral and social pressures. The second is the readiness of people, individually and as groups, to take an independently critical view of the exercise of power---by governments, parties, businesses, churches---and to express independent views on policy. *Civil society* in both these senses is suppressed under totalitarian rule. It is important for the working of a market economy and a free society.

There is no known routine for inculcating the required attitudes. The best hope is that they will gradually develop through open discussion and criticism. On the whole people want to be correctly informed. They want to be treated impartially by the courts and the police. They want enterprises that offer goods for sale or that provide employment to represent fairly what they are offering. They want politicians to put themselves up for election on fair terms.

So perhaps the first requirement for governments is that they should *not* obstruct the passing-on of information or the expression of opinion.

On the other hand, they *should* prosecute rigorously all those who seek to pay or to threaten police or judges or government servants of any rank to behave *partially*---and of course the police or judges or government servants who respond to these inducements. And there are certain commercial activities that must be *regulated* to ensure that the public are informed and that those with market-power do not misuse it.

This highlights a paradox. In different circumstances during 1997, Albania and a number of Southeast Asian economies suffered seriously because of *lack of suitable regulation* of their financial systems. But the regulation needed did not require the suppression of information or opinion. Very much the reverse, especially in Albania's case. It required openness, free comment and discussion, so that, for example, depositors could gain some idea of the risks they were individually taking, and the public at large could form a view of the risks to the whole system. On the other hand it also demanded rules of prudent behaviour by banks and other financial institutions that would be impartially observed. Where the customers individually have no way of knowing the character of what they are being offered---as often in certain aspects of health services and financial services---or where they have no choice---as often with the public utilities---or where there is a risk that suppliers will combine to deny them choice--- as in so-called restrictive practices---then the authorities will probably need to regulate: in order to make up for the *lack* of information, or the *lack* of choice, or the *lack* of capacity on the part of private individuals acting alone to maintain choice.

Institution-building for a market economy and an open law-governed society will thus need to rest on a combination of freedom of information and discussion, rigorous prosecution of corruption and intimidation, a presumption of freedom in commerical transactions, but also regulation in some cases where the customers are unable to be informed without help, or where they have no choice, or where there is a risk that choice will be denied them, or where actions that are individually advantageous to those who take them cumulatively threaten the arrangements on which the market economy relies. The regulation needed will often entail fuller disclosure as its most important element.

The Legal and Organizational Framework of a Market Economy

Laws were passed to authorize and regulate companies in four legal forms (19/11/1992); to legitimize foreign direct investment on much the same terms as domestic investment (2/11/1993); to establish the various programmes of privatization outlined in chapter 6; to provide for bankruptcy (10/1995); to reconstruct the tax system (from 1991); to separate the central bank from the state-owned commercial banks

(22/4/1992); to enhance the independence and authority of the central bank and to authorize private banks (1996); to authorize and regulate a stock exchange (March 1996) with the establishment of a Securities Commission; to allow the formation of investment funds; to regulate insurance companies; to make possible private petroleum extraction (July 1993 and February and April 1994); and to create and regulate privatized electricity companies (July and October 1995).   Most of these provisions are mentioned at greater length elsewhere in the book.

As an example perhaps of legislation in advance of the problems at which it is directed, a law on competition was approved in December 1995. This largely follows standard European practice, as specified in Articles 85 and 86 of the Treaty of Rome.   It applies to both state and private sectors. It covers the issues of dominant position, mergers, and restrictive agreements.   It has a rather wide range, in that it treats as harmful various practices followed outside the country that affect Albania's consumers and firms.   It deals with unfair business practices over and above the standard forms of restrictive practice, and the variety of anti-competitive activities covered is wider than in some other Central European countries that have also recently legislated on these matters (see Gruda & Kay, 1997). Dominant position is defined solely by whether market share exceeds 40%, and it is not clear whether the law penalizes dominant position in itself or only the abuse of dominant position.   Administration of the law is divided among several authorities.

Some idea of how far Albania was deemed to have proceeded by 1996, in relation to other transition societies, toward establishing various features of a market economy is given in the Table 9.1 from the EBRD.   No doubt some of the judgments made there will be debatable.   4* indicates the farthest advance, and 1 the lowest.   More precise meanings of the various scores on each indicator are given on the pages following the table in the source.

It appears from the table that Albania is judged well advanced in small-scale privatization and in the liberalization of its trade and foreign-exchange system.   On domestic price-liberalization it is deemed roughly as far advanced as most others or more so, but, like all the others listed, it is held to fall short of the standard characterized as 4: 'comprehensive price liberalization; utility pricing which reflects economic costs' (EBRD, 1996, p.12).   The basis for Albania's score of 3 in the last column is explained and is of some interest.   It refers to the treatment of 'investment', which appears to mean inward foreign investment.   The score is a compromise ('average') of one of 4* for 'extensiveness of legal rules on investment' and of 1 for 'effectiveness of legal rules on investment'.   The 4* on the former criterion indicates that the rules 'closely approximate generally accepted standards internationally and impose few restrictions' while the 1

Table 9.1   Progress in transition, Central Europe and the CIS, 1996

Country	Priv'e sector share in GDP (% mid-1996)	Large-scale priv'n	Small-scale priv'n	Enterprise restructuring	Price liberalization	Trade & foreign-exchange system	Competition policy	Banking ref'm & interest-rate liberalization	Securities markets & non-bank financial institutions	Extent & effectiveness of legal rules on investment
			Enterprises			Markets and trade		Financial institutions		Legal reform
Alb'ia	75	2	4	2	3	4	2	2	2	3
Ar'ia	50	3	3	2	3	4	1	1	1	3
Azerbaijan	25	1	2	3	2	2	1	2	1	2
Bela's	15	1	2	2	3	2	2	1	2	1
Bulg.	45	2	3	2	2	4	2	2	2	4
Croat.	50	3	4*	3	3	4	2	3	2	4
Cze. Rep.	75	4	4*	3	3	4*	3	3	3	4
Est'a	70	4	4*	3	3	4	3	3	2	4
FYR-Mac'a	50	3	4	2	3	4	1	3	1	3
Geo'a	50	3	4	2	3	3	2	2	1	2
Hung.	70	4	4*	3	3	4*	3	3	3	4
Kaz'n	40	3	3	2	3	4	2	2	2	2
Kyrg.	50	3	4	2	3	4	2	2	2	2
Latv.	60	3	4	3	3	4	2	3	2	4
Lith.	65	3	4	3	3	4	2	3	2	2
Mold.	40	3	3	2	3	4	2	2	2	3
Pol'd	60	3	4*	3	3	4*	3	3	3	4
Rom.	60	3	3	2	3	3	1	3	2	3
Russ.	60	3	4	2	3	4	2	2	3	2
Slovakia	70	3	4*	3	3	4*	3	3	3	3
Slovenia	45	3	4*	3	3	4*	2	3	3	3
Tajik.	20	2	2	1	3	2	1	1	1	2
Turkmen'n	20	1	1	1	2	1	1	1	1	1
Ukr'e	40	2	3	2	3	3	2	2	2	3
Uz'n	40	3	3	2	3	2	2	2	2	3

Source: EBRD, *Transition Report*, 1966, p.11

on the latter is interpreted as meaning that 'legal rules are usually very unclear and often contradictory and the availability of independent legal advice is usually very limited.   The administration of the law is substantially deficient (e.g. little confidence in the abilities and independence of the courts, no or poorly organised security and land registers)' (EBRD, 1996, p.14).   Only an oddly assorted six others score as highly as Albania on the former test (Russia, Poland, Hungary, Latvia, Macedonia, and Uzbekistan).   Only one other (the cult-dictatorship of Turkmenistan) scores as badly on the latter.   The specific comments relating to Albania under 'effectiveness of investment legislation' are as follows.

> The full text of laws relating to investment are published, usually within one month of enactment. Subordinate regulations, decrees, etc. which frequently contain substantive measures relating to investment, are in force although they are generally not published. Draft laws are usually not circulated to practitioners for comment prior to enactment. Public records in share or land registers may be up to 12 months behind current status. Despite requirement for registration, registers do not always exist. Court decisions are not generally available to practitioners. Independent professional legal advice is available. While private parties generally believe the courts will recognise their legal rights against other private parties, they do not believe that courts would enforce such rights against the state. Foreign arbitral awards are not required to be recognised and enforced by the courts, at least not without a re-examination of their merits (EBRD, 1996, p.137).

This qualified judgment on foreign-investment law can probably be extended more widely to Albania's transition. A number of laws with the right intention have been passed and regulatory authorities set up. But sometimes they are framed ambiguously so as to be difficult to enforce or use, as has been alleged with the law over sale of land, which is held to make such sale under legal forms almost impossible (IMF, 1997, pp.35-7). And supporting institutions---the courts, the records, the treatment by government---may be deficient. On the specific question of direct foreign investment, uncertainty about these institutions may help to explain why, despite permissive legislation, relatively few large investments have been made. The overwhelming *number* of inward investments have been extremely small. To judge by sample evidence, more than half by number ---concentrated among the smaller---appear to have been joint-ventures with Albanians. This may denote in part a search for security *in a context in which not much reliance is placed on the law*. For the larger investors such informal shelters may be less easily attained. Hence the clarity or otherwise of their legal positions may rate very highly with potential investors that are substantial firms.

Entrepreneurial Spirit

Here Albanians have given every sign of responding vigorously to market opportunities. In chapter 6 we mentioned the 55,000 recognized private firms (other than farms) officially known to be in existence in 1995, of which at least 40%, probably more, had been formed anew during the 1990s, not by privatization. While so many of the old state-owned industries languished or disappeared, a partly private sector of manufacturing---clothing and footwear---came to dominate in exports, among which these goods had not been represented at all under the old regime.

There is also evidence that many of the 450,000 farms have shown extensive adaptation to changed circumstances.

Consideration of risk-taking should not ignore the fact that perhaps about half a million people have at one time or another left for work in Greece or Italy, often illegally from the viewpoint of the host country, generally without any assurance of employment. These are large numbers in a population of a little over 3 million.

Business Ethics

An inevitable difficulty in a country where, for many years, all market-directed activity has been held to be criminal is to distinguish between legitimate business and crime. New boundaries have to be drawn. It may not be clear to many people what the law prohibits, and indeed the law itself may not be anywhere clearly stated. Where the law covers matters with no obvious personal implications (handling a car stolen from some anonymous person in Austria, for example, or tapping off electric power without paying for it, or selling petrol in Montenegro or heroin to be shipped to Switzerland) and is not well enforced, there may be no evident reason why the law should be obeyed.

Everywhere in the world perhaps, respectable firms from time to time make arrangements with organized criminals; sometimes respected politicians evade taxes and those in power use the means at their disposal as government to bias elections in their favour; senior civil servants accept entertainment from lobbyists; police tell lies in court and do deals with those they are supposed to be restraining. But each of these failings weakens the social structure; and, when they become routine and are no longer matters of public outcry and prosecution, the state loses its moral claims and it becomes difficult for a nation to work together for common purposes. The state risks becoming too like an instrument of exploitation on behalf of the elite or whatever segments of the elite happen to be in power.

At least until the end of 1996, organized crime did not seem to have such a powerful and pervasive hold in Albania as in some cities in Russia. But it was a presence of which people were aware, and it received a great boost in the anarchy of early 1997---possibly with encouragement from the accolades of some opposition leaders (Rama, 1997). Stolen cars were prevalent, and some of the most respectable people dealt in them. The figures give a strong impression that, from 1994 to 1996, taxpaying was becoming increasingly voluntary and ever less people were willing to pay.

Some coastal areas by the end of 1997 were said to have little gainful activity other than smuggling.   Parts of the north had for a while derived much of their income from the breaking by Albanians of international sanctions---sanctions that had been devised precisely to restrain a political leader who had been a persecutor of Albanians.   If some of the 'funds' dealt in money-laundering or smuggling or drug-handling or gun-running, they were doing what was neither systematically prosecuted nor even perhaps seriously condemned.

The Courts of Law

Mention was made above of the implication in an EBRD document that the Albanian courts may not be independent enough, or not well enough furnished with records, to be entirely reliable arbiters in civil commercial cases.   The political record to date (as recounted in chapter 4) leaves some doubt as to whether they have retained (or been allowed to retain) enough independence in criminal and constitutional cases.   There were instances that seemed to show that the judges were *not* entirely handmaids of the government in power---as when they repeatedly reduced the sentence on Ramiz Alia, or when Zef Brozi as Chairman of the Court defied the President to the point at which he was removed from office.   But it is significant that Brozi *was* removed.   And there is the case of the 32 Communist officials, imprisoned under the Democratic Party government in 1996, exonerated under the Socialist government in September 1997.

Police and Law-Enforcement

Much law-breaking seems simply to be ignored by the police.   They have been used to suppress---roughly---peaceful demonstrations in Tirana, but, together with the armed forces, they appear to have been unable to prevent much of the country from moving out of central-government control for varying periods in 1997.   They seem to have done little to suppress organized crime.   Unsurprisingly, they appear not to have acted against the Democratic Party gangs that were used in the latter part of the Berisha period to intimidate opponents.   The security service SHIK inspired hatred and fear but no confidence that it would protect life and liberty.

Information

We mentioned in chapter 4 various acts of the Berisha regime that were directed against certain newspapers, against the BBC, and generally against press freedom.   It has not been easy for Albanians to obtain access to official information.   We drew attention to the absurdity that Albanians have not been allowed to see the monthly IMF publication of Albanian economic statistics that is compiled to inform the rest of the world.   The old totalitarian assumption that *the less they know the better* simply has to be discarded if the market economy and the pluralist society are to be protected from exploitation, distortion, and the risk of financial collapse.

Political Culture

The idea of a loyal opposition, and of political opponents who routinely criticize each other publicly, but who may be on quite good terms personally and who stand together in cases of national emergency, is a difficult one to absorb.

The benefits of democracy are endangered unless political parties play within definite rules.   Their opponents must be left with a fair chance to compete for power.   Parties or individuals in government may not use intimidation or bribery, or an unequal access to any information medium, or legal or illegal attacks on the persons or liberty of the opposition, to enhance their own prospects.   As in so much else, any infringement of these rules has a tendency to become cumulative.   Those who know that they are likely to be imprisoned if they lose, will themselves be tempted to fight with no holds barred.

Berisha's Democratic Party broke most of the rules, using the courts to imprison its opponents, legislation to exclude the most active of them from political life, thugs to intimidate its critics, and its command of broadcasting to give disproportionate prominence to its cause.   It is also quite likely that there was plenty of intimidation used in the interest of the other side in the election of 1997.

Remedies

Despite the magnitude of some of the deficiencies mentioned, there are often quite straightforward remedies that a determined government can take.

First, there are spheres in which the most important role of the government is to *refrain from interfering* other than in very special circumstances.   This might apply generally to the courts and the media of information and opinion.   (Yet a government may also need to set up institutions to secure impartiality over certain kinds of issue in state-owned media.)   Toward political opponents, too, there are acts that must simply be avoided.   These self-denying rules could well be made explicit.

Then there are areas in which *re-training*---in attitudes as well as techniques---may be necessary.   This might be one part of the required treatment for the police.

Then there are necessary *procedures that must become habitual.* Mention is made above of the need to enforce registration provisions, to publish necessary records, and to consult before laws are enacted.   As with training, there may sometimes be useful foreign technical assistance in such areas.

But the really difficult task is to re-establish *law-enforcement*, and respect for law, as normal.   The problem in Albania would probably have to be tackled bit by bit, with publicity as well as firm action.   It does no harm if politicians and other members of the elite make clear that they do not regard themselves as above the law, but that is only one bit of the answer.   Public debate on television about the ethics of business and attitudes to law might play some part.   But it is primarily a matter for policing; and the rewards, selection and training of the police may well be crucial.

Summary

A market economy and a free and open society require not only a certain *legal and organizational framework* but also certain attitudes and habits of behaviour.   Aside from *entrepreneurial spirit*, they also rest on *trust*, *impartiality* in a number of spheres, and the exercise of *personal responsibility.*   These last three modes of behaviour are variously important in business, the courts, the police, the infomation media, and politics.

Albania, having moved quckly to pluralism in and immediately after December 1990, passed most of the right laws to establish the basic freedoms and formal rules and supervisory bodies for a market economy, though at times technical flaws made the law difficult to interpret and apply.   In some of these respects it was ahead of many other transitional countries.   In entrepreneurial spirit its people were prominent within Central Europe.

Yet, in a number of the aspects of attitudes and behaviour, the governments, and also the public---often led or not challenged by those in power---lacked some of the necessary habits, and widely infringed some of the unwritten rules, on which the success of a market economy and an open, law-governed society depends.

The boundary between legitimate business and crime tended to become blurred.   In the pursuit of material interest, laws were extensively ignored or flouted, with little attempt made to enforce them.

The courts, apart from being sometimes ill-equipped with the infrastructure for dealing with commercial disputes, were often under pressure to follow, or even willingly followed, the dictates of the party in power over criminal and constitutional cases.

The police and other law-enforcement agencies were also too much at the disposal of the ruling party and at the same time incompetent to deal with the disturbances that wracked Albania in 1997. The secret police were hated and feared but appear to have served no great social purpose.

Fitful attempts were made by the government to muzzle the press, and the government used state television for its own party purposes. Some information useful for making practical judgments on policy in Albania is made available to foreigners, but it is apparently thought too dangerous for Albanians to have the material for forming their own judgments.

The political culture that developed was one in which the party in power made partial use of the law and the legislative process to inactivate the opposition, and employed gangs of bullies to intimidate critics. Some of the opposition in response sought support among those, gangsters or otherwise, who had rebelled against the state.

While much of the formal institution-building has been done, the less tangible aspects of institutions have further progress to make.

There are important steps that government can take: by refraining from interfering in certain fields; by training programmes; by instituting or enforcing certain procedures; and by pursuing a serious and realistic policy for restoring respect for law.

10 Changes in Production and Trade Patterns

There have been big changes in what is produced in Albania---and big changes too in what it exports.   This chapter looks at what some of the changes are.

We also ask why they happened.   Liberalization must be a large part of the answer---but why exactly?   We suggest that there are two different kinds of reason, and that the difference is important for future prospects.

One set of changes came about because much of the pattern of production and trade that had been built up over the Communist period was *unsuited to Albania's resources* in a context in which free trade with the rest of the world was possible.   To use an economists' term, it did not fit with Albania's *comparative advantage*.   The country could get a better deal by specializing differently.   One peculiarity of the Communist system was a desire for self-sufficiency, especially self-sufficiency in grains and in certain basic industrial intermediate goods.   Consequently these kinds of good tended to be pushed beyond the point at which they would be commercially viable, however efficient the *methods* by which they might be produced.   Such   choices were likely to be overturned when private people and firms were allowed reasonably free trade with the world outside.

The second set of changes occurred in part because of another characteristic of Communist management, aggravated by features peculiar to Albania.   In command-economies, there has generally been very little incentive to use resources efficiently---not only over choice of products but also over the *methods* used *within any industry*.   There may be over-staffing or over-capitalization, obsolete techniques, slack management. Added to this, Albania's drastic switching during Hoxha's time from each of its two main supplier countries in succession, and its final renunciation of receipt of aid, increased the likelihood that it would be left with obsolete equipment in poor condition.   The result has probably been that a number of industries that were in their nature perfectly suitable to Albania's resources have found themselves uncompetitive and could not cease to be so without major new investment and reorganization.   Some events that accompanied the *collapse* of the command system may have had a similar effect.   In the reaction away from collective and state farms, farmers tended to reject crops and destroy facilities that depended on anything other than a *very small scale* of operation.   Any product that required a size of organization above the level of the household was likely to be neglected, regardless again of how suitable it might have been under different institutions.

Hence some changes can be expected *to endure*---at least until relative resource-endowments, or other conditions in the world outside, alter; while others will be best seen as *temporary*---a matter of restructuring existing enterprises or starting again from the beginning in the same industries.

Sectorally in Albania, there was a big switch of output in proportional terms from 'industry' (manufacturing and extraction) to agriculture, construction and services. Table 10.1 shows a switch of 28.3 percentage-points out of industry, matched by increases of 18.9 points in agriculture, 3.0 points in construction, and 6.3 points in services including transport. All sectors showed absolute declines into 1990 and 1991, but the declines in industry continued in each year until 1994 inclusive, while transport started increasing in 1993, and agriculture and construction in 1992. Over the four or five years ending in 1995, the EBRD's figures (1997b, pp.214-39) show nothing remotely comparable among the other transitional economies to Albania's switch of 28.3 GDP percentage points out of industry. (The nearest recorded are 18.1 points for Kazakhstan, 15.0 points for Latvia, 16.0 for Poland---all from 1990 to 1995---and 15 points for Moldova from 1993 to 1995.)

Moreover, where there was a fairly large fall in the share of industry in the other transition economies, it was usually *not* accompanied, as in Albania, by a marked rise in the share of agriculture (Armenia is the only exception). And in none of the others, except marginally FYR Macedonia, was there an *absolute* rise in agricultural output from 1990 to 1995 (*ibid.*). The figures in Table 10.1 imply that Albania's agricultural net output had already in 1993 surpassed its level of 1989, and that in 1995 it was about 25% higher than in 1989, in spite of the steep drop over the 2 years into 1991. Altogether, Albania's pattern of sectoral change was *vastly* different.

We may surmise that a part of the decline in industry represented a move out of activities which did not fit Albania's *endowments*. This part could be expected to be fairly long-lasting. But it seems likely also that a considerable part happened because of the unsuitability of *existing modes of operation*. By relying heavily from 1961 on capital goods from China, and then after 1978 breaking with China and abjuring both trade with China and aid, Albania often tied itself into obsolete equipment and methods.

So, on the one hand, the dogmatic bias toward 'industry', especially heavy industry, under the Communist regime---motivated partly by the quest for self-sufficiency---raises considerable presumptions that *some* of the manufacturing industries would not have represented an efficient use of resources, regardless of the techniques applied. There is also a presumption against much concentration on capital-intensive industry in a very-low-wage country.   Hence there was probably substantial investment in what, for an open economy, would turn out to be the 'wrong' industries.

Table 10.1 GDP by sector of origin, 1990-1995*

Percentage change over previous period:

	1990	1991	1992	1993	1994	1995
GDP	**-10.0**	**-28.0**	**-7.2**	**9.6**	**9.4**	**8.9**
Industry	-14.2	-42.0	-51.2	-10.0	-2.0	1.0
Agric're	-5.4	-17.4	18.5	10.4	10.3	10.6
Constr'n	-12.0	-30.0	7.0	30.0	15.0	12.5
Trans'n	-10.0	-30.0	-15.0	13.0	18.0	6.0
Other serv's	-8.0	-14.0	9.0	16.0	11.0	8.0

Percentage share of total GDP at constant 1990 prices:

	1990	1991	1992	1993	1994	1995
GDP	**100.0**	**100.0**	**100.0**	**100.0**	**100.0**	**100.0**
Industry	39.8	32.1	16.9	13.9	12.4	11.5
Agric're	37.0	42.5	54.2	54.6	55.1	55.9
Cons'n	6.8	6.6	7.6	9.1	9.5	9.8
Trans'n	3.4	3.3	3.0	3.1	3.3	3.2
Other serv's	13.0	15.6	18.3	19.4	19.6	19.5

*   A warning is given in the source that these figures, based on demand-side data, should be treated with caution, and that there are 'significant discrepancies' between them and some production-side data.

Source: IMF, 'Albania---Recent Economic Developments', 1997, p.44

But on the other hand, as we have seen, features of Communist economic management and of Albania's policy history suggest that perfectly suitable industries may have found themselves needing considerable new investment and changes of organization before they could be commercially viable.   The big decline in output of almost all the mining and extractive products, for example, will probably turn out to be transient, pending new management and extra capital.

So the best provisional guess is that *some* of the switch from industry to other sectors represents the assertion of comparative advantage, but that there is also an element within the change that can be expected to reverse itself if and when Albanian or foreign investors with the necessary experience are able and willing to undertake the abandoned activities.

Table 10.2 Composition of foreign merchandise trade, SITC groups, 1990, 1993-1997 (%)

	1990[a]	1993	1994	1995	1996	1997
EXPORTS *[value in million US $]*	*[322]*	*[112]*	*[141]*	*[205]*	*[244]*	*[140[b]]*
Food, drink, tobacco, live animals	47.9	14.0	14.3	7.5	8.8	11.0
Raw materials, inedible, excluding fuels	23.8	24.0	4.6	24.7	16.9	20.8
Mineral fuels, lubricants and related	7.8	8.3	26.7	2.9	4.1	1.7
Animal and vegetable oils and fats	0.0	0.1	0.5	0.7	2.2	0.0
Chemical products	0.9	4.3	3.0	1.2	1.4	1.9
Manufactures (SITC 6 & 8)	19.6	45.7	45.3	59.7	64.9	58.8
Machinery & transport equipment	0.0	3.6	3.4	1.4	1.7	5.7
Sundry products	0.0	0.0	2.2	1.8	0.0	0.0
Total	**100.0**	**100.0**	**100.0**	**100.0**	**100.0**	**100.0**
IMPORTS *[value in million US $]*	*[456]*	*[602]*	*[601]*	*[680]*	*[922]*	*[615[b]]*
Food, drink, tobacco, live animals	10.7	20.1	25.5	25.5	32.0	23.7
Raw materials, inedible, excluding fuels	5.7	0.7	2.4	2.1	1.2	1.6
Mineral fuels, lubricants and related	6.3	3.3	10.9	8.6	2.6	3.3
Animal and vegetable oils and fats	0.5	1.8	not av.	2.4	2.6	3.0
Chemical products	1.0	12.4	6.5	7.2	5.9	6.9
Manufactures (SITC 6 & 8)	26.1	23.6	18.9	31.7	32.8	39.9
Machinery & transport equipment	49.7	38.1	31.8	22.0	22.4	21.6
Sundry products	0.0	0.0	not av.	0.4	0.4	0.0
Total	**100.0**	**100.0**		**100.0**	**100.0**	**100.0**

a   The source notes that imports and exports in 1990 were largely in inconvertible currencies. Rouble values have been converted to dollars at the official rate of exchange.
b   1997 aggregates have been converted at the rate US$ 1 = 150 lekë.

Source: HEMA CONSULT, from Dept of Customs, Bank of Albania, & World Bank (for 1990-94); INSTAT (for 1995-97)

Within the industrial sector, it is difficult from published data to find out directly how the weight of the various industries has changed. A complete count in manufacturing seems to be confined to the state sector. However, use of several sources (including IMF, 1997, p.46), combined with the fact that mining and fuel production remained almost entirely in the public sector, enables us to say that output of copper and chromium ores, and of virtually all the primary energy products, fell greatly from 1991.

For manufacturing some idea of how the balance of specialization was changing can be gained from foreign-trade figures.

The dollar aggregates of imports and exports are inserted in Tables 10.2 and 10.3 in order to emphasize that equal percentages of imports and of exports in any year after 1990 by no means mean equal absolute values. If we omit the 'sundry' category, there is no class of goods in either of the tables in which Albania had a surplus in any year after 1990---*except* the category *raw materials inedible, excluding fuels* (the one including mining products) in Table 10.2.

Proportionately, however, it is clear that Albania switched in the 1990s from being an exporter of predominantly natural-resource-intensive, to one of predominantly labour-intensive, goods. Manufactures in SITC categories 6 and 8, that is manufactures excluding chemicals and machinery, came to represent about 60% by value of exports, replacing mining products, which had represented 50% to 60% in the 1980s.

Among the manufactures, *textiles, clothing and footwear*, notably labour-intensive, had come to provide 40% to 50% of total exports. This has been one of the remarkable features of Albania's transition, but it is surprising only in the speed with which it has developed. On general principles this is exactly the kind of industry in which Albania could now be expected to have a comparative advantage. Not only is it *labour-intensive* at a time when Albania has an extremely low real-wage level by European standards. It is also capable of fairly *small-scale operation*, and at the moment Albania has a bias toward the small scale. The country has not generally been attractive to the larger foreign investors, but for a variety of special reasons has drawn in a plethora of very small direct investments. There is also plenty of evidence of readiness among Albanians themselves to trade actively and to commercialize familiar activities. But there is not much sign that many individuals possess the skills and experience appropriate to large-scale directly-productive entrepreneurship in a market context, or that the climate of popular attitudes is such as to make that role easy for them. So *small-scale* as well as *labour-intensive* is where the *immediate* way ahead is likely to lie.

On the face of it other surviving light industries capable of fairly small-scale operation, such as wooden-furniture and leather-goods production, should be promising.

With those activities that are inevitably large-scale, such as mining and refining of metals, the hope does seem to rest for the time being on the fabled foreign *strategic investors*. But, given these institutional aids, there is every reason to expect the mining and metal-refining industries to revive.

Simple economic reasoning would suggest that land-intensive products do not have much future as exports in Albania, where the limited land resources are so greatly over-stretched. But even here there is always the possibility of finding niches for specialized goods given suitable advice on production standards and marketing. Land-intensive products that can be differentiated by quality and brand can be made into viable exports even where land is scarce. For example, Albania is a wine-producer, and there are plenty of recent examples of countries that have become successful wine exporters because key vineyards have taken on some of the advice which is now readily available.

Table 10.3 Composition of foreign merchandise trade, alternative categories, 1989, 1995-1997 (%)

	1989		1995	1996	1997
EXPORTS		**EXPORTS**			
[value in million US $]	*[394]*	*[value in million US $]*	*[205]*	*[243]*	*[140[b]]*
Food, live animals	19.5	Food, tobacco, beverages	13.9	17.0	20.0
Fuels, minerals, metals	54.4	Minerals, fuel, electricity	15.8	9.7	5.8
Chemical products	0.6	Chemical & plastic products	1.3	1.6	1.0
Raw materials of plant & animal origin	14.4	Leather & leasther products	3.0	4.0	5.5
Non-foodstuffs of mass consumption	9.7	Wood & paper products	7.4	4.1	6.5
		Textiles and footwear	40.9	49.2	42.8
Building materials	1.4	Construction materials & metals	9.9	11.2	10.4
Machinery & equipment	0.0	Machinery & machine tools	1.4	1.7	
		Machinery, equipment & spare parts			5.7
		Other products	6.5	1.7	2.3
Total	**100.0**	**Total**	**100.0**	**100.0**	**100.0**
IMPORTS		**IMPORTS**			
[value in million US $]	*[456]*	*[value in million US $]*	*[680]*	*[922]*	*[615[b]]*
Food, live animals	9.9	Food, tobacco, beverages	25.3	35.1	27.2
Fuels, minerals, metals	26.0	Minerals, fuel, electricity	12.7	5.5	8.2
Chemical products	12.1	Chemical & plastic products	8.5	7.2	8.5
Raw materials of plant & animal origin	15.1	Leather & leather products	1.7	2.2	2.3
Non-foodstuffs of mass consumption	7.8	Wood & paper products	1.9	2.1	3.0
		Textiles & footwear[a]	17.3	15.4	16.1
Building materials	0.8	Construction materials & metals	8.3	7.1	10.0
Machinery & equipment	28.2	Machinery & machine tools	20.4	22.1	
		Machinery, equipment & spare parts			21.2
		Other products	3.9	3.3	3.5
Total	**100.0**	**Total**	**100.0**	**100.0**	**100.0**

a   Presumably includes clothing.
b   1997 aggregates have been converted at the rate US$ 1 = 150 lekë.

Source: Statistical Yearbook of Albania 1991; INSTAT

Tourism too, though land-based, tends to use resources such as mountains and beaches that are not otherwise very productive. After an initial rise to 1993, foreign arrivals stagnated at a little over 0.3 million a year, and almost certainly most foreigners are not tourists in the usual sense. While tourist services on the ground are probably best left to the private sector, the state has a very important role, where the field is completely undeveloped, in providing infrastructure, in setting standards, in

Table 10.4   Output of various agricultural products, 1989-1996

Product (thousand tons unless otherwise indicated)	1989	1990	1994	1995	1996	Implied growth, 1989-96 (%)
Wheat	613	613	508/400	645/400	504	-18
Maize	308	227	193	216	214	-31
Sugarbeet	262	169	60	67/70	74	-72
Vegetables & watermelons	392	393	590	685/600	785	100
Dried beans	24	14	18	25	25	4
Potatoes	97	80/77	90/80	134	132	36
Green fodder	3050	2311	3520	3800	3970	30
Olives	31	10		39	28	-10
Citrus	15	10		4	3	-80
Grapes	80	91		55*	59*	-26
Meat	92	84	112	116	105	14
Wool	3	3	3	4	3	0
Eggs (million)	324	343	285	285	314	-3
Milk	460	517	803/764	968/1018	1044	127

*   These figures are derived by adding the product of vineyards and of pergolas ('vine-fruits').

Sources: Statistical Yearbook of Albania 1991; INSTAT, *Albania in Figures*, 1997, 1995; Preci, 1995; HEMA CONSULT; figures from bank sources

providing overseas marketing, and in land-use planning

Within the agricultural sector, there seems also to have been a decided shift in the pattern of production.   Unfortunately there is a variety of partly-conflicting output figures. The entries in Table 10.4 have thus to be taken with reservations. In some cases, where there are serious divergences and one figure is not clearly more plausible than another, we give more than one. Figures for 1996 (and the only or first one given in each case for 1995) are those from INSTAT.

Despite the shakiness of the figures, the picture seems clear.   There has been, since 1989, a shift out of cereals, sugarbeet and tree crops, and into vegetables, fodder and livestock.   (The other main field-crops not listed here---rye, rice, tobacco, cotton, sunflower-seeds, soya---have also declined, in some cases virtually disappeared.)

Livestock numbers in Table 10.5 do not so clearly and unambiguously show increases.   But cattle are far more important by value than the others, and their numbers increased at least modestly.   There is some sign of decline in numbers of all six classes of animals from 1995 to 1996.   We may speculate that this had something to do with the 'funds' mania.   There may have been a tendency of owners to 'liquidate' their flocks and herds. It is also believed that there has been considerable unrecorded export of live animals 'on the hoof' to Greece, where they are turned into meat. So livestock production and exports may be under-recorded, especially in 1996.

Table 10.5 Livestock numbers (thousands), 1989-1996

	1989[a]	1990[a]	1994	1995[b]	1996[b]	Implied growth, 1989-96 (%)
Cattle	699	633	670/797	842/863	806	15
Pigs	181	220	100/127	100/165	98	-46
Sheep	1,592	1,646	1,480/ 1,706	1736/ 2,209	1,453	-9
Goats	1,153	1,145	1,020/ 1,259	1,650/ 1,441	1,250	8
Poultry	5,630	5,259	3,600/ 3,206	3.900/ 4,329	4,108	-27
Horses, mules, & donkeys	177	181	226	230/ 253	226	28

a   Figures for 1989 and 1990 are in all cases from *Statistical Yearbook of Albania 1991*.
b   The first figure for 1995 and the figure for 1996 are in all cases from INSTAT, *Albania in Figures*, 1997.

Sources: SYA 1991; INSTAT, 1995b, 1997; Kunkel, 1996; HEMA
         CONSULT

The picture of rapidly rising milk output with small rises or falls in numbers of beasts is clarified when we see the substantial increases estimated in the milk-productivity of cattle, sheep, and goats; there was also a respectable rise estimated in the egg-productivity of hens (Table 10.6). An additional factor in explaining the big rise in milk output is the fact that the proportion of females among cattle apparently increased from 41% in 1989 to 60% in 1996 (sources as for Table 10.6).

How do we understand the shift away from some farming activities and into others? Again it is possible that there are two factors at work: one likely to be long-lasting, the other more transient. With the cereals, probably also sugar-beet and olives, cultivation during the Communist era had been pressed hard in the interests of self-sufficiency---pressed *unduly* hard for a world in which trade was acceptable. It has to be added, however, that the protective structure of the mid-1990s may have increased the movement out of wheat. One of the studies (Karadeloglou & Stoforos, 1997) on which this book is based suggested that in 1995 wheat appeared from comparative price data to have negative nominal protection while a number of other farm products had positive protection. Before the first day of 1997, grain and flour faced zero import duty, while import duties on a number of other farm products were positive.

Table 10.6 Increasing per-animal productivity, milk and eggs, 1989-1996

	1989	1990	1995	1996	Implied change, 1989-90 to 1995-96 (%)
Milk per cow per year (kg)	1,276	1,482	1,720	1,870	30
Milk per sheep per year (kg)	39	41	47	48	19
Milk per goat per year (kg)	75	73	83	85	14
Eggs per bird per year	98	99	109	108	10

Sources: Statistical Yearbook of Albania 1991; INSTAT, *Albania in Figures,* 1997

Absolutely it is quite likely that wheat production will rise again and surpass its 1980s level, especially since a 10% duty was imposed on grains and flour at the start of 1997.   *Relatively* we should still expect it to remain less important in rural product than during the 1980s.

Yet there may be other products for which the relative decline owes more to the move from large-scale to small-scale rural organization.   This may well have been the case with grapes grown in vineyards.   In the early 1990s the old forms of cooperation had been abandoned as discredited. There was a reaction against the regimentation of the collective and state-farm systems.   Farm infrastructure and physical capital that could not satisfactorily be used by a single family working alone were sometimes even destroyed.   Vines and fruit-trees might be cut down.   But it does not follow that the cultivation of grapes is intrinsically unsuited to Albania in an interdependent world, or that it was over-developed.   Such activities may become much more widely viable and attractive once the appropriate institutions (voluntary-cooperative or capitalist) exist to make larger-scale operation possible.   Products adapted to the smallest scale now prevail, but this may be only a transient phase.   It would not be surprising to see vineyards recovering their relative position, especially if the opportunities are taken of improving quality and marketing.

We should not neglect the other rising sectors: construction, transport, and 'other services'.   Between them these are estimated to have increased from 23.2% of GDP in 1990 to 32.5% in 1995 (Table 10.1).   The figures would imply an absolute fall in transport from either 1989 or 1990 to 1995, but clear absolute rises in construction and 'other services' to 1995 from either starting-point.   Transport maintained an almost constant proportion of GDP throughout.   The other two mounted to higher proportions than before by 1993, which they then roughly maintained over the next two years.   It seems very likely that the element of construction that rose was the private building of dwellings.   (Government capital spending had dropped to a tiny fraction of its Communist-era level.)   We might have expected transport to increase its proportion of GDP as trade became freer. It is possible, however, that such an effect has been masked by the greater efficiency, and consequently relatively lower prices for the industry's services, that have come with competition---which may well be stronger in transport than in some other sectors.

The increased importance of 'other services' is not surprising to anyone who has watched Tirana over the decade. There is a proliferation of coffee-houses and restaurants and several new big hotels. Many residences do duty as shops or workshops. There is a rudimentary travel and tourism sector that scarcely existed before: hotels, airline offices, souvenir shops, travel agents, long-distance taxis. There are six private-sector banks, however languid, and plenty of kerbside money-changers. A real take-off in tourism, which could easily happen with proper organization and marketing, might well increase further the 'other-service' sector's share.

Summary

Liberalization and privatization have been followed in Albania by a strong proportional shift of productive activities out of manufacturing and extraction into services and construction and especially agriculture. Both the extent of the fall in the share of 'industry'and the absolute rise in agriculture have been *far* out of line with what has happened in any of the other transition economies.

Within manufacturing there has been a proportional shift into labour-intensive activities, especially those that can be conducted on a fairly small scale. Almost all the extractive industries have declined radically. *Within agriculture* there has been a relative movement of resources out of the grains and most of the other field-crops and the tree-crops, and into vegetables, fodder and livestock. Over the five years after its drastic fall to 1991, farm output grew especially fast. It was estimated as surpassing its 1989 level in 1993 and exceeding it by 25% in 1995.

Manufactures, principally 'light' manufactures, came to comprise about 60% by value of Albania's merchandise exports in the mid-1990s, replacing the metallic minerals that had provided from 50% to 60% during the 1980s. *Textiles, clothing, and footwear* alone came to constitute between 40% and 50% of Albania's exports.

Some part of the changes can be explained by the 'fundamentals' of Albania's comparative advantage within the world and European economy: the relation between its land and other natural resources, its population, and its 'physical' and human capital. Abandonment of the aim of self-sufficiency, for example in foodgrains and 'basic' industrial intermediate goods, has naturally led to a move toward labour-intensive activities and toward those agrarian pursuits appropriate to a mountainous terrain and a very high density of rural population in relation to land resources.

On the other hand, some of the changes should probably be regarded as temporary, arising not because the industries concerned are unsuited to Albania's basic endowments but *either* because (i) techniques or equipment or management practices used in the past are inadequate for survival in an open economy and can not quickly enough be altered *or* because (ii) a scale of operation is required that too few Albanian entrepreneurs and too few foreigners are at present willing and able to undertake.   (In farm products some part may be due to post-transition policies that have differentially disfavoured wheat production.)   The enticement of larger foreign investors, the emergence of land transfers and of free agricultural cooperation, and the gradual development of Albanian management capacity appropriate to large-scale operation in a market economy---these changes should reasonably soon reverse those declines that have sprung only from institutional peculiarities and historical legacies. In particular, we might expect the mining and extractive sectors, and possibly also some of the tree-crops, to make a relative, as well as an absolute, recovery.

11 Public Finance

Naturally Albania's transition to the market brought a large reduction in the weight of the government in the economy.   With the advent of a private productive sector, there had also to be radical change in the means by which the state collected revenue.   The task that the authorities face in these circumstances is to ensure that the government still has the resources to fulfil its essential public functions.   Albania's rapid rise in output after its new revenue instruments had been put in place might have led to the expectation of a steadily rising capacity of the state to meet public needs. Yet this did not happen. And the prevalent judgment is that there has been a deterioration of the infrastructure of schools, hospitals, and roads, as public-sector investment has settled at a small fraction of its late-1980s level.

Changing Size of the Government Sector

In the transition of a command economy to the market we should expect government expenditure to fall in relation to national income. So it was in Albania, as appears from Table 11.1. Total government spending is given as 57% of GDP in 1989, rose to 62% in 1991 and 1992, fell sharply to 46% and 44% in 1992 and 1993, and then successively to 35%, 33%, and 31% in 1994, 1995 and 1996.

It should be mentioned that there is a choice of price-indexes for deriving the *real* (constant-price) spending and revenue aggregates.   The approach here is to use the *GDP deflator* implied by the ratio between nominal and real estimates of GDP.   But this *implied GDP deflator* rises substantially more, especially over 1993 and 1994, than the other main general-price-series available, the consumer-price index.   Both are shown in Table 11.1.   The use of the GDP-deflator means that our estimated figures for real government revenue and expenditure appear to rise less, or to fall more, between 1992 and 1995 than if we had deflated by the consumer-price index.

The aggregates are shown in Table 11.1.   The weight of the government sector in the economy, as judged by the ratio of central-government expenditure to GNP, was by 1994-96 lower than that in most West European countries.   From the *World Development Reports*, it appears to be lower than in the Czech Republic, Romania and Bulgaria around 1993 and 1994, but higher than in Russia or the Baltics about the same time, and much higher than in Singapore or South Korea.

Most of the elements in the fall of expenditure relate clearly to the changes of fundamental policy: liberalization, privatization, and the political opening to the outside world.

Subsidies, which reached a peak of about 20% of GDP in 1991 (though they had been much less, as Table 11.1 shows, in 1989), were down to well below 1% in 1995 and 1996. This resulted from a succession of decisions to raise, or to leave to market forces, a number of prices of consumer items which had been controlled up to the end of 1991. Presumably also the *strong budget constraints* imposed on state enterprises in 1992 played a large part in reducing the subsidies that had to be paid to them. Those that could not pay their way were in many cases allowed to go out of production. The big falls in outlays on subsidies occurred in 1992 and 1993. Some details are given in chapter 5. So far from being subsidized in later years, the telecommunications utility, and also the state oil company Alboil, have been major contributors to government revenue through turnover tax (and later VAT) and profit tax.

Government *capital spending* fell from about 30% to about 5% of GDP between 1989 and 1996. This is enough in itself to account roughly for the overall fall in government expenditure as a proportion of GDP. We have not been able to obtain a full account of how the changes in capital spending were made up. Presumably much of the capital spending in 1989 was on the state enterprises. There was certainly a very sharp fall in the total over 1990 and 1991. Probably an important part of the government investment that would have gone on in a normal year in the 1980s was on building of apartments, and this would virtually have ceased in or before 1993, the year in which most urban dwellings were privatized. A documented item is the change in capital spending on defence, which fell virtually to nothing: from 840 million lekë in 1989 (about 4.5% of GDP) to 22 million (all at 1990 prices) in 1992: a sign no doubt of the change of course that made Albania a more normal member of the community of nations. However, the fact that the real fall in capital spending---86% from 1989---accounts for roughly the entire *absolute* fall in public-sector outlays (and is therefore much bigger *proportionately* than the fall in recurrent spending, which was about 19% over the same period) raises a strong presumption that investment in other areas of the public sector was neglected.

Between 1992 and 1995, total *spending both on health and on education*, as proportions of GDP, fell (education from 4.4% to 3.5% of GDP, and health from 4.3% to 2.4%). As regards capital spending, which by 1992 was probably, in both sectors, substantially below the level of the 1980s (figures in the 1993 IMF *Report* suggest that in 1992 it had been only about one third as high), education seems in the period 1992-95 to have recovered rather better than health care. Over that three-year period annual capital spending on education may have approximately doubled in real terms, while that on health care increased by no more than a third. These improvements were largely due to foreign assistance. In recurrent spending, both sectors have suffered over the same period, but educational outlays have declined rather less than those on health. In education, annual non-wage recurrent expenditure slipped by nearly 40% between 1992 and 1995, and in the health sector by about 50%. The fall in the real value of education and health spending over the transition period is, as observers from an international organization, writing in 1996, put it, 'reflected in the dilapidated state of the schools and the poor state of hospitals'. The same source asserts that 'Albania entered the transition with generally good education and health indicators across the board for its per-capita income level, reflecting the priority that had been accorded to these sectors by the communist regimes'. By the early 1990s, however, the school system appeared to be in disarray, with school buildings in bad condition, and teachers and learning materials lacking. Likewise, as regards health care, 'the transition period has had a negative influence on health services. The destruction of health facilities in 1992, the shortage of essential drugs and vaccines, and subsequent lack of adeqate funds to finance the health system has caused a severe disruption.... The number of primary care access points....has significantly decreased since 1989 (as has the availability of hospital beds).'

The government, faced with the new problems of the new era, has nevertheless managed to introduce two significant *new support systems*: Social Assistance (*Ndhime Ekonomike*) and Unemployment Benefit, the latter of which has become part of the contributory Social Security Insurance system (though treated as separate in the tables in this chapter). The former at its peak in 1994 accounted for 5.5% of government expenditure (just under 2% of GDP) and reached 20% of families.

The Fiscal Deficit and its Financing

The fiscal deficit reported (Table 11.1) was very high as a proportion of GDP from 1990 to 1993 (over 30% in 1991); in other years (when it was between 8% and 11%), it would have been regarded as high, though not extraordinarily so, in Western Europe. Finland, Sweden, and Italy all recorded central-government deficits of more than 10% of GNP in 1994 (*WDR 1996*, pp.214-5). Yet Table 11.3 suggests that the deficit in Albania was rather high by the standards of Central and Eastern Europe, at all events if the countries of the former USSR are excluded. With counterpart funds excluded (see Table 11.1), Albania's deficit in 1991 (at 33.59% of GDP) would be higher than the highest in Table 11.3 (Ukraine's in 1992).

Table 11.1 National-acounting and budgetary aggregates---mainly expenditure---1989-1996 (monetary figures in million lekë)

	1989	1990	1991	1992	1993	1994	1995	1996
GDP nominal	18681	16813	16473	50700	114200	188300	225060	266200
GDP at 1990 prices	18681	16813	12156	11282	12363	13637	14932	16217
Implied GDP deflator	100.0	100.0	135.5	449.4	923.7	1380.8	1507.2	1641.5
Consumer price index		100.0	136.0	443.4	820.2	1008.7	1089.6	1220.4
Gov't exp're nominal	10604	10449	10202	23405	49958	66317	74530	81763
Gov't exp're 1990 prices	10604	10449	7529	5208	5409	4803	4945	4981
As % of GDP:								
Gov't exp're	56.76	62.15	61.93	46.16	43.75	35.22	33.12	30.71
Gov'i revenue	48.19	46.79	31.38	24.66	27.67	24.63	23.80	19.76
Deficit	8.57	15.36	30.56	21.51	16.08	10.59	9.32	10.97
Deficit before counterpart funds	8.57	15.36	33.39	27.31	19.94	12.82	10.41	11.34
Counterpart funds	0.00	0.00	2.79	5.80	3.87	2.23	1.09	0.37
External finance	0.00	0.00	0.00	0.30	5.89	4.14	2.35	0.88
Soc. insurance outlays (excl. health & unemploy't)	7.13	8.57	12.03	6.59	6.39	5.69	6.15	6.71
Soc. assist'ce outlays				0.47	1.22	1.94	1.74	1.43
Unemploy't benefit				3.24	4.17	1.13	1.22	0.81
Subsidies	8.66	15.68	20.30	8.26	2.64	1.68	0.58	0.38
Gov't capital spending	29.3	18.8	6.11	4.25	7.48*	7.22*	6.46*	4.79
Educ'n exp're				4.4	3.6	3.5	3.5	
Health exp're				4.3	3.0	2.4	2.4	
In 1990 prices: Education expenditures				497	445	447	523	
Health expenditures				485	371	327	358	

* Adjusted from Ministry figures to include items externally financed (estimated); since there appears to have been very little external financing of public investment in 1996 and none before 1992, the figures for those years are given unadjusted.   The 1992 figure is from the IMF *Report* 1994.

Source: Mainly Ministry of Finance; national-accounting aggregates from EBRD, *Transition Report Update 1997*

Table 11.2   Budgetary aggregates---mainly revenue---1989-1996
(monetary figures in million lekë)

	1989	1990	1991	1992	1993	1994	1995	1996
At 1990 prices:								
Government revenue total	9003	7866	3815	2782	3421	3359	3554	3205
Turnover tax/VAT	4224	3936	1667	526	540	359	358	553
State enter'se/ profit tax	1974	1273	355	297	432	199	164	207
Pers'al income + small-business tax				48	72	101	101	85
Import + export tax			69	335	394	454	443	470
Excises				281	471	688	689	301
Soc. insurance contributions (excl. health insurance)	922	967	1058	378	347	462	590	705
Fees				65	193	318	249	(177)
Privatization receipts						159	21	33
Agr. co-op've taxes	93	62	2					
As % of GDP:								
Turnover tax/VAT	22.61	23.41	13.71	4.67	4.37	2.63	2.39	3.41
State enter'se/ profit tax	10.57	7.57	2.92	2.63	3.49	1.46	1.10	1.28
Pers'l income + small-business tax				0.42	0.59	0.74	0.68	0.52
Import + export tax			0.57	2.97	3.19	3.33	2.96	2.90
Excises				2.49	3.81	5.04	4.61	1.86
Soc. insurance contributions (excl. health)	4.94	5.75	8.70	3.35	2.81	3.39	3.95	4.35
Fees				0.58	1.56	2.33	1.67	(1.09)
Privatization receipts						1.17	0.14	0.21
Agr. co-op've tax	0.50	0.37	0.02					

Source: Ministry of Finance; EBRD, *Transition Report Update 1997*

Table 11.3   Budget balance as percentage of GDP, certain CEE countries, 1989-1994 (a minus sign denotes a deficit)

	1989	1990	1991	1992	1993	1994 (prel.)
Poland	-6.1	0.7	-3.5	-6.1	3.4	-2.8
Hungary	-1.3	-0.1	-4.6	-7.4	-7.5	-7.9
Czechoslovakia	-2.4	-0.3	-1.9	-1.8		
Czech Republic				0.0	0.1	1.0
Slovakia				-2.8	-5.5	-5.7
Bulgaria	-0.6	-4.9	-3.5	-6.1	-11.9	-8.0
Romania	8.2	1.0	-2.4	-4.8	-1.6	-4.5
Slovenia			2.6	0.2	0.5	0.0
USSR	-8.6	-4.1	-20.0			
Russia	-16.3	-10.0	-5.7	-10.4	-9.4	-10.4
Ukraine	n.a	n.a.	-20.0	-32.0	-19.0	-11.0
Albania*	-8.57	-15.36	-30.56	-21.51	-16.08	-10.59

(from Table 11.1)
*With counterpart funds taken into account to reduce the deficit

Source: Marie Levigne, *The Economics of Transition*, Macmillan, 1995, Table A.2(a), pp.260-65; with the Albania figure added

The contribution of *grant-aid* to the government accounts (represented in the budget in the form of *counterpart funds*) reached its peak as a proportion of GDP in 1992, when it represented 5.80%, more than a fifth of what the budget deficit would otherwise have been.   It had tailed away to very little in 1996 (0.37% of GDP).

External financing of the government deficit, much of it presumably concessional and therefore having an *aid* element, began in 1992 and was at its peak (5.89% of GDP) in 1993.   It had dwindled to less than 1% of GDP in 1996.

These two elements, foreign grants and loans, made a big difference, especially over 1992-94, to the amount of domestic borrowing needed to finance fiscal expenditure.   In 1993, for example, if there had been the actual level of expenditure and of domestic revenue, but no finance or grants to government from abroad, domestic borrowing needed (much of it inevitably domestic-credit-creation) would have been about 20% of GDP. Counterpart funds and external finance reduced this amount by nearly half. The impacts in 1992, 1994, and 1995, were proportionately smaller, but still substantial (see Table 11.1).

Since there is no domestic bond market, domestic financing of the deficit has meant a combination of direct creation of base-money by the Bank of Albania and, in latter years, the sale of Treasury Bills, which have been bought largely by the state-owned banks and insurance company. Some of the implications of this are discussed in chapter 7.

Revenue Changes

The Scale of Revenue

The large reduction in government expenditure associated with the transition to a market economy would naturally be accompanied by a fall in government revenue. But the fall in revenue between 1989 and 1996 has been greater proportionately than the fall in expenditure (about 64% as against 53%); and its decline does not appear to have been a planned, orderly process. Part of it happened inevitably as a result of other major changes: the collapse of so many state enterprises meant that the turnover tax and the direct enterprise tax that they paid disappeared; similarly the dissolution of agricultural cooperatives (collective farms) ended the taxes that had been imposed on them. That revenue in real terms should have fallen drastically until 1992 and risen modestly in 1993 is not surprising. What is not so easy to explain is that, after the introduction of several new tax instruments, and in spite of the rapid economic growth recorded from 1994 to 1996, revenue increased very little in real terms from 1993 to 1995 and actually fell slightly in 1996. (Arguably the deflator we have used to express revenue aggregates in real terms might have under-stated rises and exaggerated falls, as we have suggested, between 1992 and 1994, but there would be no case for arguing this over the change between 1995 and 1996, when the GDP deflator that we have used rose less than the consumer-price-index.) Much of the increase in output and real income admittedly came from agriculture, and farmers are not subject to any direct tax. On the other hand, the increase in *domestic expenditure* over the period from 1992 to 1996 as a whole was probably greater proportionately than the increase in income because of the rate of increase in emigrants' remittances; and expenditure is also a base for tax. What the figures suggest is a progressive failure in tax collection as the economy revived.

That difficulties in tax collection should be experienced in the transition period is not unexpected. The transition to the market meant for the government not only that new sources of revenue had to be found, but also that new problems of revenue collection had to be faced. Under the old regime tax payments to the government involved merely the internal transfer of funds within the public sector: up the hierarchy from enterprises to the central authorities. In a market system, the government has to raise taxes from independent private agents---a situation giving rise to much more complex administrative problems of assessment and compliance. In fact, a completely new revenue service has to be created.

Yet it is still a serious cause for concern that, *after* new arrangements to deal with the private sector had been set in place, revenue collection apparently (from the resulting yields) became *progressively worse.*

Changes in Tax Instruments

There is a changing pattern of revenue sources evident with the transition. In 1989, four sources accounted for about 90% of revenue. These were the turnover tax, the tax on state enterprises, transfers of amortization funds from these enterprises, and social-insurance contributions. The tax on state enterprises was changed into a profit tax on companies, normally at 30% but at 50% for mining. A personal-income tax to be paid by employees, and a tax on small businesses covering the self-employed and unincorporated businesses other than family farms, all appeared in 1992. Taxes on international trade came into existence in 1991 and excises in 1992. Various fees for such items as motor registration were introduced in 1992. And in July 1996 the turnover tax (an instrument that had been going out of fashion in the world generally because of its potentially distorting effects in favouring vertical integration of firms) was replaced by a value-added tax (VAT) at 12.5% applying to all businesses with a turnover of more than US$20,000 per year. In October 1997 the VAT rate was raised to 20%. Social-insurance contributions continued, but with modifications. (See chapter 8.) Unemployment insurance has been incorporated into the system, and since mid-1995 additional contributions have been required to cover medical insurance.

International Comparisons: Revenue; Income Taxes

Albania's proportion of central-government revenue to GDP in 1996 (about 20%) is well below that of most of the countries of Western Europe, the Czech Republic, Poland, Romania, Bulgaria, Estonia or Lithuania. It is of the same order as that of the USA, Canada, Japan, Switzerland, or Russia, but it is notable that all these last five countries apart from Japan are federal states where a large part of revenue can be expected to be collected by the component states or provinces. It is similar to that of Turkey, Thailand, South Korea, Chile or Venezuela; but is higher than the rate in a number of low-income and lower-middle-income countries (*WDR 1996*, pp.214-215; all figures apply to 1994).

There has been a tendency for lowish-income countries to rely less on *income-type taxes* than high-income countries, though the picture is very varied at lower levels of average income. Factors that tend to militate against income taxes in low-income countries are the high proportion of earners in the 'informal sector' whose income is difficult to determine; the low returns in relation to the cost of collection from people with low incomes; and the sophistication needed for assessment procedures with income taxes. Changes in Albania might have been expected to work in two ways over reliance on income tax. On the one hand more people moved into the informal sector (family farms and very small businesses).

On the other hand, the fact that revenue needs could no longer be met simply by a set of internal transactions within the government machine might have meant the need to collect more revenue explicitly from the incomes of individuals and companies.

In fact, if we aggregate all the *direct* taxes (including the social-security contributions) and express the total as a proportion of total current revenue, we find that (apart from the exceptional year 1991, when the ratio was 37%) the ratio ranged over 1989 to 1996 from 23% to 32%, higher at the beginning and the end than in the middle. This range of 23% to 32% is lower than in any of the high-income countries (except Singapore) listed for 1993 in the 1995 *WDR* (no figure is given for Japan) or in South Korea, Greece or Portugal; lower also than in the Czech Republic, Romania, Bulgaria, Russia, Lithuania or Estonia; but higher than in some low-income and a few middle-income countries.

Thus, in the ratio of government revenue to income that Albania had reached by 1996 (rather more than in that of government expenditure to income), as also in the weight of income taxes in total revenue, it tended to fit rather with lower-income than with higher-income countries. Though there is variation in these ratios at all average-income levels, there are good reasons why Albania should resemble lowish-income countries in the comparatively low weight it gives to income taxes. Like many of them it has a high proportion of the workforce in very small family farms and in other one-family or one-person businesses.

Changes in Yields of the Various Taxes to 1996

Revenue collected from three of the main sources continuing from the Communist era fell drastically from 1989 to 1991 and went on falling into 1992. In successive years from 1990 to 1992, the yield from the turnover tax fell by 7%, 58%, and 69%; profit transfers from state enterprises by 30%, 72%, and 16%; and amortization receipts at rates of 18%, 89%, and 91%. In total, revenue from these three traditional sources collapsed by about 90% in three years. The fourth source, social-insurance contributions, rose in yield until 1991, but then fell by nearly two-thirds to 1992, presumably as employment went through its sharpest decline. Social-insurance contributions were still well short of their real 1989 level by 1996, though the system was now supposed in principle to cover benefit for unemployment in addition to its previous responsibilities. Meanwhile of the other three: the transfer of amortization funds had virtually ceased by 1993; and the successor taxes to turnover tax and to the state-enterprise profit tax had yields in 1993 and 1994 that were small fractions of those of their predecessors in 1989. (See Table 11.2.)

With the start of the revival in the economy in 1993, the real yields of all the main taxes (other than social-insurance contributions) rose over

1992 levels, though turnover tax by a very small proportion only.   Most continued to rise as we would expect into 1994, but surprisingly neither turnover tax nor profit tax did so, both falling quite substantially.   Still surprisingly, into 1995, most either fell in yield or remained virtually static. The exception was social-insurance, which continued a steady rise from its low point in 1993.   Into 1996, the yield of excises fell to less than half its absolute level of 1994 (the excise on petrol had been reduced, but this is not nearly enough to explain the fall); the yield of personal-income and small-business taxes taken together also fell; social-insurance continued its climb; profit tax rose by a quarter but still remained at less than half of its 1993 level; foreign-trade taxes rose slightly; and, with the replacement of turnover tax by VAT in July 1996, the yield of the two together in 1996 was about 60% up on the turnover tax of 1995.

Social-insurance doubled its real absolute yield between 1993 and 1996.   There were some small increases in contribution rates between 1993 and 1996, and medical insurance had been added to its scope in 1995, but these do not seem to explain its increase as a proportion of GDP (health-insurance receipts are excluded from the social-insurance receipts in Table 11.2).   Anecdotal evidence suggests that there may have been increasing pressure from employees on private-sector employers to register for and maintain contributions.   Nevertheless, Koliadina in a Report on the system published in August 1996 (IMF, 1996) reports that social-security contributions were very patchy except in the state sector.   In some ways it may be encouraging that, even in this relatively successful revenue device, there is great scope for improvement.   Apart from social-security, turnover/VAT and import/export were the groups with the highest absolute yields in 1996.

It is very hard to explain these year-by-year, tax-by-tax changes after 1993, against a background of rapidly rising income (and probably, for the first year or so, even more rapidly rising expenditure because of remittances), except by assuming differential and irregular administrative-political failure.

Revenue in 1997

Total government revenue for 1997 would appear, from estimates made in December of that year, to have been about 16.5% lower in real terms than in 1996.   However, real revenue in the second half of the year was about 50% higher than in the first half.   In the first half, revenue was coming in per month at a rate about a third lower in real terms than in 1996, while in the second half the rate was roughly the same as in 1996.   This comparison probably exaggerates somewhat the collapse of revenue in the first half and the recovery in the second, because there is some tendency for revenue in any case to flow faster in real terms during the second half of the year than over the year as a whole. (The seasonal pattern seems to be irregular, but rough comparison over 1993 to 1996 suggests that a factor of about 0.91 should be applied to the second-half total-revenue figures to 'de-seasonalize' them and make them representative of the rate to be expected over the year.) The final column in each of Tables 11.4 and 11.5 is derived by taking the figure for the second half of 1997 and multiplying it by 2, *without* applying the seasonal factor. Figures in those columns should be read with that qualification in mind. Nevertheless, there *was* a collapse of revenue in the first half of the year and a marked recovery thereafter.

Tables 11.4 and 11.5 use most of the same categories as Tables 11.1 and 11.2 in order to show the changes between 1996 and 1997. Figures for 1996 in the later tables are slightly different from those in the earlier ones. They were compiled later and also use the Ministry of Finance's own estimates of GDP. Each version for 1996 is as far as possible consistent with those with which it is compared. There must of course be serious doubt about the GDP aggregates, especially in such a disturbed period. The EBRD *Transition Report 1997* projects a fall of 15% in real GDP from 1996 to 1997, while the figures on which our two tables are based (drawn up in December and therefore probably two to four months later) suppose a fall of only 7%. Because it *is* later, the 7% estimate carries perhaps a shade more credibility, but there is plenty of room for error.

The collapse in revenue during the first half of the year (before the general election) was no doubt due in part to a *fall in the 'bases'* of most of the main revenue sources as trade and production became severely disrupted. But it is very likely too that there were *increased deficiencies of administration* in at least some of them, most notably perhaps customs and excises. The fact that in the second half the average 1996 rate of revenue collection was roughly restored suggests that we must look for more lasting changes that tended to boost revenue once the political troubles were over.

VAT, with its increased rate of 20% from October, was expected to have raised substantially more revenue over the whole year than had turnover tax and VAT in 1996.

Customs duties were especially hard hit in the first half of the year but in the second half seemed to be running at a rate *well above* their average for 1996. Even over the year as a whole they were down *much less* proportionately in real terms from 1996 than was the real value of merchandise-import trade (13% as against about 25%).

This suggests *either* a favourable effect of the new (in fact somewhat narrower) tariff-rate structure introduced at the start of 1997 *or* an improvement in administration *over pre-1997 standards* once the political unrest had subsided---probably the latter.

Table 11.4   National-acounting and budgetary aggregates---mainly expenditure---1996-1997 (monetary figures in million lekë)

	1996	1997 estimate	1997 second half, estimate, mult. by 2
GDP nominal	280,998	338,198	362,500
GDP at 1990 prices	16,002	14,880	15,060
Implied GDP deflator	1,756.0	2,272.8	2,407.0
Consumer price index (period average)*	1,228.0	1,638.2	
Government expenditure nominal	85,245	101,543	127,612
Government expenditurre at 1990 prices	4,854	4,468	5,302
As % of GDP:			
Government expenditure	30.34	30.02	35.20
Government revenue	18.27	16.41	19.33
Deficit	12.07	13.61	15.87
Deficit before counterpart funds	12.16	13.70	15.91
Counterpart funds	0.09	0.09	0.04
External finance	1.35	1.90	3.25
Social insurance outlays (excluding health insurance)	6.71	5.65	6.10
Social assistance outlays	1.35	1.30	1.55
Unemployment benefit	0.77	0.65	0.63
Subsidies	0.39	0.40	0.45
Government capital spending	4.54	3.70	5.58

*   CPI as implied in EBRD, *Transition Report 1997*.

Source: Ministry of Finance

Table 11.5   Budgetary aggregates---mainly revenue---1996-1997 (monetary figures in million lekë)

	1996	1997 estimate	1997 second half, estinate, mult. by 2
At 1990 prices:			
Government revenue total	2,924	2,441	2,911
Turnover tax / VAT	517	691	917
State enterprise / profit tax	193	106	132
Personal income + small- business tax	79	48	52
Import tax (customs)	439	383	516
Excises	282	95	114
Social insurance (excl. health insurance)	668	521	548
Other taxes	209	129	137
As % of GDP:			
Turnover tax / VAT	3.23	4.64	6.09
State enterprise / profit tax	1.21	0.71	0.86
Personal income + small-business tax	0.50	0.32	0.35
Import tax (customs)	2.74	2.57	3.43
Excises	1.76	0.67	0.76
Social insurance (excl. health insurance)	4.17	3.50	3.64
Other taxes	1.31	0.87	0.91

Source: Ministry of Finance

However, the rate of receipts from the third major source of revenue, social-insurance contributions, was down substantially from 1996 levels, even in the second half of the year, both absolutely and as a proportion of GDP. Reduced employment no doubt explains some part of this fall; but it seems likely from the magnitude of the change that non-compliance also increased. The fall in personal-income tax too seems too large to be explained simply by the fall in its base. And excise revenue (already in 1996 at much less than half of its 1995 level) fell further by about two-thirds in real terms.

In spite of the apparent success with enforcement of customs and VAT, there is doubtless a large scope for further increasing revenue by improving administration.

Yet, even after allowance is made for seasonal factors that tend normally to produce more revenue in the second half of the year than in the first, overall the picture gives reason for hope that, if the 1996 level of real GDP were to be restored in 1998 (or 1999), real government-revenue receipts then would be at least of the same order as in 1996, possibly higher. The apparent striking improvement in enforcement of customs, moreover, suggests that measures to increase compliance can be fruitful.

There is ground for hope but not complacency. The budgetary position in 1996 was far from satisfactory. Meanwhile, social and transport infrastructure was deteriorating. Moreover so big a deficit financed largely by money creation would be acceptable only while there was rapid growth in real income. Both considerable improvement in tax enforcement and the institution of a popular form of loan to the government must be treated as urgent.

Summary

In the transition to a market economy up to 1996, Albania experienced a fall of government outlays from about 60% to about 30% of GDP.

Simultaneously government revenue experienced an even greater proportional reduction from just under 50% to about 20%.

By these tests, the state by 1996 had a smaller role in the Albanian economy than in most of the economies of Western Europe.

The deficit between revenue and expenditure, starting in 1989 at 8.6% of GDP, rose in 1991 to 30%, returned in 1994 to 8.6%, and then gradually rose to 11% over the next two years: a high but not extraordinarily high level by West European standards.

From 1992 to 1995, counterpart funds based on grant-aid from abroad significantly reduced the deficit. From 1993 to 1995, external borrowing was important in financing it.

The part of the deficit left to be covered domestically is financed mostly by a combination of base-money-creation and the sale of Treasury Bills (mainly to the state-owned banks and insurance company). However, over 1994-96, this extra creation of money was consistent with quite moderate inflation while at the same time allowing very fast rates of output growth.   How this happened is explored in chapter 7.

The reduction in government spending during the period of transition is almost exactly accounted for by a similar absolute real reduction in government capital expenditure.   This means that capital spending *fell far more proportionately*: by an estimated 86% in real terms between 1989 and 1996, as against a fall of 19% in recurrent spending.   This is plausibly held to have a bearing on the deterioration of schools, hospitals, and roads.

There was also first a rise and then a fall in subsidies.   They rose to 20% of GDP in 1991 but declined sharply over the next two years and measured less than 1% of GDP in 1995 and 1996.

There was an increase in the number of tax instruments and there were changes (or disappearances) of those pre-existing, in order to fit better with the new economic circumstances and policy.   But the poor performance of real tax yield over the period of fast growth from 1994 to 1996 suggests that there was a progressive deterioration in the administration and enforcement of a number of the taxes.   The striking exception to this tendency was social-insurance contributions.   This is in spite of the fact that private-sector compliance with social-insurance obligations was known to be patchy.

The first half of the year 1997 saw a sharp fall in revenue, but there was then a marked recovery in the second half of the year.   The real value of revenue receipts during the second half of 1997 was very similar per month to that over the whole of 1996.   This recovery was much greater than is likely to be accounted for by seasonal factors.   It is explained to a small extent by the start of an upturn in output, but also by a rise of 60% in the rate of VAT near the end of the year and by what appears to be a real improvement in the effectiveness of customs collection.   However, the extent of decline then in other sources of revenue suggests that there is considerable scope for further tightening of enforcement.

There is also urgent need for it.   Current levels of revenue and modes of borrowing have meant deteriorating infrastructure *and at the same time* a level of cash deficit that may not always be consistent with sound macroeconomic management.   *Both* means of obtaining substantially more revenue *and* an acceptable form of borrowing from the public must have high priority.

12 Labour and Employment

There are two remarkable features of the transition of Albania's labour force to a market economy, both unique in Europe. One of them is the extent to which the population has relied on the export of workers to neighbouring countries. The other, less certain in its scale, has been an absorption by the newly privatized family-farms of labour displaced from non-agricultural activities.

As we have seen in chapter 10, the initial collapse of industrial output in Albania was greater proportionately than in any other of the transition economies. It seems likely that the loss of industrial employment was also a record-breaker.

Employment in Albania on the official estimate was 21% lower at the end of 1995 than at the end of 1989. The net fall of 307,000 jobs that this percentage decline represents was more than accounted for by the net fall of employment in industry (manufacturing, energy and mining), which on one calculation amounted to a net loss of 391,000 jobs (equal to 25% of the 1989 labourforce) between end-1990 and end-1994.

Yet, despite a rate of natural increase of population (as of 1990) of just under 2% a year, and an age-structure heavily biased toward increase in the younger age-groups, the *unemployment rate* at the end of 1995 was registered as 13%, only 6 percentage-points higher than six years earlier. (The rate of unemployment recorded had fallen almost continuously from May 1993 to the end of 1995.) In other words, quite a drastic fall in *employment* in industry and overall, over a period when the natural growth of the working-age population would have required a substantial rise if all were to be employed, led to a much more modest rise in the recorded *unemployment rate*.

The severe shock dealt by rapid liberalization had its effects ameliorated by three developments. One was unemployment benefit and the safety-net of comprehensive social assistance (discussed in chapter 8), though, as we have seen, the adequacy of these forms of support was possibly declining by the end of 1996. A second was an apparent net movement of workers from non-farming activities to agriculture. The third, and most important, was the fact that a large part of the potential workforce was able to earn abroad, principally in Greece, much higher incomes than those to which they had been accustomed, so that they massively lowered the competition for the greatly reduced job opportunities in the Albanian labour-market, while at the same time their remittances supplemented significantly the disposable incomes and investible resources of those who remained behind.

The second and third of these developments also help to explain the discrepancy between (on the one hand) the large fall in *employment*, together with the substantial *natural increase* in the population of working age, and (on the other) the comparatively small rise in recorded *unemployment* and the *unemployment rate*.

There was, according to the official statistics, an additional element: not an ameliorating factor but a further contributor to the relatively *low level and rate of recorded unemployment* in 1995 and 1996, given the *large net losses of paid jobs*. This was a fairly extensive movement of resident working-age women out of the 'labour force' (the body of people working or offering for work): so that the proportion of working-age women who were in the labour force fell from 84.6% of the total at the end of 1989 to 59.1% six years later. Such a fall in the so-called *participation rate* (the proportion of the working-age population within the country apparently offering for work) has been a fairly common experience of transition elsewhere in East and Central Europe. The peculiarity of Albania is that here it was apparently confined to women: the recorded participation rate of men actually rose. (We give below some reasons for doubt about the official figures on this matter, though it is not clear which way if any the overall picture ought to be corrected.) Though the fall in participation rate helps to keep the unemployment figures down (since by definition those not in the labour force can not be 'unemployed'), the withdrawal of women from the labour force is not likely in most cases to represent any improvement in welfare. It is very likely that many of the women concerned would gladly accept paid work if they could get it, but that they have become discouraged from trying, or for other reasons are not registered among those seeking employment.

In the same way, the absorption of surplus workers by farming, though perhaps a vital safety-valve, has doubtless not been either an unmixed blessing to the previous farm population or an adequate substitute for the jobs lost from the viewpoint of many of those displaced from industry. The extent of this is clouded by some confusions over numbers. The prevailing interpretation of present numbers seems to be the official one: that the number of workers in agriculture was about 750,000 at end-1994 and end-1995: 466,000 farms with an average of 1.6 workers each, according to one highly reputable interpreter. Figures supplied by an official in the Ministry of Agriculture give numbers in 1990 as 524,700 on the collectives and 196,700 on state farms, a total of 721,400, and indicate that the number of workers fell to 590,000 in 1992 and 1993 before rising to 750,000 by the end of 1994. This account implies a rather small net increase over the period (about 30,000) but with a dip in the meantime, which presumably betokens some movement out of agriculture during the period of disturbances and destruction in 1990 and 1991 as the old system was breaking down.   If this is correct, we take it that the farm workforce first fell to about 590,000 (quite possibly in large part because many workers emigrated) and thereafter, when privatization was effectively complete, rose by about 27% as people displaced from urban jobs moved to be with relatives in what were now family farms.

Even this modest increase must have represented, on many of the newly-formed and very small family farms, a change in which the capacity of the extra mouths often exceeded that of the extra hands.   At the same time we know that output was clearly increasing from the early days of privatization.   The influx of extra able-bodied workers, however embarrassing in the short term, may well have facilitated the necessary changes to more efficient techniques, better choice of products, and more intensive use of the land, that have to a large extent been proceeding.

Emigration, apart from the inevitable disruption caused to the lives of the migrants themselves and their families, has been a much more unqualified advantage.   In a straight material sense, most emigrants probably have a higher standard of living than they would if they had stayed in Albania.   Their movement is further important not only because it reduces the number of people competing for jobs and the number idle but also because of what they send back.   Official figures give the net private transfers into Albania in 1995 at US$384.6 million.   This represents nearly $120 for each woman, man, and child in the population over the year, or $10 a month---the equivalent of 942 lekë at the exchange rate prevailing at the end of 1995.   If this sum comprised simple transfers to Albanian families in proportion to their numbers of members, what would be received by a family of four on average would represent an addition of nearly 60% to the average monthly wage (6,406 lekë) as it was at end-1995.

Job Destruction, Job Creation, Labour Participation and Emigration

An element of fog surrounds unemployment figures everywhere.   By definition the unemployed are those *involuntarily* lacking gainful activity. But *how much* gainful activity do you need to be employed, and *how* unwilling must the lack of it be if you are to be regarded as unemployed rather than a non-participant? Arbitrary limits can be set to help answer

Table 12.1 Selected labour-market indicators, 1989-1997
(end of year, except for rows 1 and 2)

	1989	1990	1991	1992	1993	1994	1995	1996	1997
GDP at constant prices (% change)	9.8	-10.0	-27.7	-7.2	9.6	9.4	8.9	8.2 est.	-15 proj.
Industrial gross output (% change)		-14.2	-42.0	-51.2	-10.0	-2.0	1.0	n.a.	n.a.
Population (000)	3230	3282	3260	3190	3167	3202	3249	3283	
Female	1568	1595	1606	1601	1601	1586	1641	1659	
Male	1662	1687	1654	1589	1566	1616	1608	1624	
Working-age population (000)	1861	1897	1925	1849	1763	1786	1820	1850	
Female	867	886	945	937	878	886	904		
Male	994	1011	980	912	885	900	916		
Working-age population as % of total population	57.6	57.8	59.0	58.0	55.7	55.8	56.0	56.9	
Labourforce (000)	1554	1579	1544	1489	1347	1423	1304	1274	1301
Female	734	722	715	707	587	609	534		
Male	820	857	829	782	760	814	770		
Employment (000)	1440	1429	1404	1095	1046	1161	1133	1116	1108
Female	672	644	640	507	445	488	454		
Male	820	857	829	782	760	814	679		
Unemployment (000)	113	151	140	394	301	262	171	158	194
Female	62	79	75	200	142	121	80		
Male	52	72	65	194	159	141	91		
Unemployment rate (%)	7.3	9.6	9.1	26.5	22.3	18.4	13.1	12.4	14.9
Female	8.4	10.9	10.5	28.3	24.2	19.9	15.0		
Male	6.3	8.4	7.8	24.8	20.9	17.3	11.8		
Long-term unemployment as % of total unemployment					65	81	73	76	84
Participation rate (%)	83.5	83.2	80.2	80.5	76.4	79.7	71.6	68.9	
Female	84.7	81.5	75.7	75.5	66.9	68.7	59.1		
Male	82.5	84.8	84.6	85.7	85.9	90.4	84.1		

Source: Institute of Statistics; first two rows from EBRD, *Transition Report 1997*, p.214; gaps are of figures not available

the former of these questions, but degrees of willingness can not readily be measured.   The dividing-line between the 'unemployed', who are unwilling to be out of work, and 'non-participants', who are willing to be so, is exceedingly difficult to draw.

In Albania, the unemployed are officially taken to be those who are so registered and hence eligible for state benefits. Others of working age without gainful activity are non-participants. But all resident able-bodied members of farm families within the working-age range are held to be employed. Most emigration is not registered since much of it is illegal in the receiving countries. Hence there are no *official* figures of emigration stocks and flows. The Institute of Statistics, tied to data officially issued, produced a publication in 1995 on the labour market without mentioning emigration. Accurate figures on current resident numbers and on age-specific fertility and mortality would enable net emigration to be inferred, but such demographic estimates, if they exist, do not appear to be published.

With these reservations, we consider Table 12.1, which presents a selection of key economic measures for the Albanian economy and the labour market. It shows that, even in 1990, before significant reform had begun, industrial production fell quite sharply, but total employment fell only slightly, indicating a degree of labour hoarding. However, *unemployment* (*the number of unemployed*) increased to a greater extent, largely because of the increase in working-age population. Subsequently, while *employment* continued to fall from 1991 to 1993 and (after a rise in 1994) again in 1995 and 1996, the *number of unemployed* was also actually *reduced* in 1991, and then, after a big rise in 1992, continued to *fall* each year thereafter to 1996. And, even though the number of unemployed did increase in 1992, the scale of the increase was much less marked than the scale of the fall in employment. This phenomenon of *reductions* (or in one case an increase but a much more modest one) in the numbers of unemployed people in the face of substantial falls in employment can only be explained by a reduced participation rate or emigration or both, the former indeed shown in Table 12.1. It is clear that emigration and the drop in women's participation rate were the contributing factors to this phenomenon. (And of course we cannot ignore the possibility that the recorded switch of women from unemployment to non-participation may be something of an artifact of classification.)

There was a substantial increase in employment in 1994. The evidence for 1994 suggests that, when the situation in the Albanian domestic labour market improved, this had an impact on inducing non-participants to come back into the labour market. It is not clear that it had any comparable impact on attracting migrants to come back to Albania.

In what follows we try to make rough estimates of the sizes of some of the elements that had helped by the end of 1995, and indeed through 1996, to make the shock of the very rapid moves to a market economy tolerable in their effects on people's employment and unemployment. We rely for the most part on the published data provided by the Institute of Statistics

(INSTAT), largely those reproduced above in Table 12.1. These provide an internally consistent set of figures for the main demographic and labour-market variables: if not everything that we might like to have. The EBRD's *Transition Report* gives at some points quite different figures. For example, the implication of the summary table of main Albanian statistics in the 1996 *Transition Report* is that employment fell by 41% from end-1990 to end-1995, while INSTAT figures imply a fall of only 21%. However, the *Transition Report Update* of April 1997, published only five months later, implies a fall of only 12% for the same variable, by giving a much smaller fall over 1991 and a rise rather than a fall over 1990. It would be difficult to make this much smaller fall in employment credibly consistent with other data from INSTAT. While we cannot rule out the possibility that it is more accurate than INSTAT's corresponding figure, we lack other data consistent with it that could put it in context (and enquiries at the EBRD about the discrepancy between its earlier and later figures, and between both of them and INSTAT's, shed no light). Hence we are virtually obliged to use the INSTAT information if we are to make a consistent story. But the reader should remember that there are uncertainties and large differences among the sources.

From the demographic data we made two alternative projections of what the *working-age* population *would have been* if there had been no emigration. The *rate of natural increase* of the population officially reported for 1990 was 1.96%. We did not have data that would allow *age-specific fertility and mortality* to be estimated. Given the age structure, however, it seemed very likely that the working-age population (in the absence of net migration) would increase faster than total population. The lower projection (PROJW1) of the 'natural increase' of the working-age population accordingly supposed a rate of growth of 2.00%, just above the 1990 rate of natural increase of the whole population. The higher projection (PROJW2) used the actual annual growth rates of numbers of working-age men (2.81%) and working-age women (2.95%) reported for the period 1979-89, and assumed that these would have continued in the absence of net migration. A further projection (PROJT) was made of what the *total* population would have been in the absence of net migration by applying the 1990 natural-increase rate of 1.96%. The differences between these projections and the actual figures for the same dates would be estimates of the reduction due to net migration of the working-age population (or of the total population as the case might be) over the period considered.

Table 12.2 Fall in employment and rise in unemployment, 1989-1995 (changes, year-end to year-end, in thousands)

Period (year-end to year-end)	(1) Fall in employment	(2) Rise in unemployment	(3) Net loss of total population through migr'n on PROJT	(4) Net loss of working-age population through migr'n on PROJ W1	(5) Net loss of working-age population through migr'n on PROJ W2	(6) Fall in working-age population	(7) Fall in workforce = (1) - (2)	(8) Fall in workforce participation = (7) - (6)
1989-1994	279	149	357	269	357	75	130	55
1989-1995	307	58	380	276	385	41	249	208
1990-1994	268	112	345	267	339	111	156	45
1990-1995	296	21	367	274	366	77	275	198

Source: Institute of Statistics; and projections as explained in text

The projections suggest that the net loss of *working-age* population through migration was somewhere about 300,000, mostly taking place over the period 1990-94, with the net loss of *total* population probably of the order of 350,000. On the assumption that most of the net emigration up to the end of 1994 and 1995 had occurred by 1993, this is not far out of line with the figures cited by Mançellari *et al.* (1995, pp.7-8): the Greek Government's estimate of 400,000 Albanians 'working abroad' in 1993, and the Albanian Ministry of Labour's figures of a stock of 330,000 emigrants in June 1994. The result, if INSTAT's figures are broadly correct, is that the working-age population in Albania fell instead of rising over the whole period between the end of 1989 and the end of 1995 (and indeed of 1996). Emigration took all the natural increase in this age-group and more. Within this period, however, the only years in which working-age population actually fell were 1992 and 1993 (by a total of 162,000). Net emigration must have been heavily concentrated in those two years.

What is not easily credible about the figures in Table 12.2 is the implied large movement of working-age people within Albania out of the workforce over 1995, 153,000 as implied by the figures in the last column. (This column incidentally does not depend on our demographic projections but is implied directly by the INSTAT figures.) If employment fell by only 28,000 over that year, as column (1) purports to show, it is hard to believe that more than five times as many people should simply have withdrawn from workforce participation, that number being (according to the same figures) about three times as many as had withdrawn altogether in the previous four years of (in total) much more drastic employment contraction.   The suspicion probably must be *either* that, for whatever reason, more additional workers left the country in 1995 than the rest of the table suggests, *or* alternatively that the way of determining who was and who was not offering for work changed over 1995 so that the recorded fall in the workforce is at least in part an artifact of classification (i.e. that both workforce and the number of unemployed fell less than reported, and each less by the same absolute number) and that hence the *unemployment rate* (unemployment as a proportion of the workforce) rightly speaking fell *less* over 1995 than the official figures indicate.

In the study on which this chapter has been based, the contributors tried to gain some idea of the extent to which emigration had eased the unemployment that would otherwise have prevailed.   However, the figures, showing what hypothetically the unemployment rate *would have been* in the absence of emigration, have to be taken with heavy qualifications because they rest on three assumptions, at least two of which will not go close to being fulfilled.

The assumptions are, *first*, that all those who in fact have emigrated would otherwise have been added to the workforce rather than to the numbers of non-participants; *second*, that the number of 'jobs' (positions in which people can be gainfully occupied) would have been unchanged if all the migrants had simply stayed in Albania and looked for work, given an unchanged amount spent on consumption and investment in Albania; and *third* that the amount spent on consumption and investment in Albania *would in fact have been* unaffected.   It is the second and third of these that will not be entirely realistic.

Given constant spending in Albania, the extra workforce members would tend to depress wage rates, and this could be expected to have some effect in increasing the actual number of paid jobs on offer.   Some of the extra workers would move to family farms and hence be regarded as 'employed' for purposes of the statistics.   And some would probably move into self-employment, as many Albanians have done over the last few years, and again be counted as 'employed'.   If that were the only departure from the assumptions, and we imagined all the emigrants suddenly repatriated, it is clear that the number recorded as *employed* in Albania would almost certainly *rise* as a result after a longer or shorter lag.

But the third assumption is also unrealistic: elimination of emigrants' remittances would have given Albanian residents far less to spend; and this in itself would greatly have reduced the number of jobs on offer at any given set of wage-rates.   (This is explored in Mançellari *et al., 1995.*)

Table 12.3 What unemployment rates would have been on certain assumptions, end of 1994 and 1995 (%)

	End-1994	End-1995
Actual unemployment rate	18.4	13.1
Hypothetical unemployment rate in absence of		
net emigration: on projection PROJW1	31.4	28.3
on projection PROJW2	34.8	32.9
Hypothetical unemployment rate in absence of		
net emigration and net workforce-withdrawal:		
on projection PROJW1	33.5	34.6
on projection PROJW2	36.7	38.5

Source: Figures in Tables 12.1 and 12.2, and projections explained in text

Thus unemployment and the unemployment rate for 1994 and 1995 in the absence of emigration might have been *either higher or lower* than they are represented (in Table 12.3) on the assumption of an unchanged level of employment.   However, it is still of some interest to get an idea of how the lack of emigration *would have* increased unemployment *if the number of jobs available had remained unaffected.*   If the hypothetical return of the migrants would have resulted in *less* additional unemployment than indicated in Table 12.3 on the demographic assumptions made there, there would certainly be other costs incurred instead: in lower wage-levels, or in crowding of yet more people of working age onto farms, where they might count as extra workers but where they would often add more to consumption there than they would to production.

With these qualifications, simulations of hypothetical unemployment rates are presented in Table 12.3 for 1994 and 1995:

(i) on both demographic projections, PROJW1 and PROJW2;
(ii) on the assumption of no net emigration between 1989 and 1995;
(iii) on the assumption of no net emigration and no net workforce-withdrawal over the same period.

These simulations suggest that, with the number of 'jobs' (opportunities for earning income through labour) remaining constant, net emigration between the end of 1989 and the end of 1995 reduced the unemployment rate by between 15.2 and 19.8 percentage-points, and that withdrawal of working-age residents from the labour force reduced it by a further 5.6 to 6.4 percentage-points.   In the absence of *both* these adaptations, the unemployment rate on the last day of 1995 would have been between 34.6% and 38.5%.

But we stress again that the number of 'jobs' would doubtless *not* have been unchanged in number at end-1995 if emigration had been prevented or reversed.   It might have been higher or lower.   What is clear is that without emigration people in Albania at large would, one way or another, have been considerably poorer.

The changes in employment are shown split tentatively among sectors in Table 12.4, which combines INSTAT data with those from the Ministry of Agriculture.

Table 12.4   Sectoral breakdown of the fall in employment, end-1990 to end-1994 (000)

(1) Fall in total employment	(2) Fall in industrial employment	(3) Rise in farm employment	(4) Implied net rise in non-industrial, non-farm employment = (2)-(1)-(3)	(5) Rise in unemploy-ment	(6) Fall in workforce = (1)-(5)
268	391	29	94	112	156

Source: Institute of Statistics; Ministry of Agriculture

In the proportion that emigrants (those still closely enough linked to the mother-country that they are likely to send remittances) bear to the resident population, Albania is comparable to Mexico and probably far exceeds any other country in Europe.   In its demonstrated readiness for people to be re-absorbed into agriculture too, it is probably unique in Europe.   These two phenomena, with all their repercussions, have in all likelihood served to keep tens of thousands, possibly hundreds of thousands, of Albanians out of idleness and lack of earnings, with migration greatly, and the move to agriculture modestly, also increasing disposable income in total for resident Albanians.

Characteristics of Albania's Unemployment

Unemployment Turnover and Long-term Unemployment

To understand the nature of a country's unemployment it is necessary to monitor the inflow into, and outflow from, the unemployment pool. The

Table 12.5 Sectoral shares of employment, year-ends, 1994-1997 (%)

	1994	1995	1996	1997
Total employment	100.0	100.0	100.0	100.0
- in state sector	26.5	23.9	21.2	20.4
- in non-agricultural private sector	8.9	11.1	12.1	10.9
- in agricultural sector	64.6	65.0	66.7	68.7

Source: Institute of Statistics

outflow may be either into employment or out of the workforce (into non-participation, emigration, old-age, or death). From official figures for 6 months in 1993 and the 12 months of 1996, the contributors made estimates of the inter-relationships of *inflows* to the unemployment pool, *outflows to jobs*, and outflows that involved leaving the workforce (*'dropouts'*).

A finding of a significantly high *negative* monthly rate of *inflow minus dropouts* for 1993 (an average of -5.43% of the pool each month for the 5 months covered, which, since inflows are always non-negative, implies a monthly dropout rate of *at least* 5.43%) suggests that, over that year, a substantial proportion of the unemployed people simply dropped out of the labour force. Moreover, outflow from unemployment to jobs (averaging 0.89% a month for 6 months) was trivial. Therefore, although the stock of unemployed people started to fall from 1993, this fall was largely due to dropouts rather than to job creation. Given the trivial rate of outflow to jobs, we should expect the duration of unemployment to increase, and this has generally happened. The share of long-term unemployment (people who have been unemployed for more than a year) was 65% in 1993.

In 1996, as the private sector and especially the agriculture sector grew steadily, the average monthly outflow to jobs was slightly higher than for the months we have in 1993. However, this growth in output did not bring about comparable growth in jobs for the unemployed, perhaps for the following reasons. First, the growth in output might be due largely to the improved productivity per worker, as certainly happened in agriculture. Second, many of the new jobs might have been filled by people who had already been employed, or by returning migrants. The rate of net outflow in 1996 was so small (as of course was the rate of inflow too when the size of the pool was not increasing) that it is no surprise that the share of long-term unemployment should have increased in most years. By the end of 1994, this share had risen to 81%. It fell over 1995 but rose again over 1996 and 1997. While the number of registered unemployed fell by 36% between end-1993 and end-1997, the number of long-term unemployed fell by only

16%. Expanding or contracting, the pool was generally a stagnant one.

This phenomenon of low turnover of the unemployed has been common in other Central and East European economies (Boeri, 1994), and it is a ground for concern, along with workforce-withdrawal, from which it is not always easily distinguished. Transition ideally involves re-deployment of labour. When workers are instead put out of action for long periods, it is socially wasteful and personally disastrous.

Unemployment by Gender

As is clear from Table 12.1, the *unemployment rate* for women workers has been consistently higher than that for men. From end-1989 to end-1995, female *employment* fell by 32.4%, which compares with a reduction in male employment of 11.6%. It seems that women workers have been particularly vulnerable to the adverse impact of the labour-market adjustments. Women's participation rate in the labour force started higher than that of men, but it fell steadily over the reform years, whereas men's participation rate rose slightly.

Table 12.6 Average monthly rates of flow into and out of unemployment, by gender (% of unemployment pool)

1993			
Male		Female	
Inflow - Dropouts	Outflow to jobs	Inflow - Dropouts	Outflow to jobs
-6.40	0.98	-4.41	0.75

1996			
Male		Female	
Inflow - Dropouts	Outflow to jobs	Inflow - Dropouts	Outflow to jobs
1.19	1.07	-0.43	0.89

Table 12.6 presents the average monthly rate of flows into and out of unemployment for males and females in 1993 and 1996.

In 1993, the rate of *inflow minus dropouts* was significantly negative for both males and females. (More were withdrawing, by emigration or otherwise, than were entering the unemployment pool.) However, what we know from other evidence, such as that in Table 12.1, indicates that dropping-out for males primarily took the form of emigration while for females it very often took the form of moving to non-participation. Although the rate of outflow to jobs was slightly higher for males than for females, both rates were very low, indicating low turnover of unemployment for both sexes. The share of long-term unemployment in 1993 was 67% for males and 62% for females. By 1996, the number of men absent abroad had probably ceased to rise. But female withdrawal from the labour market continued nonetheless. The rises in the rates of outflow from unemployment to jobs were not large enough to make a marked impact on the size of the unemployment pool, and in 1996 (see Table 12.1) they did not prevent an increase in the average duration of unemployment.

Summary

The shock to Albania's employment in industry brought about by rapid liberalization was probably more severe than in any other transition country. Yet the Albanian workforce showed a distinctive and comparatively successful pattern of adjustments to this employment shock: principally by quite massive emigration (which brought a considerable inflow of resources through remittances) and by some movement of workers to family farms after privatization. There was also some apparent net dropping-out from the workforce into non-participation within the country, but, in contrast to other transitional economies, this, measured over the period as a whole, was apparently confined to women. Men, instead of dropping out, moved to work abroad.

As a result of these various adjustments, the level of *employment*, the *number of unemployed*, and the *unemployment-rate*, appear at times to move almost independently of each other. The actual course of the *employment* level is subject to some uncertainty, but there is agreement that employment at the end of 1996 was still substantially lower than in 1989. The *unemployment rate* as officially recorded was somewhat higher than in 1989 and at a level that would be considered high (though not extraordinarily so) in contemporary Western Europe, but it had been falling almost consistently for over three years. It rose, though by only 2.5 percentage-points, over 1997. The social-security system had been adapted and considerably expanded to take account of the existence of substantial and persistent urban unemployment, though support for both short-term and long-term unemployed was possibly becoming less adequate by late 1996.

The continuing, probably unwilling, shift of so many Albanian women to non-participation in the labour market must be a ground for concern. A further aspect of the situation that needs to be monitored and addressed is the low rate of outflow from unemployment to jobs for both men and women. The consequent increase in the share of *long-term* unemployment betokens an enormous waste of economic resources as well as a further potential source of frustration and grievance.

13 Financial Institutions

Albania's authorities in the 1990s constructed financial organizations very much according to the current prevailing wisdom, though perhaps they were slow in reforming the state-owned commercial banks. They failed on a point of regulation on which there were few close foreign precedents. It was a failure that, in the early months of 1997, seemed close to destroying the Albanian state.

Transition to the market has required the financial institutions to perform a range of new functions. A financial system in a market economy is expected to act as an intermediary between savers and investors; to allow risks to be spread and acceptably shared; to help allocate capital efficiently; to ensure that the contracts in which it is involved are honoured; to render payment simple and quick; to allow people to alter flexibly their portfolios of assets; and to protect, by regulation and supervision, against the effects of ignorance and fraud and the risk and effects of loss of confidence.

A number of these functions would have been irrelevant under the command system. Then transactions were supposed to occur either among state organs or between individuals and the state. Most decisions on investment were made bureaucratically within the state apparatus. Many of the transactions expressed in cash terms were simply accounting devices. Independence among financial agencies, which to a point is required in a market system, would have been considered subversive of policy.

Before 1992, the State Bank of Albania performed both central-banking and commercial-banking functions. There was a State Agricultural Bank and a network of savings-collection agencies. After 1991 there was an Albanian Commercial Bank which took over some of the functions of the State Bank of Albania. There were no other financial institutions apart from the state insurance company, INSIG, and the Social Security Institute. The banks' activities were confined to cash transactions and the clearing of invoices presented to banks for transfers between various public enterprises and between public enterprises and the government. Credit to enterprises was automatically extended if their funds were insufficient. But there was little provision for household access to credit. Decisions on the quantity and allocation of credit were part of the central planning process. Interest rates were determined by the State Bank of Albania and were seldom changed. All savings generated by households were channelled to the State Bank. Such was the system in existence in Albania until 1992.

As Table 13.1 shows, there have since been radical changes in the

Table 13.1   Formal institutions of the financial system, end-1996

a. Central Bank	
Bank of Albania	Central Bank pursuing policies relating to price stabiity, foreign exchange, supervision and regulation.
b. Second-Level Banks	
1. Savings Bank	Full service, state-owned bank, 17 branches and 54 representative offices.
2. National Commercial Bank	Full service, state owned bank, 30 branches and 30 representative offices. Two joint ventures with foreign banks.
3. Rural Commercial Bank (dissolved 1998)	Full service, state-owned bank; 33 branches and 160 representative offices.
4. Italian-Albanian Bank	Joint venture universal bank owned by Banca di Roma 40 per cent; National Commercial Bank 40 percent; European Bank for Reconstruction and Development 20 per cent; started in 1993.
5. Arab Albanian Islamic Bank	Joint-venture bank owned by National Commercial Bank 40 per cent; and the Arab Islamic Bank, Dallah Baraka Group and Indiviuals 60 per cent; started in 1994.
6. Dardania Bank	Private universal bank; started in 1996.
7. Tirana Bank	Albanian branch of Piraeus Bank; universal bank; started in 1996.
8. National Bank of Greece	Albanian branch; universal bank; started in 1996.
9. International Commercial Bank	Malaysian private bank; universal bank; started in 1996.
c. Financial Markets	
Tirana Stock Exchange	Started in May1996; trades Treasury Bills; intended also to trade Privatization Vouchers and Government Bonds.
d. Insurance	
1. INSIG: Insurance Institute	The sole commercial insurance provider at present; state-owned; it provides property, life and business insurance.
2. Social Insurance Institute	State owned; covers compulsory contributory social-insurance scheme.
e. Investment Banks	
1. Anglo-Adriatic Investment Fund	The sole active investment fund in Albania; started 1996. Takes part in privatization process of strategic enterprises using privatisation vouchers.
2. AAEF - Albanian American Enterprise Fund	Incorporated in the USA in March, 1995 and opened its office in Tirana in August, 1995. Investment credit, investment guarantees, equity investments and feasibility studies.
3. FEFAD - Foundation for Enterprise Finance and Development	Invests in working-capital and assets of small and medium enterprixes; started 1996.
4. SME - Small and Medium Enterprise Fund	Provides small and medium-sized businesses with initial capital; started in 1992.
5. KfW - Kredit für Wiederaufbau	Provides liquidity for small firms.
6. DtA- Deutsche Ausgleichbank	Provides liquidity for small firms.

Source: Bank of Albania

organizations. The question then arises whether the necessary supportive changes have taken place in law, accountancy, management, and governance, to support the new organizational forms.

The Bank of Albania

One of the first steps on the road to marketization was the introduction of a two-tier banking system. The State Bank of Albania was replaced by the Bank of Albania, which inherited its central-banking functions. The rest of the banking system was divided into three state-owned commercial banks: the National Commercial Bank, the Savings Bank and the Rural Commercial Bank.

The setting up of the central bank was accompanied by a debate over the powers that the Bank of Albania should have and the independence that it should enjoy. One argument is that an independent central bank acquires its credibility from setting monetary policy free from those constraints of political pressure that would operate on a bank controlled by the government. On the other hand there is a counter-argument that such important economic policies should be under the control of democratically elected representatives, responsive to the needs of the country as a whole rather that to the more narrow viewpoint of the financial establishment. Also, in a period of radical developments, it is important that the government should have a say in determining economic priorities.

Judging the Independence of a Central Bank

The independence of a central bank can be measured in three ways (Hasse, 1990, quoted in Eijffinger & Haan, 1996): *personnel-independence* (how free it is from government influence on appointments and dismissals and direct government representation on its governing bodies); *financial independence* (the extent to which it can decide, independently of the government, how far to finance government deficits); and *policy-independence* (its independence in setting the goals and using the instruments of monetary policy).

Since there are these separate dimensions, it can be difficult to compare degrees of independence between one central bank and another. It has also been argued that the actual rules relating to independence are less important than the support which the policies pursued by the central bank enjoy, not only from politicians, but also from the population at large. In this view success in Germany regarding the control of inflation flows not only from the Bundesbank's legal independence over its use of monetary policy, but also and even more from the high priority given to low inflation by the German population. The greater independence that the Banque de France has acquired in recent years arises from general political support for anti-inflation policy rather than from changed formal relationships between the Bank and the government.

Powers, Functions and Constitution of the Bank of Albania

The Bank of Albania was established under the Law of the Banking System No 7560 dated 22nd April 1992. This law established the two-tier banking system and determined the powers which the Bank of Albania would exercise and its governance. This law was up-dated in law No 8076 dated 20th February 1996, which incorporated changes reflecting experience during the 1992-1996 period.

The main statutory objective of the Bank of Albania is price stability. To support this it has the responsibility of determining the system of foreign exchange, of controlling the internal financial markets and the payments system, and of pursuing appropriate monetary and lending policies. Under the law of 1996 some of the main activities of the Bank of Albania are:

1. to formulate and implement monetary and foreign-exchange policies;
2. to act as banker, adviser and fiscal agent of the Republic of Albania;
3. to provide advances to banks;
4. to deal in government securities;
5. to make loans to the state;
6. to be responsible for the licensing, supervision, and regulation of banking and other financial institutions.

The Bank's lending to the state, represented by the Ministry of Finance, can be provided by:

1. the purchase of government securities directly;
2. the purchase of Treasury Bills by auction;
3. the purchase of government securities in the secondary market.

The law also determined that, for the years 1996, 1997 and 1998, the amounts borrowed from the central bank to cover the budget deficit would be no more that 10%, 6%, and 2% respectively of annual revenues. Because of higher-than-forecast deficits, attempts have been made to increase these percentages, and this appears to have been achieved under legislation of December 1996 (IMF, 1997, p.11). The bank was also limited by the February 1996 law in the value of Treasury Bills that it could buy itself *in the primary market* (that is, directly from the government) (*ibid.*), though the IMF Report goes on to say that these limits on financing government proved ineffective in the second half of 1996 because (a) the government found that it could commandeer interest-free loans from the state-owned commercial banks (which admittedly would not *necessarily* increase the money supply), and (b) the Bank of Albania could be induced to buy Treasury Bills *in the secondary market*, so creating extra money by the back door.

As noted above, the Bank of Albania is responsible for the supervision and regulation of the second-level banks and other financial institutions. The Bank publishes regulatory norms which the banks are expected to meet. The Bank is empowered to establish compulsory reserves of no more than 20 per cent of banks' liabilities; it determines base interest rates and the volume of long-term and short-term loans which can be made to second-level banks. It is now, however, permissible under certain limitations for second-level banks to trade with one another excess credit limits that they may have been allocated, and this trade represents in effect an embryonic interbank market.

The Bank of Albania is governed by a Supervisory Board. This consists of seven members: the Governor and Vice-governor, who are nominated by the President; the General Secretary who is nominated by the Council of Ministers; and four other members who are respectively nominated by the President, the Prime Minister, the Minister of Finance, and the Governor, all subject to the approval of Parliament. The Board is to approve the monetary and foreign-exchange policy of the Bank and any reports and recommendations it makes; to monitor its loans to the government; to determine the securities that it will hold; and to control its affiliated organizations.

There is also an Executive Committee of the Bank of Albania, which is composed of the Governor, the Vice-Governor, the General Secretary, and the Heads of Department (who are nominated by the Governor). This acts as the executive arm of the Supervisory Board.

Currently the Bank of Albania relies on direct instruments in pursuing its monetary policy. Total money supply is controlled through the limits put on the expansion of domestic credit. These limits are imposed on the whole banking system. To allow for the inflation target and the real growth expected, loan limits specific to each individual bank are set. To a point the limits may be traded among banks. Reserve requirements are also imposed. Until early 1997, these stood at 10% of all deposits. Penalty provisions are available to the Bank for enforcing the credit ceilings and reserve requirements. Certain controls over the banks' foreign-exchange positions also apply (IMF, 1997, p.17). The commercial banks also have access to a refinance facility at the Bank of Albania. There are minimum rates of interest set on time-deposits with the state-owned banks, generally ensuring that real rates are positive. Demand-deposit rates were freed at the end of January 1996 (*ibid.*).

The issuing of Treasury Bills from July 1994 has allowed financial institutions and other firms and individuals in principle to participate in the beginnings of a short-term money market, but it is believed that traders in Treasury Bills now are entirely, or almost entirely, state-owned enterprises, mainly banks.

It is clearly hoped that an increasing amount of lending will take place, on terms influenced by demand and supply, and at interest rates determined in the money markets, though influenced by central-bank intervention.

These developments are at an early stage, and their progress will depend on the successful reorganization of the whole financial system.

How Independent is the Bank of Albania?

As has been suggested, examination of legislation alone does not provide a definitive answer to this question.   In limiting, year by year in advance, the amount of government deficit that could be financed by central-bank credit, the parliament aspired to tie the hands of both government and Bank in this very important area.   Before the election of June 1997, there was speculation over who would win in case of conflict between the Bank and the government over Bank financing of the large deficit projected.   The legislation seems designed to give the Bank a fairly high degree of independence, which was internationally fashionable in the 1990s.   Yet such intentions are not necessarily fulfilled in times of constitutional conflict and political unrest.

The strength of the parliamentary and popular position of the government has a bearing on how far it can stretch its powers.   The executive in Albania was in a strong position in the second half of 1996 and in a much weaker one in the first half of 1997.   Yet even in this latter period it was possible for the President to dismiss the Governor of the central bank.   Perhaps a clue to how this could happen is provided by the fact that, though the move caused concern abroad, it was not generally criticized, even by oppositionists (then highly vocal) within the country.

Generally in a transitional economy, a central bank, if it chooses to be more conservative and restrictive than the government desires, can rely on at least tacit support from the multilateral organizations, notably the IMF. This can no doubt be an important element in any power-conflict.

A certain amount may also depend on the actual expertise present in the central bank and on popular and media perceptions of its effectiveness. Before the collapse of the 'pyramid funds', the Bank of Albania could reasonably claim a fair measure of success in its anti-inflationary policy, which appeared to have brought inflation down to manageable levels without preventing rapid recovery of output and income.   After the collapse, its achievements inevitably looked more dubious.

Second-Level (Commercial) Banks

These were established by legislation on 28th April, 1992.   The sector has been dominated by the three state-owned banks: the National Commercial Bank, the Savings Bank, and (until its dissolution in early 1998) the Rural Commercial Bank.   The other banks (joint ventures with foreign banks or wholly-foreign-owned) are small in comparison.

The functions required of them are radically different from those of

banks in the previous regime. In a market system banks are expected:
1. to attract savers by offering competitive rates of interest;
2. to provide security of deposits by operating profitably;
3. to resolve the conflicting maturity and risk requirements of borrowers and lenders;
4. to provide a payments mechanism;
5. to allocate resources according to the expected returns that investments offer.

Bankers have to acquire the skills and techniques (i) to avoid bad loans and (ii) to provide an effective mechanism for monitoring loans made and ultimately for enforcing any contract (which may involve restructuring an enterprise or forcing it into bankruptcy).   Consistent failure to operate profitably will result in the failure of the bank as depositors lose confidence in its ability to meet its liabilities.

In a thoroughly market-oriented system commercial banks cannot rely on the authorities, namely the central bank, to bail them out if they should get into difficulties. The central bank will provide lender-of-last-resort facilities for *profitable, but temporarily illiquid,* banks. But it is not the central bank's function to bail out *insolvent* financial institutions. Where this rule is followed, banks are ultimately subject to a 'hard-budget' constraint.

Inherited Problems of the Commercial Banks

At present the banking system in Albania is some distance from meeting these objectives. This is in no small measure due to its legacy from the previous regime. As well as inherited loans in arrears, and the lack of market discipline in making and securing repayment of new loans, there are other weaknesses which play a part.   These include *illiquidity* due to the accumulation of loans in arrears; *large margins* between lending and borrowing rates (around 7 percentage points about the end of 1996*); no interest received* on the amount, equal to 10% of deposit-liabilities, held in the form of obligatory reserves with the central bank; requirements to provide certain *services to the state free of charge*; difficulties *over altering lending practices or cutting employment costs*; and *insufficiency of capital* provided by the state as owner even for meeting capital-adequacy requirements.

Capital Needs of the State Commercial Banks

Estimates of the extra sums reported as required in mid-1997 for the three state-owned commercial banks to meet their existing uncovered obligations, and also to have adequate capital on the criteria established by the Bank of Albania, are given in Table 13.2.   'Budget obligations' are those bad debts owed to the banks on which the government pays them 1.5% interest. 'Capital needs' represent the accumulated losses of the banks. The figures allow for the required capital-adequacy ratios adjusted for the appropriate risk-coefficients. On top of the US$108.8 million given in the total, there was also a need for resources to make good the damage to the banks in the riots associated with the failure of the pyramid funds. This makes a total required of about US$120 million to establish the banks on a sound footing.

Table 13.2   Further capital required by banks, mid-1997 (US$ m.)

	Savings Bank	National Commercial Bank	Rural Commercial Bank	Total
Budget obligations	20.5	38.9	6.1	64.5
Capital needs	28.6		15.7	44.3
Total	**49.1**	**38.9**	**21.8**	**108.8**

Source: Official estimates

Table 13.3 Banking institutions: balance sheet, 31/12/1995, 31/12/1996 (lekë billion)

Assets	Dec. 1995	Oct. 1996	Liabilities	Dec. 1995	Oct. 1996
Reserves	10.30	11.59	Demand deposits	17.35	28.91
Foreign assets	23.47	32.25	Time & saving deposits	28.12	34.06
Claims on central government	108.52	114.71	Foreign-currency deposits	20.08	32.43
Claims on non-financial public enterprises	3.09	3.48	Foreign liabilities	1.14	1.33
Claims on private sector	8.35	10.49	Central-government deposits	75.92	65.31
			Capital account	9.76	12.13
			Other (net)	1.36	-1.63
Total	**153.74**	**172.52**		**153.74**	**172.52**

Source: International Financial Statistics, April 1997

Recent Position of the Banks: Deposits and Loans

What Table 13.3 shows is (i) the domination of both sides of the balance sheet by the government sector, (ii) the significant amount of foreign currency depositing and lending, (iii) the relative shortage of reserves and capital, and (iv) the relatively small part played by the non-financial public-enterprise sector and the private *sector.* 'Claims on Central Government' appear to be largely Treasury Bills.

Table 13.4 Banks: structure of non-government deposits
(% of non-government deposits)

Each of banks at end-1996; totals all 8 banks at ends 1994, 1995, 1996

	NC	S	RC	IA	AAI	D	T	NG	'94	'95	'96
Demand	78.6	22.8	48.3	87.9	100	96.8	97.6	43.5	47.1	44.4	58.9
Time	21.4	77.2	51.7	12.1	0	3.2	2.4	56.5	52.9	55.6	41.1
	100										
Public sector	19.1	5.8	6.0	0.1	0.0	9.2	0.0	0.0	33.2	28.4	13.3
Private sector	65.6	18.6	40.4	66.2	42.9	40.3	83.1	21.3	11.6	15.7	48.5
Indiv'ls	15.3	75.6	53.6	33.6	57.1	50.5	16.9	78.7	55.3	55.9	38.2
	100										
In lekë	70.0	70.8	85.5	13.1	10.3	3.0	4.2	1.2	68.3	68.6	69.7
In for'n currency	29.7	29.2	14.2	86.9	89.7	97.0	95.8	98.7	31.7	31.4	30.3
		100									
Deposits of each bank as % of eight banks' total	57.49	32.57	6.54	1.75	0.54	0.22	0.76	0.14	% rise Dec 94 to Dec 95: 46.9	% rise Dec 95 to Dec 96: 59.1	100

NC = National Commercial Bank; S = Savings Bank; RC - Rural Commercial Bank; IA = Italian-Albanian Bank; AAI = Arab Albanian Islamic Bank; D = Dardania Bank; T = Tirana Bank; NG = National Bank of Greece.

Source: Supervision Department, Bank of Albania

Table 13.4 goes on to show the relative sizes of the main banks---the three state banks accounting for over 96% of all deposits among the eight at the end of 1996---and the importance of various kinds and sources of deposit to each bank.

From Table 13.4 the following observations can be made.
1. Most private-sector banks were dominated by demand-deposits.
2. The Savings Bank, the National Commercial Bank and the Rural Commercial Bank were the main homes for time-deposits.

3. The bulk of deposits arose from the private (i.e. corporate) and individual sectors, as would be anticipated since they are the main savings-surplus units.

4. It is noticeable that deposits in private-sector banks were almost wholly in foreign currency. They were not making much contribution to lek-denominated business.

Examination of the maturity-structures of the banks' total time-deposits at end-1995 and end-1996 shows that:

1. There are few deposits beyond one year;

2. There are substantial deposits in the range 9-12 months. However, there was a significant reduction in that category during 1996 and a corresponding rise in the two shortest categories (up to 3 months). It is normally a sign of uncertainty when deposits shift to a shorter term.

The amount of long-term lending which the banks undertake, seen against the short-term character of deposits, suggests that there is a great deal of maturity-transformation taking place, with potential liquidity problems in case short-term deposits are not renewed.

Analysis of lek as against foreign-currency deposits, and of demand- as against time-deposits, shows that, over 1996, there was a substantial increase in demand-deposits in lekë, largely from the private sector. In foreign currency too, a switch to demand-deposits is apparent, with again the private sector as the main source. Both these trends would suggest a growing uncertainty concerning the financial system. However, what happened between these dates cannot be understood in isolation from the pyramid-fund mania at the end of 1996, which may have involved both withdrawal of deposits for the purpose of investing in the funds and deposits made by the funds themselves. After the collapse of the funds, it was reported that deposits of private individuals in the state banks increased.

Separation of the figures for private and joint-venture banks from state banks indicates the following.

1. Virtually all loans from private and joint-venture banks are in foreign currency and at short term.

2. The bulk of state-owned banks' loans are for the long term.

3. Only state-owned banks lend to the public sector.

4. In contrast to the private banks, the state-owned banks are largely active in lekë, although they do have significant foreign-currency lending.

Bank Loans in Arrears

The major concern regarding the commercial banks relates to their loans in arrears, which hinder privatization and the introduction of market discipline.

As one might expect, most of the arrears are on short-term loans and to the household and private (corporate) sectors (see tables in Stewart & Xhafa, 1997). It is also notable that at the end of 1996 most (79%) of the loans in arrears had been outstanding for more than six months.

On one interpretation of certain figures from the Supervision Department of the Bank of Albania, it would appear that, at the end of 1996, of loans made *other than to government* by the three state-owned banks and the Italo Albanian and Dardania Banks combined, 48.8% of total loans outstanding were in arrears. (The Rural Commercial Bank, though holding only about 14% of the eight banks' total deposits, accounted for nearly half of these arrears of non-government borrowers from the five banks.) If this interpretation is at least roughly accurate, such a large incidence of arrears on loans, combined with a lack of capital, is a major weakness in the system and a major hurdle to future improvements.

But the arrears are not only a large problem in themselves; they may also be symptomatic of a serious deficiency either in banking practice or in property law. According to further evidence (Table 11 in Stewart & Xhafa, 1997), arrears of loans from the same five banks increased by more than 30% over 1996; so they do not appear to be entirely a hangover from an earlier time. The loans in arrears will have to be dealt with, if there is to be significant progress in reforming the Albanian financial system. And, if it is to any extent failures in current law or practice that have significantly contributed to these arrears, these failures will also have to be addressed.

Restructuring and Privatizing the Banks

The banks need substantial additional capital. This will not come from foreign sources unless:
1. the balance-sheets of the banks and the enterprises that are their debtors are cleaned up;
2. there is improvement in provision of information so that decision-making can be better informed;
3. management is allowed to manage in the long-term pursuit of profit.

In practice, privatization (management committed to a major private-sector shareholder) may well be necessary to ensure that the banks lend on commercial criteria with due attention to the possibility of default and with appropriate security. Altogether, elimination of other possible ostensible options (bankruptcy or liquidation for the state banks, *large* injections of government money) leads to the need for privatization with a 'strategic investor'. But that requires first the cleaning of balance-sheets. Decrees and legislation were already in place by the end of 1996 to deal with this combined operation. (For details see Stewart & Xhafa, 1997.) Since then, to the same end, one of the three state banks (the Rural Commercial) has been liquidated and its liabilities and performing assets transferred to the Savings Bank. Also, under legislation (Law Nr 8339) of 30th April 1998, an agency with a limited life-span has been formed to take over the bad debts of the Rural Commercial Bank and to buy any bad debts of the other two state banks incurred by the last day of 1997, provided all ways of recovering the debts have been exhausted. This does of course inescapably involve an injection of government money.

International projects, mainly funded by the EU, have been floated to help in bank restructuring and privatization. A Counsellor from the US Treasury has also been attached to the Ministry of Finance for the purpose.

As of August 1997, there was a proposal, originating in discussion with the multilaterals, to appoint an Administrator for each of the state trading banks. The Administrator would have sweeping powers, subject only to high-level government veto, and extending to liquidation of the bank if no other path to commercial viability were available---or alternatively to privatization. It was considered likely then that, for the first few months, each bank's existing Executive Director would be appointed as its Administrator, with a foreign firm taking the role thereafter.

In April 1998, the Executive Director of the National Commercial Bank had been appointed as its General Administrator. Privatization of that bank was still planned for the end of 1998, but no foreign institution had yet been selected to be Administrator during the actual process, and, despite one round of advertisement, no candidate for 'strategic investor' had been accepted. Privatization of the Savings Bank was planned for the end of 1999, and in that case an Irish bank had been chosen as Administrator.

In a paper given in December 1997, Arben Malaj (then Finance Minister) and Fatmir Mema set out requirements for reviving the financial system. They emphasized especially the need for a scheme to guarantee the bank deposits of the public (Malaj and Mema, 1997).

Tirana Stock Exchange

The Tirana Stock Exchange began its operations in May 1996. The market trades in Treasury Bills, which are a major source of government deficit funding. The aim had been that privatization vouchers and government bonds would also be traded, but vouchers have in fact been traded informally through other channels, and government bonds have not so far existed apart from those devised for such purposes as dealing with the bad debts of banks. Until now it has not been possible in practice for companies in Albania to issue common stock. The only purchasers of Treasury Bills are the three state banks, INSIG and the Social Insurance Institute. In order to be saleable, Treasury Bills have needed to offer something like 2 percentage-points in excess of the average bank deposit rate of interest.   Banks have been induced to buy them partly because otherwise they have in recent times had very restricted sources of earnings; in mid-1997 their brief virtually forbade lending to new customers.

Insurance

The Insurance Institutes are state-owned and still face no competition, but there are plans to open the market to domestic and foreign participants.
1.   INSIG - The Insurance Institute
This state-owned entity covers commercial insurance of all kinds: car, property, life assurance.   Premiums are set by the state and there is very little incentive to undertake insurance for private individuals.   Being effectively a monopoly, INSIG is highly profitable and a source of tax revenue.

2.   Social Insurance Institute
This covers insurance through the state for old age, unemployment, sickness, invalidity, and maternity.   There are compulsory contributions.   (See chapter 8 for details.)

3.   Provision has been made in law for additional, privately-financed occupational pensions within larger companies in order to provide a supplement to public provision.   As of mid-1997, there had been no company which had agreed to provide these benefits.

Investment Funds

Of the six investment banks or funds listed in Table 13.1, only one, the Anglo-Adriatic, was said in 1997 to have been active.   It had accumulated a large number of privatization lekë and vouchers on behalf of individuals. A mid-1997 estimate, as mentioned in chapter 6, had it holding these assets to a *face-value* of just over 10 billion lekë, on behalf of 41,182 people.   But remember that in late 1997 the face-value was about 30 times the market-value.

The 'Pyramid Funds'

The exact nature of these funds, whose effects went close to destroying the Albanian polity, still has an element of mystery.   How far were they really pyramid funds in the strict sense?   How did they survive for considerable periods paying real-interest-rates drawn from the realms of fantasy?   How and why did they suddenly become a major national phenomenon in 1996? If a report by the accountants Deloitte & Touche, who were appointed administrators for five of the funds, is published, we may know more.

What was their business? We have to consider the possibility that the funds might have been intermediaries between lenders and borrowers (reflecting the inadequacies of the formal system); or mainly producers and traders on their own account in the non-financial sector; or honestly but crazily conceived devices to benefit their customers; or simply swindles. If intermediaries or producers and traders, they *might* be dealing more or less in illegal activities (drugs and arms, other smuggling, money-laundering). The IMF Report (1997, p.31) has them acting to only a small extent as *intermediaries* in on-lending funds to the private sector. Those that invested in Albania seem to have done so mainly on their own account. On *money-laundering*, some of the people likely to have the best evidence give rather oblique testimony. One of the current supervising authorities is reported (*Albanian Daily News*, 1/4/1998, p.7) as saying that there was no evidence of money-laundering for the five recently under scrutiny (Vefa, Silva, Leka, Cenaj, Kamberi) but that they had *pretended* to be money-laundering because that impressed depositors. Malaj and Mema (1997, p.3) say much the same: that the popular belief that some of the funds were laundering money increased their credibility. But the former Governor of the Central Bank, Kristaq Luniku, is reported (*Albanian Daily News, ibid.*) as saying that Albanian *banks* were 'washing-machines for dirty money'. The first two of these statements are not very clear exculpations of the funds; the third does not actually accuse them.

The most important funds can be grouped into three classes according to the assets they were found to have when they were closed or failed. Sude (the first major fund to fail) and Gjallica (centred in Vlorë and associated in the public mind especially with senior Democratic Party politicians) were both reported at the time to have had nothing that could be traced in the banking system (*Keesing*, 41454). It was obviously hard for the public not to see them as swindles and we have to allow for this possibility---even if the front-woman for Sude (after whom it was named and who for some time was said to be the only person arrested on account of the funds' failure), or the president of Gjallica, or the politicians, may not fully have understood what was going on.

At the other extreme, Xhaferri and Populli (formally charitable foundations) were found in late-January 1997 to have between them US$ 300 million in cash and bank deposits (*Keesing*, 41454). This appears to have been enough to repay about half of what had been deposited by their more than 200,000 customers. Both owed their origin to one man. They had come on the scene very late and promised huge rates of interest, amounting (in one offering at the end) to 49% compound a month for a 3-month period, the equivalent of an annual rate of 12,200%. Who but a very rational cynic could resist? If you believed what you saw and only what you saw, and asked no questions about how it was possible, then this was clearly the philosopher's stone. It has been suggested that they were 'pure' pyramid funds, with the receipts used only to make payments to past lenders, and the funds' continuation depending on a rapidly accelerating rate of new depositors. It is plausible that the promoters may have been honest, but if so they must have been completely naive in all matters except marketing.

The case of the Vefa, Silva, Leka, Cenaj, and Kamberi funds is different again. Some of these had been running for several years, and Vefa, the company that operated the largest of the five, had publicized itself flamboyantly as a pillar of development and public spirit. When their assets and liabilities were analysed, the administrators, Deloitte & Touche, reported (*Albanian Daily News*, 3/4/1998, p.7) that claims on them amounted to US$347.9 million, while 'the maximum sale value of their assets' was only US$50 million, about one-seventh. They had claimed to have US$467 million in assets (*Economist*, 9/5/1998, p.112). Vefa alone, with 90,000 depositors, accounted for about two-thirds of the assets of the five and over 70% of their liabilities. Individual funds might be able to pay back between a quarter and a twelfth of the claims upon them. These five funds, or some of them, make up a large part of the story before 1996. Originally they had paid interest at 4% to 5% a month (IMF, 1997, p.31). A monthly rate of 5% amounts to 80% a year. This would have represented a negative *real* rate if paid over 1992 and 1993 (when the annual rate of consumer-price inflation averaged 110%), and a positive real annual rate averaging 46% over 1993 and 1994, or 62% over 1994 and 1995---very high, though perhaps not quite out-of-this-world over limited periods for shrewd traders in a time of fast development. Yet, with such high rates, the suspicion that illegal activities entered into the portfolio is difficult to banish. Then, in 1996, the story goes, the true pyramid funds entered, offering even higher rates, and the established companies moved up to 6%, and then to 8% or 10%, a month (*ibid.*). Perhaps at this time Vefa and the others had at least to maintain something like their current rate of receipt of deposits in order to avoid cash-flow problems and to pay what they had promised. But to achieve that they now needed to offer interest-rates so high that in effect they had to become pyramid funds themselves. (Honest buccaneers, we might say, over-optimistic but with relics of rationality, found they were obliged by competition to behave like crazy fantasists in order to keep afloat.) Vefa, at the most conservative end, is said to have stuck at 8% a month, the equivalent of 152% a year (in real terms 112% a year if the inflation rate was 19%). We speculated in chapter 2 that the Dayton Agreement of November 1995, in relieving Yugoslavia of trade sanctions, may have removed one important source of income for these funds, so that maybe even the game they had played before had become more difficult. It was announced in May 1998 that another accounting firm, Coopers & Lybrand, would investigate a further twelve funds (*Economist*, 9/5/1998, p.112).

Once the pyramid principle had taken over in 1996, the craze took on in exactly the way that could *for a while* keep the pyramids afloat. After a temporary lag over the May 1996 election, the rate of depositing with the funds increased again and went on increasing. One estimate (Hoxha, 1997, p.31) is that the rate of depositing of US$ 0.5 to 0.6 million a day in July rose to US$ 3.5 to 4.0 million a day by the end of August.

The elements of mystery and uncertainty over how it all happened emphasize just how unprecedented the experience was. Though there are claims that the IMF gave warnings, there was probably no international advice packaged up and ready for just this contingency. Action much before 1996 could have seemed over-zealous. No immediate harm seemed to be coming to Albania from the pre-1996 funds and the environment of international illegality that probably nurtured them. Then the process took off quickly and unexpectedly in 1996 into its pyramid form. Once that was recognized, it was politically speaking already late for clean decisive action. A radical policy, ever more urgent in the people's interest, became more and more likely to be a loser for any politician who indulged in it. The election of May 1996 no doubt enhanced the government's case for doing nothing. Then, the later action was left, the more traumatic it would be. Firm moves calculated to mitigate the impact of the eventual collapse would upset the misplaced confidence on which the funds depended and would be hugely unpopular. The snare was activated. Any attempt to escape would be acutely painful.

There is surely a moral in these events, but it needs to be teased out. If *all* borrowing institutions had been *effectively*---from say 1994---subject to *regulation and supervision*, this might have averted the disaster altogether. We also suggested in chapter 2 that the lack of *political openness* was an important factor in allowing the pyramids to develop unchallenged. That is plausible if openness is taken to include an impartial and independent state broadcasting system, an uninhibited press, and an educated class that is not afraid to express its ideas and criticisms freely in public. Yet we have to admit that there is no guarantee that this alone would have sufficed to avoid all major grief. It could hardly have made much difference before the true pyramids came on the scene, and after that there would be some real damage whenever the process was stopped---and hence understandable concerns about rocking the boat. Serious *suppression of sanctions-busting and of other infringements of international law and propriety* might also have prevented the taste and expectation of inordinately high interest-rates from developing. Again, the damage could have been much reduced by timely *courage* and a sense of *cross-party solidarity in emergency* on the part of politicians.

All the plausible lessons are salutary ones, but to state such conditions highlights how difficult in the circumstances preventive action before the start of 1996, or corrective action after that, would have been. Even with hindsight, we can not be sure that any readily imaginable increase of wisdom and virtue on the part of the Albanian authorities and opinion-leaders could have completely forestalled a catastrophe of some degree.

Summary

The transformation required in Albania's financial system to adapt it to the needs of a market-economy was little short of revolutionary. The governments did most of what was prescribed as far as they were able. But events that no one expected took them unawares.

Changes that have taken place include the introduction of a two-tier banking system, with central-banking functions separated from those of commercial banks. The Bank of Albania has acquired many of the functions of a market-economy central bank, with a degree of autonomy. In Albania the government has hitherto relied more or less heavily on the central bank to finance deficits directly by base-money creation, though laws have been passed requiring it (though rather ineffectively) to reduce that reliance. Tax evasion, and a lack of financial instruments apart from Treasury Bills, seriously restrict the government's financing capability.

The financial system is still dominated by the banks, and, despite the setting up of foreign-owned and joint-venture banks, the (now two) state-owned banks still constitute the great preponderance of the sector. Other officially recognized financial institutions (the state-owned insurance company, the Social Security Institute, and one active and several dormant private investment companies) are negligible as commercial intermediaries.

Time-deposits are almost entirely with the public-sector banks, and few have more than a year to maturity. The bulk of public-sector banks' loans are long-term. They are largely active in lekë but have made some foreign-currency loans. Most private-sector banks' liabilities are dominated by demand deposits; all of them deal overwhelmingly in *foreign-currency* deposits and loans; and virtually all their loans are short-term.

Deposits in state banks (the overwhelming bulk of all deposits) come mostly from central government, far less from the private sector, and only to a very small extent from state enterprises. Only the Savings and National Commercial Banks have lent to state enterprises.

Loans in arrears have recently formed large shares of the loans made to the private sector and public enterprises and were specially important in the portfolio of the Rural Commercial Bank before its dissolution in 1998. Arrears have also been significant for the remaining two state-owned banks. In mid-1997, most loans in arrears had been so for longer than six months, and the total of loans in arrears was still increasing substantially over 1996.

There is legislation in place for restructuring the state banks and the financial requirements are known. As of early 1998 action had begun to provide the two remaining state banks with balance-sheets expunged of non-performing loans---with the help of an institution that had begun by taking over non-performing assets of the Rural Commercial Bank. Such a restructuring involves inevitably a significant input of public money. Unless the state commercial banks are reorganized and privatized, the benefits expected to result from the discipline of the market system will not be realized. The private banks have so far not provided any real substitute.

However, even with evidence of good intent over the banks' balance-sheets, there were still difficulties early in 1998 over attracting suitable 'strategic investors'.

The pyramid-funds scandal shows the importance of having an effective financial system accessible to the population at large and enjoying its confidence. Paradoxically the failure of these informal 'banks' provides an opportunity for the authorities to attract depositors and borrowers to the official sector. If the banks are to be attractive to depositors, there will need to be reasonable assurances of their soundness, so that people can be confident that their deposits are safe. Formal deposit-insurance arrangements would help.

Albanian banks are essentially universal providers of finance. This is inevitable given the lack of alternative sources of long-term debt or equity finance. This form of financial system, successful in Germany and Japan, probably presents the most appropriate model for Albania. It might be appropriate also, however, to consider a credit-union type of financial organization in order to allow saving and borrowing activity to reach a greater proportion of the population while reducing the adverse-selection and moral-hazard problems of small-scale financial activity.

For the economy to become more integrated and for financial markets and institutions to interact effectively, an improved payments system is needed to give greater speed and greater certainty about time-of-completion. This is a precondition for reliance on indirect monetary-policy instruments.

Legal and educational measures to support an improved financial system will also be necessary. More clearly defined property rights and a mechanism for using collateral assets in financial transactions are required. Also bankruptcy law and practice will need to be clarified, and also made operational by the relevant training of accountants and lawyers.

In enterprise governance, and specifically in bank governance, procedures will have to be updated to provide effective market discipline.

The emergence of the pyramid funds and their collapse gives occasion to a number of possible lessons: the need for political openness; the value of courage and cross-party co-operation among politicians in emergencies; possibly also the case for insisting on international legality; certainly the need for careful regulation and supervision of all borrowing institutions.

Markets unaided do not provide sufficient discipline. Regulation and supervision require the development of standardized accounting procedures and a regime of supervision which is reliable and has sufficient authority.

The radical changes needed should be concurrent so that the total system can operate effectively. There are large resource implications.

14 Foreign Resources

Official aid and direct private investment are only two of various forms in which foreign resources may enter a country. This chapter considers aid briefly and direct investment at much more length. The imbalance springs in part from the different amounts of information available to us, but it is perhaps justified by the peculiarities of foreign direct investment in Albania.

Official foreign aid *committed* to Albania was of the order of 15% of GDP over each of the years 1994-96; in 1992 and 1993 it was a considerably higher proportion than that. Though only a little over half the aid committed altogether over 1991-96 was actually *disbursed* within the period, aid has clearly formed a large part of the inward transfers and capital movements that have allowed the country since 1991 to consume and invest substantially more in value than it has produced. The pattern of aid changed over the period from a high concentration in 1992 on food and commodity and 'balance-of-payments' categories to an overwhelming dominance in 1996 of flows described as for development and investment, but since 1992 technical assistance has remained important throughout. (See Table 14.1.)   Technical assistance itself has been described as becoming over the period less 'general' and more specific to particular projects and operations.   Very probably there was a switch back to the more emergency-type help in 1997.

The amount of foreign direct (private) investment that Albania received has been modest by the standards of Central European transitional economies.   Over 1989-96 it was immensely smaller per head of population (US$93 all told) than in Hungary, the Czech Republic or Estonia, and still quite clearly smaller than in Slovenia, Latvia, Poland, or Slovakia. But it was markedly higher than in FYR Macedonia, Romania, or Bulgaria, and higher than in any of the CIS countries except Kazakhstan, Azerbaijan, and Turkmenistan (all of them well-endowed with mineral resources).   For 1996, the peak year so far, the value of the inflow was reckoned as 3% of GDP (EBRD, 1997b, p.126).

In 1996, the gross foreign-direct-investment (FDI) inflow, as recorded officially (ACFIP, 1997, p.7) and apparently as used in these EBRD comparisons, was only about a quarter of the value of official aid committed.   Yet in assessing the relative importance of the two forms of finance we should note the fact just mentioned that nearly half of the aid committed was normally not actually disbursed, and also that these official FDI figures omit investment for trade and for offshore exploration.

Moreover, the form---often very small-scale---in which much of the FDI appeared in the early and mid 1990s may have suited the country's needs rather well.   Both FDI and official aid could, of course, bring far more than simply 'capital'.

Beside FDI, private foreign capital inflows included loans and portfolio movements.   We do not have figures for the aggregate amounts of these flows to Albania, but the consolidated presentation of inflows by the EBRD (1996, p.114) estimates that, for the transition countries as a whole over 1991-95, these two categories of gross private inflows were between them more than twice as great as FDI.

From late 1993, Albania's policy toward foreign direct investment was extremely open and permissive, and the volume increased in 1995 and again in 1996.   Then inevitably the events of 1997 seriously stemmed the flow; they may be expected to cast a shadow over new investment prospects for some time.   In 1998 the kind of investment typical of the earlier years would still be valuable, but there is also a pressing need for a quite different style of investor to take managing shares in the remaining large state enterprises.   For all forms of inward investment, several years of convincingly restored law and order would be the best inducement.

Administration of Aid

From the time aid began, in 1991, until 1994, aid coordination was divided among three Ministries.   In mid-1994, the Department of Economic Development and Foreign Aid Coordination was established under the Council of Ministers for the programming, negotiation and coordination of aid, and for information about it.   The line Ministries were to be responsible for its actual use.   Policy over aid is clearly conditioned by the Economic Programme of the government and by the Public Investment Programme.   It is held by some that the lack of a single system for recording and tracking foreign aid has been a weakness and has almost inevitably allowed inefficiency in its allocation.

Aid: Forms, Timing, Functions

Aid covers both *grants* and *loans*.   If loans are to be counted as aid, they must be *soft*, that is charged at less than commercial rates.   They may be either *soft loans* in the usual sense or *concessional trade-credits*.   In 1991, 75% of the aid received by Albania was in the form of grants.   The proportion fell to 52% in 1995 and 38% in 1996 as the country's economic position brightened.   From the EBRD's table (1996, p.114) it seems likely

**Table 14.1 Aid commitments received, by function, 1991-1996
(US$ million in current prices)**

	1991	1992	1993	1994	1995	1996	Tot. 6 yy	%
Bal'ce of pay'ts	0	94.3	65.9	36.9	48.8	6.6	253	13
Techn'l assist'ce	4.9	78.2	74.6	45.4	55.2	57.4	316	16
Human-itarian	175.4	0	24.0	9.5	0	0	209	10
Food aid	13.5	136.4	73.4	12.4	0	0	236	12
Comm-odity aid	26.8	81.7	2.6	1.1	0.4	0	113	6
Devel't/ invest't	0	58.8	82.0	165.7	261.7	324.6	893	44
Total	**220.7**	**449.3**	**322.5**	**271.0**	**366.2**	**388.6**	**2018**	**100**
Total dis-bursed	**n.a.**	**n.a.**	**n.a.**	**n.a.**	**n.a.**	**n.a.**	**1076**	
GDP in curr't $ at 100 lekë=$1	*	*	1142	1883	2251	2662	*	
Aid comm'd as % of GDP	*	*	28	14	16	15	*	

'n.a.'= not available; figures in cells marked * are omitted as likely to be misleading.
Source: Official figures

that Albania's proportion of grants to loans for these years was higher than the average for the transition economies.

The changes in the proportions of the various categories of aid received, as shown in Table 14.1, are not unexpected, for a country that was in very severe distress over 1991 and 1992 but made a fast recovery thereafter. 'Long-term' categories (technical assistance and development / investment) take up about 60% of the aid in current dollars over the whole period, and virtually all of it in 1996. Some of the humanitarian, food and commodity aid (mostly in earlier years) provided items included in the state budget, and hence enter the budget accounts as 'counterpart funds'.

Rules on Foreign Investment in Albania

The main law regulating foreign investments in Albania is Law Nr 7764 of 2/11/1993, *On Foreign Investments*. Under its provisions foreign investments in Albania need no preliminary authorization. They are freely allowed under the same conditions as investments by nationals, except in regard to land ownership. Thus, if a foreign investor wants to invest in Albania, he will do so under virtually the same conditions as an Albanian, and he does not require the permission of any Albanian authority.

A foreign investor may act on his own or in co-operation with an Albanian partner, public or private. He must, however, be registered as a juridical person, that is adopt one of the four types of company or association recognized by Albania's company law (Nr 7638 of 19/11/1992). In order to be registered, all forms of company must present their statutes and a variety of other documents to the District Court of Tirana.

After being registered in the Business Register, a company must also be registered at the Taxation Office. Some fairly minor taxes or fees have to be paid on registration, and a contract for social-security has to be concluded. Once this is done the company receives a licence from the Taxation Office and is free to operate a business in Albania.

What is to be stressed is the simplicity of these procedures. Provided the formal requirements are fulfilled, no person or institution may refuse a potential foreign investor the right to operate.

If a foreign investor wants to co-operate in a joint-venture *with a state-owned enterprise*, further documents must be provided by the state organ that has the state enterprise concerned under its jurisdiction, and the approval of the National Privatization Agency must be obtained.

If a foreign firm wants to create a joint-venture *with a private person* in Albania, the procedure is the same as for formation of a company.

All persons, natural or juridical, undertaking any economic activity in Albania are subject to the Albanian tax system, which is the same for foreign subjects as for nationals. Under the profit tax there are concessions for new enterprises and for profits reinvested, and foreign-owned enterprises are equally eligible for these favours. Albanian fiscal legislation has no special provisions for foreign investors.

The foreign investor is free to transfer abroad at any time the profit realized in Albania on his capital, or indeed to transfer his capital itself, without being subject to any tax obligation or any obligation to the Albanian state arising from the act of remittance. Disputes with the government may be submitted to the International Centre for Settlement of Investment Disputes. The only relevant restriction on foreign investors is that they may not ordinarily buy land in Albania, but even this limitation is waived if their investment on the land is sufficient.

Foreign Direct Investment, 1991-1995

Information Sources

We rely here for quantitative information on two samples of FDI covering
the years from 1991 to 1995, at some points extending to 1996.   Neither
covers the whole population, but using both sheds useful light.   Both deal
only with initial investment and ignore reinvestment of profits and follow-
up investments.   Sample 1 is from ACFIP and is generally cited officially.
But its published aggregate *values* explicitly leave out investment in trade
and in offshore oil and gas exploration (though trade is included in some
other ACFIP data), and in some cases information on companies included
appears to be imperfect.   Sample 2 was assembled by Spiro Brumbulli
from records at District Taxation Offices, where all new companies,
including those involving foreign investment, must register.   This,
however, also excludes offshore-exploration investments, and in addition
investments in the financial sector.   Though comparison of his figures with
ACFIP's suggests that he tracked a very large part of new FDI from 1991
to 1995 in the categories he aspired to cover, not all Taxation Offices
would cooperate, and some had kept records imperfectly.   In particular it
was not always possible to know the year in which a company had been
registered.   Detailed results from his research are presented in the paper on
which this chapter draws (Brumbulli & Dunlop, 1997).   So Sample 2
presents evidence on much of the very small investment in trade ignored by
the aggregate values of sample 1, but its incompleteness may introduce
other biases.   Because it does not include several Districts in the extreme
south that have much of the country's ethnic-Greek population, its author
suspects that it may under-represent investment from Greece.

Beside these elements of known incompleteness, there are
discrepancies in the tables that follow where we should not expect them.
To some extent the figures given have to be regarded as pointers.   Viewed
in this spirit they can tell some fairly consistent stories.

Table 14.2 Companies involving FDI, to 1995 (numbers)

Sector	Joint-ventures	Wholly foreign-owned	Total	% of total
Agriculture	26	7	33	1
Transport	64	48	112	4
Construction	71	53	124	5
Services	77	67	144	6
Industry	292	123	415	17
Trade	1,002	592	1,594	67
Totals	**1,532**	**890**	**2,422**	**100**

Source: ACFIP, *A Guide to Business in Albania*, 1997, p.15

Table 14.3 FDI value (excluding trade, offshore exploration), 1991-1996 (US$ million, current prices)

Year	1991	1992	1993	1994	1995	1996	**Total**
Amount	9*	20*	58	53	70	90	**300**

* These figures are slightly different from those reported in Table 7.5

Source: As for Table 14.2, with 1996 figure updated on ACFIP advice

Table 14.4 Sectoral breakdown by value of major foreign direct investments, 1991 to July 1995, ACFIP data (US$ million, current prices)

Sector	No. of firms	Total investment	Foreign component	Share (%) in foreign component
Agriculture	5	28.1	15.1	5.5
Construction	22	211.0	162.3	58.8
Fisheries	2	1.1	1.0	0.4
Food-processing	4	9.6	8.5	3.1
Hotels	1	10.1	5.0	1.8
Light industry	29	95.3	79.2	28.7
Mechanical	2	0.8	0.5	0.2
Poultry	1	2.6	0.3	0.1
Services	5	0.5	0.4	0.1
Trade	4	3.4	1.9	0.7
Wood industry	2	3.7	1.9	0.7
Total	**77**	**366.3**	**276.1**	**100.0**

Source: Data from ACFIP, extracted by S Brumbulli

Numbers of Investors, Value, and Timing

ACFIP reports 2,422 companies formed by the end of 1995 as involving foreign investment. These clearly *do* include those investing in trade, two-thirds of the total *number*. Table 14.2 shows their distribution among the main sectors and how many were wholly foreign-owned.   Table 14.3 would suggest that these companies, 828 in number (that is, excluding the 1,594 involved in trade) provided altogether US$210 million of inward direct investment over the five years.   But Table 14.4 appears to be saying that *77 of the largest of these companies alone* (with 751 smaller ones omitted) had brought in US$276 million even before the end of 1995. (The few firms included that are described as involved in trade make a negligible contribution and do not explain the discrepancy.)   Moreover, to compound the apparent inconsistency, 32 firms with substantial foreign investment are said to have been omitted from the sample in Table 14.4 because information on them was not adequate for identifying their sectors. If these entailed the same amount of foreign capital on average as the other 77, the foreign-component figure for the 109 would be US$391 million.

Part of the explanation seems likely to be that Table 14.4 covers *proposed* investments recorded that were not necessarily *realized*.   Data from Sample 2 in various tables below also refer to foreign investments as recorded when the companies were registered, and these relate similarly to *intentions* rather than *realizations*.   To examine this possible source of discrepancy, Brumbulli followed up 240 registered companies that had reported projected foreign investment in 4 Districts.   He found that 45 companies, representing 18.8% of the companies and 25.5% of the registered capital, had undertaken no activity whatever at the time of investigation.   If discounts of this general order can be applied to the US$276.1 million investments in Table 14.4, they at least reduce the gap with Table 14.3---but plausible reconciliation between the two through an adjustment of that order requires us to assume that the 2,345 (i.e., 2,422 *minus* 77) investments excluded from Table 14.4 are on average *extremely* small.

If Table 14.4 gives a reliable picture of the sectors of the *larger* foreign investors to mid-1995, it would seem that *their* investments were overwhelmingly in construction and light industry.   But remember that, if we take the implications of the numbers strictly, the firms detailed there exclude 751 (presumably mostly smaller) firms with foreign investment *other than in trade*, and also 1,594 in trade.   Information from Sample 2, in Tables 14.5 and following, is based on 1,798 firms registered before the end of September 1995.

Table 14.5 FDI from tax registrations (sample 2), 1991 to September 1995 (values in US$ million at current prices)

Year	No. of firms	Foreign capital by year	Foreign capital cumulative
1991	10	1.24	1.24
1992	62	4.91	6.15
1993	241	38.35	44.50
1994	422	22.36	66.86
1995	238	115.69	182.55
199x*	825	64.14	246.70
Total	**1,798**	**246.70**	

* This covers cases in which the year of registration could not be established.

Source: District Taxation Offices, reported in Brumbulli & Dunlop, 1997

On the assumption that the number of firms in Table 14.2 is similarly based on registrations rather than realizations, these 1,798 (designed to be a complete tally from most, but not all, Districts) may be taken as 74% of the total 2,422 firms.   Of the sample 1,010 were joint ventures and 788 wholly foreign-owned (66% and 89% respectively of the totals in these categories shown by Table 14.2).

Table 14.5 conforms roughly with Table 14.3 in pointing to a rise in the value of incoming FDI in each year except 1994, when there was a slight decline.

Extent of Foreign Ownership

The proportion of foreign investments registering that were wholly foreign-owned, as judged from sample 2, increased suddenly in 1993 if we reckon by numbers of firms, or suddenly in 1995 if we reckon by weight of foreign investment.   Over the years after 1992, there was a swing toward 100%-foreign-ownership by number of firms, but much more markedly by amount of investment.   In 1992, wholly-foreign-owned firms made up 19% of the firms and 14% of the foreign investment projected.   By the end of September 1995 these figures had changed to 44% and 73%.   Those with 50% or less foreign ownership, though comprising 29% of the firms at this time, accounted for only 3% of the foreign investment.   Of investors recorded as first registering in 1995 itself, those wholly-foreign-owned accounted for 98% of the new foreign investment recorded for that year. Increasingly, it seems, investors tended to be bigger, and the bigger investors tended to be wholly-foreign-owned.

Table 14.6 Size of firm and foreign capital per firm (sample 2), 1991 to September 1995

Year	Number of firms	Average size of firm: capital in US$ million	Average amount of foreign capital in US$ million
1991	10	0.18	0.12
1992	62	1.16	0.08
1993	241	0.21	0.16
1994	422	0.07	0.05
1995	238	0.49	0.47

Source: District Taxation Offices, as reported in Brumbulli & Dunlop, 1997

Size of Investing Firms

It is clear that the average size and amount of foreign capital per firm both increased sharply in 1995. (See Table 14.6.)

The inflation of lek prices, mainly in the first two years, makes the size-categories not entirely consistent in meaning. Also the fact that the figures are in current-price dollars means that their sums over the five years have to be taken with slight reservations. But probably neither of these anomalies affects the main lines of the picture conveyed.

Clearly the overwhelming bulk of the initial foreign capital was in the 30 big firms, which comprised less than 2% of the total number of firms covered in the sample.

By the end of 1996 there were a few well-known foreign companies in Albania. Coca-Cola was in operation, as were Rogner (Austria, US$20 million in investments), Rekor (Greece, US$13 million), Al Kharafi (Kuwait, US$30 million), Di Vicenzo Estero (Italy, US$10 million).

Distribution by Sectors of the Economy

It was difficult to classify the firms in sample 2 rigorously by sector. A clear specification was not always given at the time of registration, and in any case a firm may be involved in more than one sector. Sometimes a firm may be registered as a 'production company', which does not unambiguously denote the sector. Or a firm may be registered for both trade and construction. For these reasons, some of the classifications in what follows (based on tables in Brumbulli & Dunlop, 1997) may be dubious.

Table 14.7 Firms with foreign investment, by size of firm (sample 2), 1991 to September 1995

Year	Size of initial total capital (lekë m.)	< = 0.1	> 0.1 < = 10	> 10 < = 50	>50 < = 100	> 100	Total
1991	No. firms	4	5	1	0	0	10
	Foreign capital (US$ m.)	0.007	0.404	0.827	0	0	1.238
1992	No.	19	37	4	1	1	62
	For. cap.	0.016	0.736	1.183	0.578	2.400	4.913
1993	No.	90	118	18	6	9	241
	For. cap.	0.068	1.982	3.100	2.305	30.894	38.349
1994	No.	282	106	21	7	6	422
	For. cap.	0.258	1.725	5.173	3.447	11.759	22.362
1995	No.	193	37	3	1	4	238
	For. cap.	0.167	0.459	0.414	0.688	113.966	115.694
199x	No.	473	330	9	3	10	825
	For. cap.	0.380	4.613	1.808	2.101	55.244	64.145
Tot'l	No.	**1,061**	**633**	**56**	**18**	**30**	**1,798**
	For. cap.	**0.896**	**9.919**	**12.505**	**9.119**	**214.263**	**246.701**

By number (% in each size-class)

1991	40.0	50.0	10.0	0.0	0.0	100.0
1992	30.6	59.7	6.5	1.6	1.6	100.0
1993	37.3	49.0	7.5	2.5	3.7	100.0
1994	66.8	25.1	5.0	1.7	1.4	100.0
1995	81.1	15.5	1.3	0.4	1.7	100.0
199x	57.3	40.0	1.1	0.4	1.2	100.0
Total	**59.0**	**35.2**	**3.1**	**1.0**	**1.7**	**100.0**

By initial foreign capital (% in each size-class)

1991	0.6	32.6	66.8	0.0	0.0	100.0
1992	0.3	15.0	24.1	11.8	48.8	100.0
1993	0.2	5.2	8.1	6.0	80.6	100.0
1994	1.2	7.7	23.1	15.4	52.6	100.0
1995	0.1	0.4	0.4	0.6	98.5	100.0
199x	0.6	7.2	2.8	3.3	86.1	100.0
Total	**0.4**	**4.0**	**5.1**	**3.7**	**86.9**	**100.0**

Source: District Taxation Offices, as reported in Brumbulli & Dunlop, 1997

By far the largest number of firms in sample 2 has been in trade: about 63% of the total. This fits closely with ACFIP's comprehensive figures in Table 14.2.   But by value total initial foreign investments in trade have been only US$26 million out of US$246.7 million in the sample, with a foreign component of US$19 million, 7.7% of total foreign capital initially invested.   Trading firms with foreign participation are thus numerous but small. Their main activity has been the import of finished consumer-goods. The first moves into the market economy were apparently concentrated on trade, because firms engaged in foreign trade had not existed at all, and there was great potential demand for a variety of goods: foodstuffs, industrial inputs, household goods, among others. Another reason for the lure of trade was its ease of operation. In the existing conditions of excess demand, there was no great need for managing ability or professional standards. Many people thrown into unemployment could take up trade of some sort. There was also often a high rate of return on importing, and opportunities for speculation. Trade turned out to be one of the most profitable sectors.

Construction has also been very attractive to foreign investors. Though the number of construction firms with foreign capital has been relatively small---84 all told in sample 2, 4.7%---the foreign component of their initial capital represents 53% of the total initial foreign capital. Construction investment had come apparently from 1993 on, the great bulk of it in 1995. Construction is also by far the most important sector among the large foreign investments recorded in Table 14.4. The construction firms in which foreigners have participated clearly tend to be large by Albanian standards. Construction is necessary for the restoration of the economy, and, as in many other countries, people are very willing to put extra resources into housing. The sector can be expected to continue attracting foreign investors.

'Production' is another important category. This seems to indicate mainly small-scale manufacturing. If we add together light industry, food industry, wood industry, and mechanical, from Table 14.4, covering relatively large investments, we get a total of 37 firms. The total number of firms in light industry, wood industry, food industry, and 'production' in sample 2 comes to 292. If these sets of categories cover roughly the same sectors, and those not included in the ACFIP figures are in the three smallest size-groups of Table 14.7 (with roughly-speaking less than half a million US dollars initial total capital), then it would appear that there were by late 1995 (in the Districts covered by sample 2 alone) something like 255 firms in manufacturing at this small-to-smallest end of the scale which had drawn some direct foreign investment. The proliferation of small firms in manufacturing is a pointer to the vibrancy of the Albanian economy's response to the market. The fact that there is such widespread foreign participation in them is an unusual feature, doubtless also a strength, which has probably depended on personal connections of Albanians, through emigration or otherwise, with small entrepreneurs in neighbouring countries, especially Italy.

The importance of the 'service' sector is also worthy of note, with 13.6% of the foreign investment in sample 2, even though it excludes hotels, tourism, and restaurants. Here the proportion of firms is less than that of investment, though there is no great representation of the sector among the larger firms recorded in Table 14.4.

Foreign investment in agriculture does not appear in sample 2 except in 1992 and 1993. This is surprising in that it means that the only foreign investments occurred during and just after privatization of farm land, when conditions would have been most unsettled. But there are only 5 firms listed in agriculture here, which may very probably be the same as the 5 large firms that appear in Table 14.4 This suggests that the nature of the investments may have been somewhat exceptional, without much direct connection to normal family farming.

Country of Origin

As elsewhere in Eastern Europe, neighbouring countries have predominated among the sources of FDI. Tables 14.8 and 14.9 show investments by country of origin as revealed in sample 2. Table 14.10 shows country of origin for the small number of larger investments as recorded by the ACFIP.

The picture is dulled somewhat by the fact that such a large proportion of the investment recorded by the Tax Offices is of unknown origin. The ACFIP figures, however, confirm the overwhelming importance of Italy and then Greece. The Tax Office sample (sample 2) puts Greece well below Kosovo in amount of foreign-investment capital provided. On this point the ACFIP figures in Table 14.10 probably give a truer impression for the following reason. It appears likely, from comparisons made earlier in this paper, that the ACFIP data for this limited number of firms cover the great bulk of the FDI by value. They show Greece accounting for about 60% as much inward investment as Italy, with Kosovo very far behind. The discrepancy between the two samples on this point is probably accounted for by the limitations of the Tax Office sample. It happens that Tax Office records for Korçë and Vlorë Districts in the south are especially defective in information about country of origin. Gjirokastër and Sarandë Districts, also in the south, are not even included at all in the sample. Since it is in the southern areas that ethnic-Greeks are concentrated and connections with Greece strongest, it seems likely that Greek investment is heavily represented in the 'unknown country of origin' category in Tables 14.8 and 14.9 and in the investment entering the Districts excluded from those tables. Greece is almost certainly the second-most-important source-country. However, the evidence does suggest that Kosovo, with its largely ethnic-Albanian population, is the third-highest investor, despite the fact that it rates less than 0.5% of the value of the (larger) investments in the ACFIP sample (Table 14.10). In Tables 14.8 and 14.9, Kosovo's proportion of initial FDI (in nominal-dollar terms, *among the investments with nationality identified*) is 6.0% and its proportion of firms 6.8%. We conclude from its much lower representation in the ACFIP data than in sample 2 that Kosovo FDI is mostly small-scale. But it is not minute: the 57 firms in sample 2 identified as having Kosovo capital when they were registered had an average of US$205,000 each.

Countries of origin included among the 'Others' category are the USA, China, Switzerland, Turkey, Kuwait, some other Arab countries, Croatia, Slovenia, Canada, Sweden, and Russia.

**Table 14.8 Foreign investments by country of origin (sample 2),
1991-1995 (firm numbers; US$ thousand, current prices)**

Country	No. of firms	No. of firms	No. of firms	No. of firms	No. of firms	No. of firms	No. of firms
	1991	1992	1993	1994	1995	199x	Total
Neighbours of which:	7	29	132	210	93	130	601
Italy	*4*	*14*	*69*	*125*	*64*	*70*	*346*
Greece	*2*	*6*	*26*	*53*	*19*	*43*	*149*
Kosovo	*0*	*4*	*22*	*19*	*5*	*7*	*57*
Macedonia	*1*	*5*	*15*	*13*	*5*	*10*	*49*
Others	1	10	35	73	50	63	232
Unknown	2	23	74	140	95	632	966
Total	**10**	**62**	**241**	**423**	**238**	**825**	**1,799**
Country	Foreign capital	Foreign capital	Foreign capital	Foreign capital	Foreign capital	Foreign capital	Foreign capital
	1991	1992	1993	1994	1995	199x	Total
Neighbours of which:	1,083	3,110	21,620	9,018	105,822	41,634	182,287
Italy	*80*	*2,721*	*19,777*	*4,527*	*105,630*	*29,986*	*162,721*
Greece	*858*	*59*	*1,732*	*4,357*	*183*	*393*	*7,582*
Kosovo	*0*	*215*	*75*	*120*	*4*	*11,243*	*11,657*
Macedonia	*145*	*115*	*36*	*14*	*5*	*12*	*327*
Others	7	409	410	1,513	8,239	1,568	12,020
Unknown	292	1,394	16,319	11,833	1,632	20,943	52,413
Total	**1,382**	**4,913**	**38,349**	**22,364**	**115,693**	**64,145**	**246,846**

Source: District Taxation Offices, as reported in Brumbulli & Dunlop, 1997

It is notable that there is little investment from countries in Western Europe apart from Italy and Austria, and little from North America. It would seem that investors in the world at large are not yet much aware of Albania as a place to establish long-term business. This is understandable, since it is small, and so far poor by European standards.

Table 14.9 Foreign investments by country of origin (sample 2), 1991 to September 1995, in US$ current prices (% from each country)

Country	1991	1992	1993	1994	1995	199x	Total
Neighbours of which:	78	63	56	40	91	65	74
Italy	*6*	*55*	*52*	*20*	*91*	*47*	*66*
Greece	*62*	*1*	*4*	*19*	*0*	*1*	*3*
Kosovo	*0*	*4*	*0*	*1*	*0*	*18*	*5*
Macedonia	*10*	*2*	*0*	*0*	*0*	*0*	*0*
Others	1	9	1	6	8	2	4
Unknown	21	28	43	53	1	33	21
Total	**100**	**100**	**100**	**100**	**100**	**100**	**100**

Source: Table 14.8 above

Table 14.10 Foreign investments by country of origin, 78 larger investments, ACFIP source, 1991 to July 1995

Country of origin	Number of firms	Initial foreign capital invested, 1991 to July 1995, % of total in sample (summed in current $ US)
Italy	45	51.8
Greece	28	30.8
Kuwait	1	9.8
Austria	1	7.4
Germany	1	0.1
Kosovo	1	0.0
France	1	0.0
Total	**78**	**100.0**

Source: Albania Centre for Foreign Investment Promotion

Most of the investment has been from countries that have had some prior connection with Albania---where there are emigrants from Albania or people who have ethnic or cultural links. With some stretching of the terms, Kuwait might arguably come into this category because of the Islamic association, which does in this case seem to play some part in the motivation. Geographical proximity also seems to have some bearing. If any of the investments are associated with criminal activity, proximity and prior connections may be especially relevant. But it has also been suggested that, for legitimate small-scale trading or service or manufacturing activity, a foreign investor would need a local contact with whom some trust was possible. Because of migration and other links, small investors from Italy, Greece and Kosovo were much more likely to be able to find such contacts than similar investors from elsewhere. It has also been pointed out that numerous producers in Italy, especially those from the South, are used to the idea of relocating not only their trading but also their manufacturing to other countries around the Mediterranean.

For whatever reasons foreign investors do not seem to have participated significantly in privatization sales, at least until the end of 1996. The only important exceptions are some mining-related operations. Though not conclusive, it is perhaps significant that World Bank figures on privatization for 1994 and 1995 (*World Debt Tables*, 1997) show no foreign exchange as being earned by the Albanian government for its privatizations over those years. It is certainly hoped that there will be much wider interest when the banks, utilities, and more of the mining and energy enterprises, are privatized. The authorities are actively concerned to attract large foreign investors with relevant experience into taking controlling shares. To date, Albania has not undergone the privatization of large-scale enterprises on a scale seen in some other transition countries such as Hungary, the Czech Republic, Slovakia, and Poland. Quantitatively, the FDI flow into Albania may increase with subsequent privatization. In fact, the major items to be privatized in and after 1998 will await interest from a suitable large foreign investor. But the style of spontaneous, and often small-scale investment that characterized the mid-1990s will probably take some time and reassurance before it revives.

Geographical Distribution within Albania

There is some tendency for particular kinds of investment to be found in particular parts of the country. (Foreign investment of sample 2 is cross-tabulated by District and sector in Brumbulli & Dunlop, 1997.)

Tirana District received 85% of the foreign direct investment covered by sample 2. As the capital, Tirana attracts foreign investors in most sectors and forms: construction, trade, light industry, construction materials, services---small business and large. Tirana's favoured position is presumably explained partly by the fact that it has the most complete infrastructure; partly by its concentrated and comparatively wealthy population (about 0.5 million) and the resulting domestic market; partly by the fact that it is the administrative, cultural, and trade centre.

Apart from trade and rather small-scale production, the other Districts have aroused foreign-investor interest mainly in those sectors in which they inherited some specialization from the planned economy. So the Districts of Berat, Korçë, Vlorë and Shkodër, which had developed the production of ready-made garments and shoes, have attracted foreign investment in these activities. Similarly, FDI in timber processing has gone principally to

Elbasan; in agricultural processing, to Kavajë; in mining, to Bulqizë.

Motivation of Foreign Direct Investment in Albania

The interpretation commonly made that geographical proximity and cultural affinity are important in attracting FDI projects to transition economies appears consistent with observation of the countries from which FDI which has been attracted to Albania. One of the most notable characteristics of FDI in Albania is its geographic **concentration by source country**, with two countries accounting for the great preponderance of all foreign investment. These are its immediate neighbour Greece, which according to one source contributed some 20.7% of all the identified firms making foreign investments between 1991 and 1995, and Italy (48.1%) the closest 'major' economy, and one with which it has connections stemming in part from the Italian invasion of 1939. (Pointers from cases where origins are identified in the incomplete figures reported in Tables 14.8 to 14.10 suggest that, by number of firms, Italy provided 42% or 58% of those with nationality identified, and Greece 18% or 36%; and that, by amounts of foreign capital in current-price dollars, Italy provided 84% or 52%, and Greece 4% or 31%, with Greece almost certainly very much under-estimated in the first figure in each case for reasons already explained.) Indeed, as shown in Table 14.8, countries defined as 'neighbours' (Greece, Italy, Kosovo, and Macedonia) account for 72% of all foreign firms identified by nationality in sample 2. (These percentages, and those cited just above them, exclude the 'Unknown' category in Tables 14.8 and 14.9 from their denominators.) Albania has attracted some, but very little, FDI from elsewhere, and virtually none from the other large Western economies.

Another characteristic of FDI in Albania relevant to the present point is its **sectoral concentration** (as measured *by numbers of firms*) in the trading sector. This concentration suggests that the aim of the majority of investments has been to distribute consumer products within Albania. *By amount of foreign investment*, however, the concentration has been principally in construction and light industry (taken as a combination of the categories 'Light industry', 'Wood industry', 'Food industry', and 'Production').

Finally, the size of the majority of FDI projects in sample 2 (94% are in the two smallest size-bands, with capital of roughly US$100,000 or less, and 59% have capital below about US$1,000, the minimum limit for which incorporation is required) suggests that the great majority of all *firms* that have received FDI have been **small-scale trading operations**, further reinforcing the supposition that they have been located in Albania not because of any comparative advantage in labour costs or other factor costs, but in order to serve the local, in this instance the country, market.

From this we can conclude that most FDI in Albania, at least until the end of 1995, was concerned with *meeting the demands of the domestic market*. In this it was like FDI in most other transition economies in Central Europe. It probably differed from the pattern in Hungary or the Czech Republic, however, in having a higher concentration on *trade and distribution* as distinct from production. Yet a further peculiarity of Albania in Central Europe was that *some* FDI could be regarded as *resource-based.* There were some foreign investments in the mineral sector and in oil-gas exploration; and, insofar as FDI contributed to the clothing and footwear industry, it was involved in an important source of exports, whose particular advantage was low-cost labour.

Finally, one other motive has at least to be considered. It is notable that so many very small packages of investment come from the two countries to which Albanians have in the last few years migrated in large numbers, and some also from the two neighbours with significant Albanian-speaking populations. We have at least to raise the question whether, as with China in the 1980s (but on a much smaller scale), there has been some degree of influence from a *familial or patriotic* motive, and expatriate Albanians, or relatives of Albanian nationals, have been drawn to invest in the country because of cultural or family linkages. However, the best-informed opinion is that actual investment by expatriate Albanian nationals or former-nationals has not been important---but at the same time that the concentration of investment from Italy and Greece and Kosovo is not due solely to geographical proximity: a number of small investors from those countries have found it easier than those from elsewhere (because of migration or of past and present cultural links) to establish the connections that are necessary within Albania. Cultural and historical linkages seem to have been important elsewhere in Central Europe during transition.

FDI in 1997

An estimate from a Bank of Albania source (personal communication) was that FDI entering the country in 1997 amounted to US$48 million. Given the traumas of that year, this figure looks surprisingly high against the US$70 million and US$90 million of the previous two years (Table 14.3). But they are not comparable. The 1997 estimate was based on imports of machinery and equipment. This was assumed to be mostly brought in to replace items damaged in the disturbances. However, that would make it 'follow-up' rather than initial investment, and follow-up investments are not included in either the ACFIP or the sample-2 figures cited elsewhere in the chapter.   If *all* the FDI of 1997 was of this character, it would have rated a zero against the figures for 1991 to 1996 in Table 14.3.   It is perhaps encouraging that replacement of damaged equipment was proceeding, but the evidence as described does not mean that the flow of new FDI had revived.

Summary

Official aid *committed* to Albania in the mid-1990s amounted to about 15% of GDP.   In 1992 and 1993 its ratio to GDP was considerably higher. However, only a little over half the aid committed over 1991-96 was actually *disbursed*.   The forms of aid switched from a predominance of emergency-type flows in the early years of the decade to items with longer-term motivation by 1995 and 1996.   Technical assistance was important throughout but tended over time to become more closely tied to specific projects and operations.   Quantitatively, even in 1996, aid disbursed was probably more important than 'initial' foreign direct investment, which is estimated as amounting to about 3% of GDP in that year.   But the value of both depends on much more than the tally of dollars.

New initial foreign direct investment generally increased in both numbers of firms and amounts of foreign capital from 1991 to 1996.   At the beginning most firms were joint-ventures, but the proportion wholly-foreign-owned increased until in 1995 the overwhelming bulk of new foreign capital was in wholly-foreign-owned companies.

The great majority of the *firms* embodying FDI have been in trade, which was specially important with those entering in the early years.   The biggest share of *foreign capital* has been in construction and then in various forms of light industry.   More than half the firms involved seem to have been extremely small---below about US$1,000 in initial capital.   Regional distribution of foreign investment *in manufacturing* (with investment in any industry often locating where that industry was concentrated in the Communist era) suggests that much of it has gone into the re-structuring of pre-existing enterprises rather than into new ventures.

Neighbouring countries have been overwhelmingly important in the sources of FDI: mainly Italy, Greece, and Kosovo in descending order. Austria and Kuwait have each provided at least one investment of significant size.   Though a few big names in world investment have set up subsidiaries or branches, investment from countries without historical or cultural links to Albania has been very meagre.   The concentration of the sources of FDI in neighbouring countries, coupled with the importance of investment in trade and construction and the small size of most of the units involved, suggests that its motivation is mainly concerned with the local market---but much of it is directed at channelling in goods and services that have not been available before, rather than at producing within the country in order to gain access against protection barriers or geographical distance. It is mainly *trade-and-distribution-based* rather than *market-access-based* in the senses of the terms used by Dunning.

This concern with the local market, rather than natural-resource-based or labour-based investment for export, or with stages of production that are integrated into a multinational network, is fairly typical of FDI entering the transition economies.   But there is a somewhat different balance of activities in Albania from that of Hungary and the Czech and Slovak Republics, where more of the FDI has been in manufacturing rather than in trade and services.   At the same time, there is in Albania the *beginning* of *resource-based* foreign investment, some of which is likely be motivated by exporting.   This has been seen in natural-resource industries (minerals and petroleum). There has also been foreign investment in the important and growing clothing and footwear sector, which makes use of Albania's cheap labour and is partly directed to export.   These latter developments raise the possibility that FDI will help Albania to exploit its apparent comparative advantage in certain natural resources and low-cost labour.

It is probable that much of the small-scale FDI entering Albania until the end of 1996 was able to do so because of the presence of Albanians within the source countries or past or present cultural connections.   It has been argued that a small-scale foreign operator would need a partner in Albania with whom he could cooperate; and small investors from Italy, Greece and Kosovo would find it much easier to locate such partners than investors from other countries.   If this is so, it might be regarded as having at least faint echoes of China in the 1980s, where inward investment was heavily dominated by overseas and 'compatriot' Chinese who clearly depended considerably on acquaintance or cultural connections.

It seems that, in spite of its welcoming legislation and (since late 1993) simple procedures for admitting foreign investors, Albania has not yet made its name on the world scene as a place to invest. This may be partly the result of its small population and low average income. It may also owe something to the character of the government's privatization up to the end of 1996, which had not had much to offer to large foreign firms with no special reason for being in Albania.

'New' FDI probably ceased, or nearly so, after the early months of 1997, though replacement of equipment on the part of foreign firms and joint-ventures seems to have continued.   We may guess that a resumption of the kinds of foreign investment that characterized the mid-1990s will require a prior period of relative law and order and reassuring political stability.   The government will also strive to attract 'strategic investors' to participate in, and manage, banks, utilities, and mineral and oil operations.

15 Events of 1997

Central Tirana in December 1996 had the air of a boom town. The streets were full of cars. New apartment blocks and offices were visibly shooting up. Booths and kiosks, and even more rudimentary selling-points, were ubiquitous. Small restaurants and coffee-shops had sprouted wherever there was space and potential custom, and they seemed to have occupied every square foot of the parks to the west of Bulevardi Deshmorët e Kombit. Live turkeys were present in abundance at the vegetable market just opposite the Vefa holding company's headquarters. Vefa itself had festooned the town with bunting to advertize a festival for its fifth birthday. Jewellers'shops were numerous and apparently unprotected. Even in the cold weather, there was plenty of life in the central square and boulevard during the early evening.

In retrospect, there seems to have been a prevailing euphoria during that culminating month of the Albanian miracle. Yet ominous signs had begun to appear. One of the smaller funds, Grunjasi, had already failed (Hoxha, 1997, p.31). Early in December the Sude fund, a major player, fronted by Sude (Maksude Kademi), had 'temporarily' suspended payment.

The first days of the new year were quiet. Sude, a lone mother of two living at the flat of her sister and brother-in-law in Tirana, had promised to resume payment on the 15th January. But when that day arrived she announced over a megaphone that she was bankrupt (*AO*, 3, 1, January 1997, p.3). (She later claimed that she had not known what happened to the money that she had received. Someone with whom she was unacquainted collected it at the end of each day and brought what was needed next morning.) At about the same time, Gjallica, one of the largest of the funds, said to owe US$385 million (Hoxha, 1997) or US$145 million (*Keesing*, 41504), suspended payments, again with an undertaking to resume. On the 16th January, as crowds in Vlorë stoned the city hall in protest at the trouble with Gjallica, the government froze the assets of two other giants, Xhaferri and Populli (*AO*, 3, 2, February 1997, p.3), from whose bank accounts and offices it recovered US$300 million (*Keesing*, 41454). Sude and Gjallica were reported to have no traceable money in the banking system, though elsewhere Gjallica was said to have US$28 million in assets. Altogether in January, nine funds failed (*ibid.*).

Now hundreds of thousands of households realized that they had very probably lost much or all of their deposits, in some cases virtually the whole of their assets. So, from mid-January, the disasters had begun, and with them mass protests that could be violent themselves or violently suppressed.

For convenience, we divide the story of the rest of this momentous year into four parts, punctuated by three events that each represented an important step toward recovery. The first of the three was the formation of the coalition government (the Government of National Reconciliation), which was sworn-in on the 12th March. The second was the entry of the multinational force (Operation Alba) which began on the 11th April. The third was the parliamentary election of 29th June and 6th July. (To avoid frequent citations in what follows, we mention that, unless other sources are given, the factual information in this chapter comes from either (i) the 'Chronology of the Main Events', later called 'Chronicle---Flash--- Chronicle', in the *Albanian Observer,* volume 3, 1997, nos. 1-6; or (ii) *Keesing's Record of World Events,* with successive months of the year covered on pages 41454, 41504-5, 41556-8, 41596-8, 41653-4, 41703-4, 41747-8, 41789-90, 41834-5, 41876, 41933, and 41979 respectively. Events are dated so that they can readily be traced in one or other of these sources. Those after late June come exclusively from *Keesing.*)

From Unrest to Anarchy: 16th January to 12th March

The stone-throwing demonstration at the city hall in Vlorë on the 16th January was the first of a series of disturbances that tended to grow in severity through the rest of January and February. 3,000 came out on Tirana's Skanderbeg Square on the 19th, and there were mass protests in Shkodër and Durrës on the 23rd. On the 24th, there was 'rampage' of 5,000 in Lushnje, where Foreign Minister Shehu was attacked the following day. On the 26th, the level of violence rose: crowds, according to the report, set fire to government and Democratic Party buildings 'across Southern Albania'; the army was called out to protect the Bank of Albania and television headquarters; thousands of demonstrators clashed with police in Tirana.

Vlorë became the centre of unrest. The announcement on the 4th February of the collapse of Gjallica (which had promised to resume payments on the 5th) led to futher violent demonstrations in Vlorë. There on the evening of the 5th February 1,000 demonstrators and 200 police stoned each other and many shots were fired. From then on there were daily marches in Vlorë. There too, on 10th February, two died in or after battles with riot police, and two days later a policeman was shot dead. On the 20th, 46 students in Vlorë started a hunger-strike to press for reimbursement. On the 16th there were protests in Fier and Sarandë. Apart from those in Tiranë and Shkodër, protests and rioting until the end of February seem to have been concentrated in coastal Districts in the centre and south. The government tried to control and suppress them, but the police were not always prepared to be very active, and Vlorë particularly was clearly out of control. An impression was created on the part of the police of brutality, and of enmity toward the public, but not to much effect in restoring order.

Political initiatives until the end of February seemed ineffectual. Parliament on the 23rd January passed a law to ban pyramid schemes, with penalties of 20 years in jail for promoters. As buildings began to go up in flames on the 26th, the President was given emergency powers. Ten opposition parties on the 30th constituted themselves the Forum for Democracy and promised more protests across the country. They called for the dismissal of the government. On the 11th February the Forum asked specifically for peaceful demonstrations every day from noon until 2 p.m. Several times before the very end of February government spokesmen asked the opposition to join in talks but without result. On the 8th February, each side asked to other to join in talks, but again there was no meeting. In attempts to win back support, President Berisha on the 31st January promised compensation to depositors, and in a visit to Lushnje on the 18th February he promised to free the area from all taxes for two years. On the 4th February, the authorities starting paying out to depositors the remaining funds of Xhaferri and Populli, expecting to give Xhaferri depositors 52% of what was owed them and Populli depositors 60%.

By the middle of February fears had arisen over the survival of the longer-running funds such as that of Vefa. Vefa had reduced its interest payments to 3% (*AO*, 3, 2, February 1997, p.12) but had apparently put a stop to withdrawals of capital. On the 17th, Vefa's chief, Vehbi Alimuçaj, appeared on television to reassure investors in his own and certain other funds that their deposits were secure, and that these funds were not linked to the pyramids. He claimed to have received US$500 million in credits from foreign firms. Two days later Vefa announced that it would immediately start repaying clients who had deposited US$5,000 or less. Yet there were clashes outside Vefa's Tirana headquarters on the 20th.

Six weeks after the start of the protests they showed no sign of abating. There was no scheme announced that could have seriously mitigated the suffering of the depositors. The opposition parties were if anything encouraging the unrest. The government for its part showed no sign of wanting to bring its opponents into partnership. There had been plenty of destruction of property and a few deaths. However, the situation, even in Vlorë, seems to have been one of recurrent disturbance rather than anarchy.

But two important changes appeared on the last day of February. Weapons were seized by the mob from a police armoury in Vlorë, and in consequence there was a gun-battle through the night in which three civilians and one secret-policeman were killed; protesters set fire to the police headquarters. Over the next couple of weeks raids on government armouries became common. Not only guns but also tanks, helicopters, and ships were taken by the dissidents. A state of emergency was declared by parliament on the 2nd March, with public gatherings of more than four people banned, and authority for the security forces to disperse crowds with gunfire; but by now it was too late. On the 4th March, the Army announced that 'red rebels' were in control of Vlorë and Sarandë. Over the next few days two further southern cities, Tepelenë and Gjirokastër, followed. Police and troops commonly fled. There was burning and looting. This was anarchy. Much of the country (by the end of March, it was said, about a third) had ceased to be under the government's control.

The second new development on the 28th February was that representatives from the Democratic and Socialist Parties met each other for the first time since the election of the previous May. The Socialists called for a technocratic government and early elections. The very next day, as roads and railways were blocked by rebels in the south, the President announced that the government would resign and that its successor would be appointed after consultation with other parties. The Meksi government in fact resigned on the 2nd March. Yet, in what seems in the circumstances an amazing move, Sali Berisha, who was the chief target of blame, was re-elected unopposed by the National Assembly as President of Albania on the 3rd. On the 8th, the President announced the suspension of military action against the rebels and offered an amnesty. Though this had no effect, an agreement was signed on the 9th between the President and the leaders of all parties that there should be a government of national unity and fresh elections by June.

A further important element was that on the 8th March, Franz Vranitzky, the former Austrian Chancellor, came to Tirana as envoy of the OSCE. He was to play an important part in throwing international weight behind the adoption of electoral arrangements that were acceptable to all parties. It was said that Vranitzky, and Netherlands Foreign Minister Van Mierlo (representing the European Union), helped to mediate in negotiation of the agreement of the 9th. In another foreign move for mediation, the Italian Ambassador, Paolo Foresti, held talks with the Vlorë dissidents on the 10th.

On the 11th March, rebel leaders in the south declared that they had formed a National Committee for Public Salvation, which demanded Berisha's resignation by the 20th and its own inclusion in negotiations on the new government. On the same day the President appointed as Prime Minister Bashkim Fino, a southern Socialist Party figure, who had been Mayor of Gjirokastër. The new government was sworn in on the 12th and won a vote of confidence in the Assembly on the 14th. It included 6 DP members, 5 Socialists, and 9 members of 7 smaller parties. The DP held the Ministry of the Interior, but no members of the outgoing government were included.

Anarchy with Negotiation: 13th March to 11th April

The new government faced extending anarchy. Over the 11th, 12th, and 13th March, looting, including the plunder of armouries, spread to Tirana, Elbasan and the north. In the northern Tropojë area, Berisha's home base, rebels who seized weapons, in contrast to those of the south, vowed to defend the Berisha regime. Police and troops were reported in one place to have fought each other. From the 12th, there were gun-battles in the streets of Tirana, together with mass looting. Rinas, the only international airport, was blocked. Deaths were reported in Elbasan, Mjeke, and Shkodër. On the 13th, the prisons were opened in Tirana; all state buildings in the northwestern town of Lezhe were said to have been fired, as was the government-bank building in Shkodër.

Yet it is fairly clear in retrospect that the formation of the coalition government was an essential step in the return to normality. Constitutionally power remained in the hands of the Democratic Party, which controlled the Assembly and the Presidency and hence by law could dismiss the government. But, with the disintegration of the security apparatus, real power depended on bridges to the rebels and to the international community. The erstwhile opposition parties still had credentials with the southern dissidents. Thus Fino and the government possessed important bargaining-power. Broadly the international community was committed to resolution through conciliation. This again strengthened Fino's position. While Vranitzky on frequent visits seems to have negotiated primarily with Berisha, it was members of the government who conducted talks with Italian and other EU Ministers.

On the day that it was sworn-in, the Fino government called for military assistance. A meeting of NATO Ministers in Brussels on that day was reported to be unenthusiastic, but EU Foreign Ministers, when they met on the 15th and 16th March, agreed to send a military and police advisory force. On the 26th and 27th the OSCE met to discuss Albania, and made a proposal to the UN Security Council for a multi-national peace-keeping force. The Council on the 29th authorized individual states to send troops to help Albania restore order, and the Albanian parliament made legal provision for the force on the 30th. Eventually Italy, France, Greece, Spain, Romania, Turkey, Austria, Denmark, and Slovenia agreed to take part.

Meanwhile violence and destruction continued. Armed bands were said to be terrorizing Korçë. Those holding power in the south seem to have been a mixture of semi-popular informal authorities and organized criminals. There was no territorial government, and individual villages had to defend themselves. Opposition leaders generally sought favour with those controlling the southern towns, sometimes but not always making exceptions of those who were essentially gang bosses (see Rama, 1997, for examples). On the streets of Tirana, with the formation of government-supporting vigilante groups, and popular peace rallies on the third and fourth Sundays in March, a measure of public order was restored. Rinas airport was re-opened on the 20th.

Mass attempts to migrate to Italy by sea, such as had been common six years earlier, were resumed. It was said that 10,000 had crossed by the 19th March. A ship went down with 80 people on the 28th. With Albanian approval the Italian Navy tried to check the flow. However, the Prodi government in Italy remained actively sympathetic to Albania throughout, as to a great extent did the Simitis government in Greece.

Fino made his first visit to the south as Prime Minister on the 1st April and met rebel leaders in his home town. He announced then that the SHIK, the secret police of the post-Communist regime, had been disbanded, though subsequent arguments over the headship of SHIK imply that this had not in fact happened. Next day he met Romano Prodi, the Italian Prime Minister, in Vlorë, and he went on to Athens for talks with Prime Minister Simitis, together with Van Mierlo and Vranitzky. On the 5th, however, gunmen apparently sympathetic to Berisha prevented Fino from visiting the northern city of Shkodër.

On the 9th April, the Assembly approved the lifting of press restrictions, and two days later some papers that had been silent for a month resumed publication.

The Multinational Force (MNF), 'Operation Alba', was to be led by Italy. Advance troops landed on the 11th April to secure Rinas airport.

Over these extremely disturbed few weeks since early March, there had been little visible improvement on the ground. Nevertheless the principle of conciliation and negotiation, rather than suppression by force, had been established; and the active involvement of the European and world community had been achieved.

Restoration of Enclaves of Normality: 12th April to 6th July

The advance guard of the MNF at the airport was followed by larger numbers of Italian, French, and Spanish troops that entered on the 15th April. Soldiers of other nations would arrive over the succeeding weeks. The force was to secure ten towns. The first units went to the centre and north, but on the 17th a small Italian contingent entered Vlorë and began talks with Osmani, 'the self-styled commander of the Committee of Public Salvation'. He said that he had assured the Italians of his support.

On the 17th April, Vranitzky said that the leaders of the main parties had agreed to the holding of an election on the 29th June. This was a target toward which political activity could now be directed. The form and conditions of the election remained hotly contentious between Berisha and his opponents. There was a recurrent fear that Berisha, and the Assembly he commanded, would insist on conditions that led the former opposition parties to refuse to play. This was the outcome that had to be avoided if the election was to provide any resolution. Through May and June there were repeated warnings to the parties---from the EU, Italy, Greece, Germany, the USA---that they must agree to participate in the election and make sure that it would be seen as legitimate.

The main disputed issues over the election were the following: the personnel of the central electoral commisssion; whether there would be international observers; how the seats in the Assembly would be divided between constituency members and those elected on proportional rules; and what the proportional rules would be. (As we mentioned in chapter 4, the additional seats in 1992 were allocated so as to make the proportions of the parties' seats more nearly equal to the proportions of their popular votes; while in 1996 they were allocated simply to reflect the proportions in which the constituency *seats* had been won, so that they made no difference to the proportions of seats held. There was also a question over the threshold proportion that a party would need before it was eligible for one of the additional seats.)

On the 9th May, ten parties including the DP and the Socialists signed a contract agreeing that there would be elections before the end of June and apparently approving the system to be used. Yet four days later the agreement on the system had apparently collapsed, with the Socialists threatening to walk out of the Assembly if the DP's version of the electoral law was passed. After Vranitzky's return on the 14th, a new compromise was reached, and a law was approved by the Assembly on the 16th. Disputes over the conduct of the election continued, but again on the 22nd Vranitzky announced that all main parties had agreed to contest it. On the 26th, a 17-person Central Electoral Committee was announced, with a DP chair and Socialist vice-chair.

The final arrangement distributed the additional seats simply according to the proportions of *votes* (figures are cited in Rama, 1997), with a threshold of 2%---far from a proportional system *overall*, but likely to give the front-runner less of an advantage than the 1996 system favoured by Berisha. Paradoxically, the features for which Berisha and the DP had held out could by no means be guaranteed to benefit them. In fact, they did better on the system actually used than they would have done on the one they had preferred, and would have done far better again on a topping-up with a genuinely proportional objective as practised in Germany. It seems more than likely that the President was mainly concerned to provoke the other parties into boycotting the poll.

A further group of prominent DP members had broken away in April to form the Movement for Democracy. At some time towards the end of May, about 37 parties seemed to be in the field, but they had grouped themselves into a much smaller number of alliances. There was a six-party Union of the Right; a nine-party Union for Democracy including the DP; and a five-party group including the Socialists.

What to do about the funds and their depositors continued to occupy some attention, but the impression gained from news items is that what had happened was already seen as irreversible. Berisha was apprently under some pressure from the multilaterals to authorize a thorough investigation (*AO*, 3, 6, June 1997, p.13). Nano, as leader of the Socialists, promised full compensation (*AO*, 3, 6, June 1997, pp.9, 17), but Berisha had promised the same, and at much the same time Arben Malaj, the Socialist Finance Minister in the coalition government, explained why compensation was impossible (*ibid.*, p.13). Maybe not much attention was paid any longer to such promises.

Pending the election, it seems that little was actively done to end the effective fragmentation of the state. A reasonable degree of order was secured in certain towns, and also along certain routes, such as that between Tirana and Durrës; but movement north or south of Tirana, as in much of the rest of the country, was held to be dangerous. A traveller could face criminal gangs, as well as soldiers, police, and representatives of local committees---all highly armed, undisciplined, and on guard against each other. By mid-May, however, Tirana itself was free of regular gunfire, and, in spite of a 9 p.m. curfew and the presence of numerous armed police and foreign soldiers, life there appeared to be fairly normal. Across the country, even in places under government and MNF control, acts of violence continued. A grenade was thrown at the President near Durrës shortly before the election. A figure commonly cited is that 2,000 people altogether were killed in the first half of the year.

On the 25th April, Berisha announced that he had replaced the Governor of the Bank of Albania, Kristaq Luniku. Luniku, who seems to have enjoyed a certain measure of international respect, claimed to have warned the government repeatedly from late 1995 about the funds. He had pressed for the approval of bills apparently to control them. He had asked, he said, that their operations be suspended while they were investigated to discover whether they were able to pay the interest-rates they offered (*AO*, 3, 5, May 1997, p.18). In public, however, he seems to have confined himself to complaints that the funds with their high interest-rates had attracted depositors away from the banks. Why the President dismissed the Governor at just this time is not clear, but he probably calculated rightly that Luniku's absence from Albania over the previous six weeks would deprive him of much political support and leave him in a weak position to complain.

It was decided that the election would be combined with a referendum on restoration of the monarchy. Leka Zogu, who had left Albania as a baby a few days old in 1939, son of the first-generation Albanian monarch

King Zog, campaigned for a restoration as a path to national unity.

Six days before the poll, the leaders of the two main parties were induced to meet in Rome in order to pledge themselves to campaign peacefully and to respect the result.

Re-establishing the State: from 7th July

The election was held in two rounds: on 29th June and 6th July, with a futher two run-offs on the 13th. A second poll between the two front-runners was held in each constituency in which no candidate had scored over 50% the first time. There were 115 constituency seats and a further 40 that went to parties that had scored 2% or more of the initial vote, in proportion to their votes. The result was a very decisive win for the Socialist Party, with 52.75% of the vote (79+22 seats). The Democratic Party was second with 25.70% (17+11 seats). Of eight smaller parties represented, one received just over 3% of the vote, 5 between 2% and 3%, and 2 less than 2%, and there were 3 independents elected (figures cited in Rama, 1997; *Keesing,* 41747-8, gives one more seat for the Democratic Party). It was estimated that 73% of the electorate voted. OSCE observers described the conduct of the poll as 'acceptable', though there was some violence. In the referendum, 33.26% voted for a monarchy and 66.74% for a republic.

On the 23rd July, Sali Berisha removed one important obstacle by resigning as President, following the precedent set by Ramiz Alia in 1992. The next day the Assembly elected as President of Albania Rexhep Mejdani, a distinguished academic physicist, who, since August 1996, around the time of the Socialist Party's apparent nadir, had been its Secretary-General. Until that time he had not been active in politics and he had never been a member of the old ruling party, the PLA. He was expected to bring the party closer to victims of Communist persecution (*AO*, 3, 7-8, July-August 1997, p.9). The Assembly then proposed Fatos Nano as Prime Minister. On the 25th, Nano's government---comprising 14 members of the Socialist Party, 3 of the Democratic Alliance, 2 of the Social-democrats, 1 of the Human Rights Party (PMDN), the one Agrarian Party member, and 1 independent---was sworn-in. Bashkim Fino remained in the government as Deputy Prime Minister. (For details on the members of the government, see *AO,* 3, 7-8, July-August 1997, pp.9-13.)

Rama (1997) draws important conclusions about Albanians' voting behaviour from the 1997 election, which he illustrates with examples. They may be paraphrased briefly, perhaps modified slightly by our own interpretations. First, Albanians had clearly swung considerably between parties from election to election. Second, they appeared to be voting mainly for parties rather than for locally prominent individuals (what we might interpret as a typically European, rather than US-Philippine-Japanese, pattern). Third, there was no evidence that religious allegiances affected voting or choice of candidates: Muslim-majority electorates chose Orthodox and Catholics; a Catholic-majority electorate chose a Muslim. Fourth, cultural background and ethnic nationalism played little part: Albanian-Albanian constituencies were faced with Greek-Albanians and elected them; parties with an Albanian-ethnic message got minimal support. Finally, there was no strong north-south contrast between the allegiances of the two major parties. On this last point, Rama's conclusion may be debated, but the evidence he cites is important---that, in the 26 constituencies he counts as northern, 12 Socialist and 12 DP candidates were elected, most of the Socialists winning in the first round (that is by absolute majorities) and most of the DP only in the second. While he admits by implication that the south voted overwhelmingly Socialist, and the whole of the rest of the country very differently from those 26 northern constituencies (only 5 other DP candidates can have been elected by any of the remaining 89 constituencies), he writes off this big difference as due to the 'fraudulent' character of the polls in the south. Maybe. He appeals to other results, which he does not specify, to support the claim. Yet, even if he is over-stating the case, the results he quotes are enough to show that there is no clear division in which 'north and south' equates to pro- and anti-Berisha or anti- and pro-Socialist. Rama's conclusions about the electors' behaviour, even with some qualifications over the last, provide on the whole good omens for the survival of the Albanian state and for the future health of Albanian democracy. He himself is less optimistic about the behaviour of the *politicians* in both main factions.

The election and its aftermath have revealed that there is no clear operational distinction in economic policy between the major parties. Once the crucial decisions were made in the early part of the decade, economic realities, pragmatism, and pressures from the multilaterals and donor governments, have doubtless tended to push both in the same general directions. Ideas of 'left' and 'right', still much used in Albania, refer to history and symbols rather than to current policies.

The central task of the new government was to restore law and order and the writ of the state. The last member of the MNF left on the 11th August, though a small number of Italian and Greek officers remained under different auspices to help re-organize the army and the police. At the time killings were said to be reported almost daily. On the 3rd August, the new Minister of the Interior, Neritan Ceka, said he would rid the roads of gangs and robbers within 60 days. While this has still not been entirely realized at the time of writing in mid-1998, there seemed to be a perception of greater safety in travel established even as early as August 1997. On the 17th of that month, Ceka ordered the return of all looted weapons by the 30th September, on penalty of 5 years' imprisonment.   Shortly before that deadline he was to announce that 45,000 weapons had been handed in, but 600,000 were estimated as still outstanding.   On the 12th August the government said it had sent Interior Ministry troops to the four southern cities of Vlorë, Sarandë, Gjirokastër, and Tepelenë, to restore order and confront the criminal gangs.   Two days later it was reported that police had taken control of the port of Vlorë and had arrested the supporters of the 'most powerful Vlorë warlord'.   Since the widespread dissemination of guns, a higher level of violence in personal disputes has been alleged.   A very public example occurred when a Socialist Member shot and seriously injured a DP Member on the floor of the National Assembly on the 18th September.

On the 23rd October, the Assembly passed a bill authorizing a commission to investigate the armed rebellion.   President Mejdani, who, in spite of taking a less active role than his predecessor, could display a certain independence, returned the bill to the Assembly, which, however, passed it again on 12th November.   A further constitutional issue arose over a parliamentary attempt to allow the government to audit and administer private companies in certain cases.   This was to provide for ensuring transparency in any future cases similar to those of the pyramid funds.   The Constitutional Court raised objections, and the Assembly on the 19th September amended the Constitution document to allow the legislation to be enacted.

How has the new government performed over democratic propriety, openness, and the rule of law?   It is early for passing a definite judgment. A more liberal, and extremely simple, press law was passed on the 4th September, effectively removing the restrictions of the 1993 Act.   An agreement between the two main parties on balanced television reporting of political issues led Pjetër Arbnori, former political prisoner and former Speaker, to end a hunger-strike on the 8th.   By one means or another it was arranged that 32 former Communist officials who had been sentenced to prison in 1996 for crimes against humanity should have their convictions overturned by the Supreme Court on the 29th September; and on the 14th October the Prosecutor-General dropped the charges against Ramiz Alia and others under the 'genocide' law passed in 1995.   Both moves were made on the grounds that the crimes had not existed when the alleged acts had been committed.   While these events might be interpreted as further illustrating the responsiveness of the Courts and of law officers to political pressures in the interests of the current government's friends and associates, it can be said on the other side that the ground alleged is a plausible one; the law on genocide was fairly blatantly introduced by the previous government for its own party advantage; and both reversals could be seen as overturning acts done for party-political rather than juristic reasons.   So far, to the best of our knowledge, the Nano government has not followed its predecessor's example in selectively prosecuting its defeated opponents.

There have been allegations, however, of political appointments to posts in which capacity and integrity rather than allegiance should be the criterion.   Without intimate knowledge of the cases it is difficult to judge such criticisms.   They may or may not apply to the replacements made in August of the Army Chief of Staff, the head of SHIK, and the Governor of the Central Bank.   It has also come to be accepted that a number of personnel right down the hierarchy are changed with a change of ruling party.   Apart from waste of skills and experience, a danger here is that a change of government comes to seem a matter of livelihood for too many people, with corresponding intensity of feeling in the contest.

On the 5th August, the Greek Foreign Minister agreed that a large number of illegal Albanian migrants should receive temporary work-permits.   This followed a draft presidential decree issued by Greece in late January (*AO*, 3, 2, February 1997, p.18).   While the provisions as foreshadowed in that draft decree were criticized from the migrants' standpoint (mainly because of the temporary and arbitrary character of the permits), the legalization represents a large concession in a field vital to the welfare of Albanians; and its value will depend on how it is administered.

By the end of the year, if not before, it was clear that 'the state', with whatever weaknesses and imperfections, was restored.   Organized crime was not by any means beaten.   Armed bands could still attack towns in broad daylight.   But the system of independent fiefdoms that had existed for a while in the south was gone.   Most people certainly did not want a continuance of the anarchy that had arisen as a by-product of general anger and mistrust of the previous government.

The Economy in 1997

What is remarkable about the indicators for 1997 is the recovery in the second half of the year.   When most of the pyramid funds' depositors discovered that they would stop receiving interest and would not recover all or any of their capital, several things happened.

First, hundreds of thousands of people realized that they had much less wealth (net assets) and a lower expected-future-income stream than they had believed.   This meant that they would spend less, on consumption or investment, than they had previously planned to do or indeed had been doing.   There was no corresponding increase in wealth for anyone else: the 'subjective' loss that occurred for so many was not accompanied by a (subjective or objective) gain for anyone else.   So, overall, there was virtually certain to be less 'real' spending unless some countervailing influence was introduced.   That would mean less spending on imports, but also less on goods and services produced within Albania.   And that in turn would mean less income for Albania's residents---less for those running shops, transporting, manufacturing, working in restaurants, taxi-driving, possibly even farming. They in turn would spend less, and that would reduce the incomes of others again, and so on. It is not inconceivable that this effect could largely have been prevented or reversed by action in compensation that to an extent restored people's views about their wealth. But doing this without undue creation of money or undue commitment of future government revenue would at best have been tricky.

Table 15.1 Exchange-rates and price-levels, 1997

	Sept. 1996	Dec. 1996	Jan. 1997	Feb. 1997	Mar. 1997	Apr. 1997	May 1997
Lekë per $US (end of month)	107.8	103.1	128.1	144.1	148.5	148.3	175.1
Consumer Price Index (average over month)	141.6	144.2	146.5	154.3	175.9	173.3	175.1
% rise in CPI from Dec. 1996			1.6	7.0	22.0	20.2	21.4

	June 1997	July 1997	Aug. 1997	Sept. 1997	Oct. 1997	Nov. 1997	Dec. 1997
Lekë per $US (end of month)	178.7	145.2	155.7	147.4	143.7	145.4	149.8
Consumer Price Index (average over month)	184.5	182.3	183.4	186.4	195.8	200.2	204.8
% rise in CPI from Dec. 1996	27.9	26.4	27.2	29.3	35.8	38.8	42.0

Source: INSTAT; Bank of Albania; *International Financial Statistics*

Second, there was almost inevitably a fall of confidence in the lek. The stability of the floating rate against the dollar had depended on confidence (apparently justified over more than four years) that the rate was somehow right or that the authorities would act to maintain it. This belief could not withstand a sudden loss of confidence, in which people wanted to shift out of lekë, or emigrant workers or investors became more reluctant to bring in foreign exchange. Already on the 31st January the lek had fallen against the dollar by 20% since the start of the year, to 128.1. At its lowest point near the end of May it was alleged to have reached 194 to the dollar before the Bank acted to support it (*AO*, 3, 6, June 1997, p.8). Its lowest month-end figure recorded was 178.7 to the dollar at the end of June.

After July the lek rose notably.   The number of lekë to the dollar was below 150 at the ends of each of the last five months of the year.   A remarkable stability of the dollar exchange-rate seemed to have been re-established.   Over the last three months of the year the daily market rate varied between 142.17 and 154.44.   The range of the daily rate against the mark was proportionally even less---from 82.06 to 86.13.   But the trend in lekë to the dollar was again slightly upward from November 1997 to April 1998---to the point where it was nudging 160.   Insofar as the fall in the lek in the first half of 1997 was purely a matter of confidence, it might perhaps have been avoided or reversed by prompt action, which in the circumstances would have depended on fairly firm international support. But strong international support for threatened currencies of small countries (or even of some large ones such as Indonesia or Thailand) is not as a rule provided quickly or without conditions.   The depreciation in turn probably led to a further loss of confidence.

The depreciation would also inevitably lead with some delay to a rise in domestic prices.   The Consumer Price Index rose 42% over the year 1997.   This was unpleasant for a population that had become used to fairly stable prices, but it is a long way short of hyper-inflation.   People noticed particularly the rise in the price of bread, aggravated no doubt by the 10% duty imposed on imports of wheat and flour at the start of the year.   By mid-1998 there were already signs that the inflation-rate had slowed.   The rise in the index for the first five months of 1998 was at an annual rate of 20.4%, little higher than that over 1996.   Between December 1996 and May 1998, by which time it seemed that the price level was flattening, the rise had been 53.5%---very close to the proportion by which the number of lekë to the dollar had risen.   There might be debate over *how exclusively* the depreciation of the exchange-rate and the accompanying rise in domestic prices can be attributed simply to the fall in *confidence* in the lek, but confidence must have played a large part.

These first two effects were essentially *financial*, depending on shocks to people's beliefs and to their trust in the system.   Arguably measures to correct them were possible in principle, though they may well have been beyond the reach of the Albanian authorities acting alone.   But the disturbances inspired by the financial crisis led then to adverse impacts on the *real* economy which no financial conjuring could have reversed.

So, to move to a third ill-effect, the crisis, by making movement around the country dangerous, blocked internal and international trade.   As an indicator, merchandise exports in current-dollar terms during the first half of 1997 stood at only 31% of those for the whole of 1996; for imports the proportion was 28%.   For 1997 as a whole, we have only figures in lekë, and the real and dollar value of the lek fluctuated greatly over the year; but crude comparisons such as those given in Table 10.3 (converted this time at the actual average market rate over the year of 149 lekë per dollar) make 1997 merchandise exports and imports 58% and 67% those of 1996. So there was *some* recovery of foreign trade in the second half, but much less striking than the recovery in government revenue outlined in chapter 11.

Fourth, and most important for the long term, there was much destruction of government buildings, including what were clearly social facilities, and privately-owned factories, and also plundering of state and private property---much of which would have to be replaced in order to restore the previous level of potential material welfare.

We have two preliminary estimates of the fall in real GDP from 1996 to 1997. The EBRD *Transition Report* (EBRD, 1997b, p.214) puts it at 15%; a Ministry of Finance estimate made in December, probably two or three months later than the EBRD projection, says 7%. By the way it is defined, GDP gives an over-favourable picture of change at a time when much productive capital has been destroyed: it does not take account of the *depreciation* of capital goods. Even allowing for this and adoptng the 15% figure, we may still judge that Albania's economy suffered *surprisingly* little. Though what happened in the first half of 1997 was *not* a civil war, its impact on production and trade might well have been similar. A projection made in November 1997, apparently accepted by the IMF, was that growth in GDP from 1997 to 1998 would be 12% (*Keesing*, 41933). This would mean, on the worse of the two estimates for 1997, very nearly returning to the 1996 level---and, on the better one, clearly surpassing it.

It is said that some people had stopped working in 1996 in response to the funds; peasants sold or slaughtered their beasts; and families sold their houses. Malaj and Mema (1997) say that 3,000 families had sold their houses. The selling of houses to invest in the funds might well impoverish the families concerned, but it would not diminish the housing stock. On the other hand any increased propensity to sell livestock might well lead to increased slaughter and reduced breeding, and hence to reduced numbers. But, if there was a tendency to stop work or slaughter beasts in 1996, this is likely to have been reversed in 1997, which in itself would dampen the fall, or boost the later recovery, of GDP.

According to the figures (Table 12.1) employment fell over 1997, but by only 8,000 (in fact *less* than employment *fell* over 1995 or over 1996), while unemployed numbers rose by 36,000; but at the end of 1997 unemployed numbers were still well below those of the end of 1994. The unemployment *rate* was up over the year, but by only 2.5 percentage points, to 14.9%, again well below that of the end of 1994. But remember that, as emphasized in chapter 12, employed numbers, unemployed numbers, and unemployment rates seem to move to some extent independently of each other. This is because withdrawal from the workforce (always a dubious statistic) and emigration (not directly recorded) loom so large. The fact that so much 'employment' is inferred from resident farm-family membership is one of the reasons why there may be doubts about the reliability of the figures or at least of the interpretation to be put on them.

As mentioned in chapter 11, government revenue recovered considerably in the second half of 1997. (See Table 11.5.) Though it was down from 1996 by about 17% in real terms for 1997 as a whole, the second half of the year taken alone showed an average real monthly rate of revenue collection very similar to that of the whole of 1996. Seasonal factors seem likely to account for a part of this difference (a *regular* seasonal pattern is difficult to pin down), but the recovery (stemming mainly from VAT and customs) seems to be far greater than that would explain. A decision to raise the VAT rate from 12.5% to 20% was made in early October (*Keesing*, 41876).

Inward transfers (public and private) in the first half of 1997 ran at only 27% of the value for the whole of 1996, and a central-bank source has told us that the level of *private* remittances for 1997 as a whole was below the annual average estimated for 1993-95. Probably the pyramid funds had attracted cash that some emigrants now preferred to deposit in Greece or Italy, or else to convert into goods.

We have mentioned that probably *new* foreign inward investment virtually stopped after the first couple of months of 1997, but recorded imports of equipment have led to the rough estimate that about US$48 million worth of investment, presumed to be mainly for replacement of what had been destroyed, had come in over the year.

Various new arrangements for aid and international support were made in the second half of the year. Donors' conferences in Brussels and Rome, 17th to 21st October, approved aid of US$600 million (*Keesing*, 41876). A series of agreements with the IMF (5th September, 7th October, 7th November) involved a number of commitments on the Albanian side and also an IMF credit (*Keesing*, 41384-5, 41876, 41933), whose importance lay mostly in the signal that it gave to donor governments and investors.

It is notable that (according to a communication from a central-bank source) Albania's foreign reserves actually *rose* over 1997, by US$44 million.

So, in several respects, there was quite a swift rebound towards economic normality after the mid-1997 election. People on the whole in mid-1998 must have been poorer than two years earlier, objectively as well as subjectively. Yet macroeconomically the system was again under control; and recovery of output seemed to be imminent. GDP per head may well return to its pre-disaster level by 1999. But one of the negative elements that GDP ignores is deterioration or destruction of capital goods. The GDP changes will take no account of the fact that, as a one-off result of the events of 1997, the public infrastructure---of schools, hospitals, roads, and the like---will probably be in distinctly worse shape even than before. Collecting a far higher proportion of the tax revenue due---and devising ways for government to borrow from the public---assume even greater urgency.

Summary of Observations from the Events of 1996 and 1997

Le Corbeau honteux et confus
Jura, mais un peu tard, qu'on ne l'y prendrait plus.

Jean de la Fontaine

The trauma of the pyramid funds and the subsequent rebellion and anarchy may be of some use if the right lessons are drawn about the characteristic behaviour of the Albanian people and the courses open to them. We make some suggestions stemming from what is recorded in this chapter.

1. Nothing in the social inheritance of the people of Albania makes their state inherently liable to break up. No significant body of people (other than possibly organized criminals) wants to see the state fragmented or other groups expelled from it.

2. Albanian people generally recognize the need for government but have no automatic respect for actual governments and expect the government of the day to protect them against man-made disasters. There are elements among them who will express resentment by destroying social property.

3. Albanian electors are *no less* inclined than those elsewhere in Europe to vote on national issues and parties as distinct from local issues and personalities, and are *less* inclined than electors in a number of European countries to vote according to religious or cultural affiliation or habit, or out of group-hostility.

4. In Albania, as in many modern states, the machinery of government and law-enforcement has not been well adapted to deal with widespread popular protests and demonstrations.

5. When it appears that according to prevailing public opinion a government has failed in some vital respect, law and convention need to be such as to ensure that it resigns promptly and submits itsdelf to the judgment of the electorate.

6. In a post such as that of President of Albania, there is a vital role for someone who will act as a trusted and impartial umpire over the political process---one who is not personally involved in the government's decisions, or ordinarily in its appointments, but who can interpret the rules, mediate between rival parties, and call elections in emergencies. Hence perhaps the desire of the Socialist Party and two of its allies for a 'prime-

ministerial' rather than 'presidential' system (*Keesing*, 41747-8).

7. For a government to cheat in elections or bias election coverage tends to generate ill-feeling and dissidence.

8. Using the law to punish defeated political opponents renders the stakes in an election too high and makes difficult the cooperation between rival politicians that is sometimes necessary.

9. The practice of replacing more than the very top layer of officials after a change of government not only risks the loss of expertise but also raises the personal stakes in an election for too many people.

10. Attempts by the government to control news and comment block an important safety-valve and weaken a possible shield against disaster.

11. For a country of Albania's size and special situation, European and international support can be particularly useful, and this enhances the case for playing according to accepted European conventions.

12. Tolerating activities that are contrary to domestic law or to international law and commitments, even when such activities seem harmless to Albanians in the immediate present and indeed appear to generate income, runs the risk that the state and society will come to be controlled or unduly influenced by organized criminals and discredited abroad.

16 Prospects and Priorities

Twice in seven years Albania has faced the abyss. Twice it has managed to pull back. Its first recovery owed much to bold and sensible policies and astonished the onlookers. Political failures played a crucial role in its second fall in 1997.

Now in 1998 the country seems set to make a second recovery. Most of the forces that produced the Albanian miracle of the mid-1990s are probably still there to be released. And Albanians at large have shown that, given the chance, they are only too happy to renounce anarchy and have every intention of staying together.

Yet falling and rising again should not become a habit. The 1997 disaster revealed unpleasant features and left unhappy legacies. The ease with which criminal bosses could gain control of cities, the fact that so many weapons have been disseminated and that travel remains more dangerous than before, the wasteful and self-defeating results of burning and looting, the destitution of so many honest people, and the return of larger numbers to severe poverty and insecurity: much of this will remain to be regretted even if fast growth overall resumes.

In the new environment entailed by 'transition', a number of adjustments have to be made, as the 1997 events made clear. Governing has largely to proceed by consent. People understand well enough what democracy means, and they know now that, if government does not respond, they can bring it to a halt---even though in general they have no desire to do so. No faction can expect to ensure its position in power indefinitely. Give-and-take with neighbouring countries, and attention to the rules and conventions of Europe, are necessities in the world in which Albania has chosen to take its place. Moreover, to secure a number of features of life that are valued, adequate resources have to be channelled to the state (for example, to pay for most education and health services) or to the relevant private agents (for example, to pay for housebuilding, which needs special financial institutions for its flow to be efficiently maintained).

We suppose that now much of the country's leadership has a fairly clear idea of priorities---for making life more secure, and more comfortable, and fairer, and more open to creative activity, and in every good sense more human. But we shall set out here what we consider important both in certain broader public issues and in particular points of economic policy.

It seems at least arguable that, until the pyramids appeared, opening to the market had worked *better* to increase potential material well-being in

Albania than in any other transition country in Europe or in the former Soviet lands. We tried in chapter 2 to work out why this was so. Given minimally suitable conditions, there is every reason to believe that small-scale producers, principally farmers, and a whole range of service-providers, and an increasing number of light-manufacturing enterprises, will continue steadily improving and expanding what they do, and that housing will progressively become more adequate. But how to maintain those conditions? And how to achieve the other elements of prosperity and well-being?

First and utterly crucial is the maintenance and enhancement of law and order. This is eminently desirable for its own sake and also essential for reassuring foreign investors. Bandits must be off the roads. Producers and traders must be given every opportunity to escape from protection rackets and every incentive to expose them. The police must be incorruptible and reasonably competent, and a sufficient number of them trained in non-violent crowd control. Modern methods of tracking stolen property might be explored. This is all urgent, but none of it will be achieved easily or quickly. Even more difficult is providing a reasonable assurance that there will be no more sacking and burning and looting. For that, political mechanisms need to be strengthened. The government's policy for reconstructing mining and hydrocarbons, banking and insurance, and the utilities, depends on enlisting *strategic investors*. Neither investors of this kind, nor the kind of investor, large or small, that has entered spontaneously in the past, is likely to be attracted unless there is security of property.

Second, for a number of reasons, attention must be paid to institutionalizing the rule of law, electoral fair-play, accountability of government, and openness. Rules and conventions governing the state-owned media, the law courts, the electoral commission, the role of the head of state, and the universities, may have parts to play. A certain amount has been done and projected in these directions since the 1997 election. Some suggested requirements are mentioned in the 'Summary' section at the end of chapter 15.

Third (a challenge admittedly involving dilemmas over values as well as great practical difficulties) there should be movement toward a serious policy on the kind of illegality whose main *immediate* victims and ill-effects lie *outside* Albania: the illegal drug and arms trades, sanctions-breaking, smuggling of all kinds, dealings in cars stolen abroad, money-laundering to conceal international crime and fraud.   These are tempting sources of income, but they bring curses to the host country too in the kind of people and activities they attract, in their strong tendency to corrupt the police and government generally, and in the obstacles they raise to international cooperation.   To become the crime haven of the region is

that growth, the less limiting this constraint would need to be.

Eighth, as suggested toward the end of chapter 6, certain changes in the arrangements for the use of vouchers in *mass-privatization* could reduce the uncertainty associated with bidding, increase the market-value of the vouchers, and cause the process to provide a wider and more equitable distribution of assets among the public.

Ninth, changes in the details of the law on land-ownership and transfer are clearly needed to render sales of land easier, so making possible consolidation of strips, and also facilitating movement of families away from the land (and consequently increasing the average size of, and income from, holdings) as urban opportunities increase.

Tenth, the state of Social Security and Social Assistance payments needs attention, as the proportional gap between urban Unemployment Benefits and Social Assistance on the one hand and the minimum wage on the other widens, while rural recipients get at best a small fraction of the urban payments. One ameliorant suggested for the very difficult problem of dealing with rural social security was that more informal, community-based methods might be used in rural areas to provide at least one stage of the process of determining who is in particular need.

Eleventh, or perhaps higher, we might have mentioned the need for privatizing (in whole or in part) the utilities, the metal and hydrocarbon industries, and the state-owned financial sector. But the need is fully recognized by both government and opposition; the basic approach appears sound; what is lacking in most cases is the willing partner. First catch your strategic investor.

Twelfth, again a high priority but hardly necessary to mention, is effective supervision and regulation over the whole of the financial sector. This can be fiendishly hard to do in a watertight fashion. Part of the trouble in 1995-1996 was the difficulty of recognizing the *boundaries* of the financial sector when the landscape was changing. *Now* of course it is clear that the authorities must be extremely alert to what is actually happening, and legislation has to adapt itself quickly to deal with new phenomena.

Albania's revealed capacity for economic growth may rightly be the envy of the other transition countries. But certain practices and policies are needed for that growth to be reliably sustained and to be directed into the just and comprehensive promotion of human welfare.

Bibliography

Newspapers, Periodicals

Albanian Daily News, Independent Albanian Economic Tribune Ltd., Tirana.
Albanian Observer, Adrion Ltd., Tirana.
Economist, Economist Newspaper Ltd., London.
International Financial Statistics, IMF, Washington, DC.
Keesing's Record of World Events, Cambridge, England, and Washington, DC.

Books, Articles, Annual and Occasional Series

AAS 1995 [Albania, *Annual Agricultural Survey 1995*], Tirana.
ACFIP [Albania Centre for Foreign Investment Promotion] (1997), *A Guide to Business in Albania*, Tirana.
Aslund, A. and Sjoberg, O. (1992), Privatisation and Transition to a Market Economy in Albania', *Communist Economies and Economic Transformation*, vol. 4, no. 1, pp. 135-47.
Bachtler, J.F. and Downes, R. (1994), 'Regional Socio-Economic Development in Albania', Report to the European Commission DG1, European Policies Research Centre, University of Strathclyde, Glasgow.
*Bachtler, J.F., Kristo, I., Llaci, Sh. and Rooney, M.-L. (1997), 'Regional Socio-Economic Development in Albania', Paper submitted to the European Commission under ACE project no. 94-0714-R, Department of Economics, University of Strathclyde, Glasgow.
Boeri, T. (1994), 'Labour-Market Flows and the Persistence of Unemployment in Central and Eastern Europe', in OECD, *Unemployment in Transition Countries: Transient or Persistent*, Paris.
Brancati, G. (1996), 'The Albanian Economy during the Communist Regime', in T.Perna *et al.*, *Passage to the West*, Publishing House of IFAW, 'Dora d'Istria', Tirana.
*Brumbulli, S. and Dunlop, S. (1997), 'Foreign Direct Investment during Albania's Transition', Paper submitted to the European Commission under ACE project no. 94-0714-R, Department of Economics, University of Strathclyde, Glasgow.
Carter, F.W. and Turnock, D. (1996), *Environmental Problems in Eastern Europe*, Routledge, London.
Cooper, R. (1996), *The Post-Modern State and the World Order*, Demos, London.
*Davies, J.R., Kule, Dh., Levine, N., Mançellari, A. and Pitt, D.C. (1997), 'Albania: the Privatization Experience', Paper submitted to the European Commission under ACE project no. 94-0714-R, Department of Economics, University of Strathclyde, Glasgow.
Duka, R. (1992), 'Mining and Metallurgic Industry in Albania: Prospects for

Future Development', in *The Transition to Market Economy in Albania*, Dynamis, Quaderno 13/92, Istituto di Ricerca sulla Dinamica dei Sistemi Economici, Milano.

EBRD [European Bank for Reconstruction and Development] (1994), *Transition Report 1994*, London.

EBRD (1996), *Transition Report 1996*, London.

EBRD (1997a), *Transition Report Update*, April 1997, London.

EBRD (1997b), *Transition Report 1997*, London.

Eijffinger, S.C.W. and Haan, J.D. (1996), *The Political Economy of Central Bank Independence*, Princeton Special Papers No.19, May 1996, Princeton, NJ.

Garnaut, R.G. and Clunies-Ross, A.I. (1983), *Taxation of Mineral Rent*, Oxford University Press, Oxford.

Goss, C. (1986), *Petroleum and Mining Taxation*, Policy Studies Institute and Royal Institute of International Affairs, London.

*Grieve, R. and Clunies-Ross, A.I. (1997), 'Albania : the Public Finances, 1989-96', Paper submitted to the European Commission under ACE project no. 94-0714-R, Department of Economics, University of Strathclyde, Glasgow.

*Gruda, S. and Kay, N. (1997), 'Albanian Industry and Competition Policy', Paper submitted to the European Commission under ACE project no. 94-0714-R, Department of Economics, University of Strathclyde, Glasgow.

*Hallwood, C.P. and Mac Donald, R. (1997), 'Recent Nominal and Real Exchange Rate Experience in a Transitional Economy: the Case of Albania', Paper submitted to the European Commission under ACE project no. 94-0714-R, Department of Economics, University of Strathclyde, Glasgow.

Harxhi, E. (1995), *An Invitation to Albania*, Besa, Tirana.

Hashi, I. and Xhillari, L. (1996), 'Privatisation and transition in Albania', Paper presented at a Conference on 'Albania Economy Towards Free Market' Tirana, 13-14 December 1996, Staffordshire University Business School, Stoke-on-Trent.

Hashi, I. and Xhillari, L. (1997), 'Privatisation and transition in Albania', University of Staffordshire Business School Economics Section Discussion Paper, December 1997.

HEMA CONSULT, Consultant's report, precise provenace unknown, possibly 1995.

Hoxha, A. (1997), 'Why did it Happen?', *Albanian Observer*, vol. 3, no. 3-4, March-April 1997, pp. 30-1.

IMF [International Monetary Fund] (1996), 'Albania---Recent Economic Developments', IMF Staff Country Report, 1996, Washington, DC.

IMF (1997), 'Albania---Recent Economic Developments', IMF Staff Country Report, April 1997, Washington, DC.

INSTAT [Albania, Institute of Statistics], (1995a), *Albanian Labour Market in Transition*, Tirana.

INSTAT (1995b), *Albania in Figures 1994*, Tirana.

INSTAT (1996a), *Reporter of Economic Enterprises 1991-1995*, Tirana.

INSTAT (1996b), *Albania Human Development Report*, Tirana.

INSTAT (1997), *Albania in Figures 1996*, Tirana.

*Karadeloglou, P. and Stoforos, C. (1997), 'Policy Analysis in Albanian

Agriculture Using a Sectoral Model', Paper submitted to the European Commission under ACE project no. 94-0714-R, Department of Economics, University of Strathclyde, Glasgow.

Koliadina, N. (1996), 'The Social Safety-Net in Albania', IMF Working Paper, Washington, DC.

Kornai, J. (1995), 'The Principles of Privatization in Eastern Europe', in K.Poznanski (ed.), *The Evolutionary Transition to Capitalism*, Westview Press, Boulder, Colorado.

Kunkel, D.E. (1996), 'Albanian Agriculture in Transition', Paper presented at a Conference on 'Albania Economy Towards Free Market' Tirana, 13-14 December 1996.

Lavigne, M. (1995), *The Economics of Transition*, Macmillan, London.

*Love, J., Duka, R. and Minxhozi, L. (1997), 'Changes in Albanian Production and Trade Patterns', Paper submitted to the European Commission under ACE project no. 94-0714-R, Department of Economics, University of Strathclyde, Glasgow.

Malaj, A. and Mema, F. (1997), 'The Informal Market and its Impact on the Albanian Economy', Paper presented at a Conference on 'Bank System Reforms, Bank Loans Portfolios and Enterprise Restructuring', Tirana, 12-13 December 1997.

Mançellari, A., Papanagos, H. and Sanfey, P. (1995), 'Job Creation, Job Destruction and Temporary Emigration: the Albanian Experience', Paper prepared under a European Commission TEMPUS project, June 1995, and presented at a Conference on 'Albania Economy Towards Free Market' Tirana, 13-14 December 1996.

Mema, F. (1997), *Privatizimi në Shqipëri* [Privatization in Albania], University of Tirana Faculty of Economics and Shtëpia Botuese Toena, Tirana.

Mima, F. (1994), 'Financial Aspects of the Law', Paper issued by the Social Security Institute, Albania, Tirana, undated, probably 1994.

Ministry of Public Economy [Ministry of Public Economy and Privatization, Albania] (1997), 'Privatization Strategy of State Owned Companies in Primary Importance Sectors', Tirana, December 1997.

Muço, M. (1996), 'An Overview on the Economic Reform in Albania', in T.Perna *et al.*, *Passage to the West*, Publishing House of IFAW, 'Dora d'Istria', Tirana.

PIP [Public Investment Programme, 1996-8] (1996), Albania.Council of Ministers and Department of Economic Development and Aid Co-ordination, Tirana, March 1996.

Preci, Z. (1994), 'Decollectivization and Agricultural Transformation in Albania', Reform Round Table Albania Document No. 1, Albania Center for Economic Research, Tirana.

Prifti, P.R. (1978), *Socialist Albania since 1944: Domestic and Foreign Developments*, M.I.T.Press, Cambridge, Massachusetts.

*Qirici, S. and Clunies-Ross, A.I. (1997), 'Adapting Social Security and the Social Services', Paper submitted to the European Commission under ACE project no. 94-0714-R, Department of Economics, University of Strathclyde, Glasgow.

Rama, S.A. (1997), 'Failed Transition, Elite Fragmentation and the Parliamentary Elections of June 29, 1997', *International Journal of Albanian Studies*, vol. 1, no. 1.

SYA 1991 [Statistical Yearbook of Albania 1991], Tirana.

*Stewart, W.J. and Xhafa, H. (1997), 'The Challenge of Albania's Financial Sector', Paper submitted to the European Commission under ACE project no. 94-0714-R, Department of Economics, University of Strathclyde, Glasgow.

UN [United Nations], *Energy Studies Yearbook*, New York.

UN (1995), *Human Development Report Albania*, New York.

World Bank and European Community (1992), *An Agricultural Strategy for Albania*, World Bank, Washington, DC.

World Debt Tables [now called *Global Development Finance*], World Bank, Washington, DC.

WDR 1996 [World Development Report 1996], World Bank, Washington, DC.

WDR 1997 [World Development Report 1997], World Bank, Washington, DC.

*Yin, Y.P., Qirici, S. and Clunies-Ross, A.I. (1997), 'Labour-Market Adjustment in Albania's Transition', Paper submitted to the European Commission under ACE project no. 94-0714-R, Department of Economics, University of Strathclyde, Glasgow.

Zymberi, I. (1991), *Colloquial Albanian*, Routledge, London.

*   Copies of papers so marked, which formed the studies on which the book is based, may be obtained from A.I.Clunies-Ross, Economics Department, University of Strathclyde, Glasgow G4 0NL, Scotland.

Index

agriculture
  collectivization 9
  farm income 32-3
  farm numbers 176
  output and growth 22
  privatization *see* privatization,
    farmland
  production pattern 22, 156-8
  productivity 33
  share in GDP 9
  workers, density 33
  workforce 7, 176-7
Ahmeti, Vilson 61, 66
aid, foreign official 59, 164-6,
  208-10, 242
airports *see* transport
Ali, Pasha of Tepelenë [Ali Pashë
  Tepelena] 48
Alia, Ramiz 54, 56, 58, 59, 61, 62,
  64, 235, 237
Alimuçaj, Vehbi 229
Arbnori, Pjetër 62, 237

balance of payments 117-9
Bank of Albania *see* central bank
banks 60, 190-200
  central *see* central bank
  commercial 194-200
benefits *see* social security
Berisha, Sali 49, 62, 64, 65, 68,
  230-1, 233, 235
bonds, government 120, 166, 190,
  200, 247
Brozi, Zef 66, 146
Bufi, Ylli 60, 61

Ceka, Neritan 61, 63, 236
central bank 62, 191-4
  constitution 192-4
  independence of 194
China, analogies with 21-2, 81, 224

constitution 59, 68, 233, 243-4

Council of Europe 52, 62, 69
courts of law, government relations
  with 61, 64-6, 146, 238
CSCE *see* OSCE

Dukagjini, Lekë 48

education 8, 165-6
election results 59, 62, 63, 68, 69,
  236-7
electoral system 61, 69, 233-4
emigration 15-16, 21, 58, 66, 180-5,
  239
  effect on labour market 180-4
emigrant remittances 16, 21, 117-9,
  177
employment 175-88, 241-2
  and emigration 175-7, 180-4
  labourforce 40, 178
  number employed 61, 79, 188-9,
    241-2
  participation-rate 176-9, 186
  regional distribution 40-2
  sectoral distribution 40-1, 185
  unemployment 64, 178-9, 183-7
    long-term 178, 185
  wage-levels 130-1
European Community and Union 52
exchange-rate 23, 60, 64, 108-11,
  119, 239-40
  real 23, 112-4

finance, public *see* public finance;
  tax
financial system 189-207
Fino, Bashkim 230-2, 235
foreign direct investment 17, 44,
  208-9, 212-26
  motivation 223-4
  policy and law 60, 142-4, 211
  regional pattern 44, 222-3
  scale 213-5, 216
  sectoral pattern 213, 216-9
  source-countries 219-22

foreign trade *see* trade, foreign
Foresti, Paolo 230

GDP, growth and decline 4-5, 7, 56,
    61, 62, 64, 113, 242
  explanations of fast growth 20-4
  explanations of collapse 24-30
Genocide, Law on 68
Gjinushi, Skënder 68
Greece, relations with 55, 66, 68,
    70, 232, 236, 238
growth, economic *see* GDP

health indicators and services 8,
    162-3
housing 85-6, 91, 95, 242, 247-8
Hoxha, Enver 54, 58, 62
Hoxha, Nexhmije 57, 61, 64

institutional development 4, 15,
    139-49, 238-9
investment, foreign *see* foreign
    direct investment
irrigation 34
Italy, relations with 230-3, 236

Kademi, Maksude [Sude] 227
Kastrioti, Gjergj [Skënderbej] 48
Kosovo 49, 51, 68

labour *see* employment
liberalization 3, 11-12, 72-81, 143
  finance 78-9
  foreign exchange 60, 80
  foreign investment 80
  foreign trade 77-8
  hard-budget 75-6
  labour 79-80
  prices, domestic input 76
  prices, essentials 77
  prices, farm 77
  prices, non-essentials 76-7
  subsidies 77
Lleshi, Haxhi 66
local government 37-9
Luniku, Kristaq 202, 234

Malaj, Arben 200, 202, 234

Mejdani, Rexhep 58, 235, 237
Meksi, Aleksandër 62-3, 230
mining and minerals 34-5, 105,
    152-4
minorities 47
monetary policy 108-10
  instruments 111
  targets 108-9
money-laundering 202
money supply and velocity 19, 115
multinational force (Alba) 232-7
Myftiu, Manush 61, 66

Nano, Fatos 49, 55, 57-8, 60, 65,
    68, 234, 235

OSCE [Organization for Security
    and Cooperation in Europe]
    52, 57, 232

parties, political 57-62, 64, 68,
    233-4, 235
    241
Pashko, Gramoz 60, 63
pensions *see* social security
petroleum 34
political chronology 52-71, 227-39
pollution 43, 46
population
  density 31
  growth 10, 35
  life-expectancy 36
  regional distribution 37
press and media, government
    relations with 67-8, 69, 146-7
    238
price-level, inflation 18, 64, 114,
    238-40
privatization 3, 12-13, 61-2, 83-106,
    143
  auctions 86, 89, 93
  banks 99-9, 194-200
  'Decree 203' 89-90
  electricity 96-7
  farmland 22, 60, 84-5, 90-1, 95
  housing 85, 91, 95
  mass- 87-90, 93-5, 101-3, 106
  minerals 97, 104

petroleum 97
political impact of 22-3
small units 84, 92-4
small and medium enterprises
   85-6, 92-4
strategic investors 97-8, 101,
   103-4
telecommunications 98-9
utilities 83, 99-100
voucher- 87-90, 93-5, 101-3, 105
voucher-market 89
Prodi, Romano 232
production, patterns of 150-60
prosecutions, politically motivated
   28, 64-8, 147-8
public finance 161-74
deficits, financing 163-6, 172
expenditure changes 162-4, 172
revenue changes 165, 167-73,
   242
taxes *see* tax
pyramid funds 18-19, 24-9, 70,
   201-5, 227-9, 234

railways *see* transport
reform 56-7, 60, 62-3 *and see*
   liberalization; privatization
regional government *see* local
   government
religion
ban on 9
religious traditions 48
reserves, foreign 16, 117-9, 242
roads *see* transport
Ruli, Genc 60

safety-net *see* social security
Selami, Eduard 68

Shehu, Tritan 228
Simitis, Costas 232
SHIK (security police) 67, 232, 238
shipping *see* transport
smuggling 17, 23-4
social security 4, 14-5, 23, 60,
   122-38
adequacy 131-3
benefits and pensions 127-30
budget 131, 164, 172
contributions 122-6
medical 123
rural and urban 127-8, 133
wage-levels and 130-1
stabilization 13-15, 17-21, 239-42
Sude *see* Kademi, Maksude
stock exchange 200-1

tax 78, 119-20, 168-73, 243
topography 31-2
trade, foreign 10, 16, 77-8, 117-19,
   153-5, 240-1
transition
elements 2-4
impetus 52-3
success in CEE countries 4-5
transition economies defined 2
transport 43-7
Treasury Bills 109-10, 166, 200-1

Van Mierlo, Hans 230-2
voting behaviour 235-6, 243
Vranitzky, Franz 230-4

Zogu, Ahmet [King Zog] 49, 53, 54,
   234-5
Zogu, Leka 234-5

256